S0-AFX-838

FAIR HOUSING

A Guidebook for
Owners and Managers
of Apartments

Fair Housing

A Guidebook for Owners and Managers of Apartments

Introduction

As Americans, we enjoy some of the best housing in the world. And as Americans, we usually take for granted our ability to choose suitable housing based on our preferences, our ability to pay, and our housing and credit history.

However, it was not always so: the landmark Fair Housing Act dates only to 1968. Federal protections for persons with disabilities, and for families with children, are even more recent, having been added to the Fair Housing Act in 1988.

Yet, today, anyone who attends housing industry meetings will find that the principles of fair housing are thoroughly ingrained in the thoughts and actions of professional owners and managers. Everyone agrees that residents and applicants are entitled to be treated consistently and on the basis of their individual situations. Similarly, everyone believes that it is not only illegal but immoral to base our treatment of residents and applicants on our own stereotypes, myths, or fears.

So, if everyone agrees on general principles, what is the need for a guidebook like this, why does it cover so many topics, and why does it go into such detail? Here are a few of the answers:

- As we implement fair housing, the relatively simple principles of fair housing begin to interact with a bewilderingly complex array of housing markets, properties, residents and applicants, an environment in which nothing is simple.

- The principles of fair housing sometimes contradict, or seem to contradict, other strongly held American values, and it is not always easy to determine what is legal, let alone to determine what is right and moral.

- There are a variety of fair housing laws (federal, state and local) with differing applicability to different apartment properties.

- Many aspects of fair housing practice stem from laws and regulations that, although simple and definitive in the abstract, are subject to varying interpretations in the real world. This means that case law becomes relatively more important than in most other areas of apartment ownership and management. It also means that the cutting edge of fair housing practice is always changing.

The purpose of this guidebook is to help apartment owners and managers translate their support of fair housing in principle, into the consistent day to day reality of fair housing in the properties they own and manage.

This process begins with an understanding of the various fair housing laws. Next is an assessment of each property for potential fair housing challenges. We suggest policy approaches that will provide a firm foundation for each property's fair housing efforts. The guidebook also presents a wide range of fair housing issues, including issues at the cutting edge of fair housing practice.

We also include citations for landmark cases, plus a variety of appendices containing useful information that is sometimes not easy to find. Finally, the guidebook includes insights from expert owners and managers who have faced these issues and developed particularly effective approaches.

We hope that this guidebook will contribute to the continuing advancement of fair housing principles and practice in the apartment industry.

© 2000 by the Compass Group, LLC and
The National Affordable Housing
Management Association.

All Rights Reserved.

Published in Washington, D.C. 20005 by

The Compass Group, LLC

and

The National Affordable Housing Management Association

Manufactured in the
United States of America.

Author, Title, Subtitle

The Compass Group,

Fair Housing

A Guidebook for Owners and Managers of
Apartments

ISBN

0-9669944-2-6

Portions of this book have appeared previously in *The NAHMA Fair Housing Guidebook For Owners and Managers of Housing Recieving Federal Financial Aid, Third Edition.*

Publication Information

Fair Housing: A Guidebook for Owners and Managers of Apartments

A question and answer guidebook covering nondiscrimination laws as they apply to the rental of apartments.

First Edition
July, 2000

Published by:
The Compass Group, LLC
1275 K Street, NW
Suite 925
Washington, DC 20005
www.compassgroup.net
inquiries@compassgroup.net

Copyright

All rights reserved. No part of this book (except appendices) may be reproduced in any form or by any means, or stored in electronic form, except by the express, written permission of the publisher. The entire text (except appendices and quotations from federal regulations and legal cases) is jointly copyrighted by The Compass Group, LLC, and The National Affordable Housing Management Association.

Copyright 2000

The Compass Group, LLC

The National Affordable Housing Management Association

Disclaimer

This publication is designed to provide accurate and authoritative information in regard to the subject matter covered. It is sold with the understanding that the information herein is of a general nature. If legal or other expert assistance is required, the services of a competent professional should be sought.

The information contained herein is based on sources believed to be accurate and reliable. However, no representation or warranty is made as to such accuracy. Readers should refer to primary sources whenever appropriate, and should make certain that information has not been affected by recent developments.

This guidebook is an introduction to certain important issues involved in fair housing for the rental of apartments in the United States. It is not exhaustive of the issues and requirements. It reflects the authors' professional experience, research and opinions, which may or may not agree with those of other commentators or experts in the field. The reader must appreciate that the correct course of action will turn on particular facts and circumstances that surround a particular property, its geographic location, and the evolution of case law.

Acknowledgements

This Guidebook represents a significant enhancement of material previously published in the NAHMA Fair Housing Guidebook - 3rd Edition. Those who contributed to that seminal work, therefore, are to be thanked again. They included NAHMA members Terry Ross, Phil Carroll, Don Beebout, Bobby Griffith, Lee Brown, Randy Lenhoff, Brian Sellars and Charlie Wilkins. Contributors outside of NAHMA included Patrick Sheridan and Doug McDowell of the Rural Housing Service, and Steve Rosenblatt of Spectrum Seminars.

The original Guidebook, which served as a foundation for this work, has been extensively updated and expanded, thanks to the efforts of so many. The primary authors of this effort have been Anker Heegaard, Charlie Wilkins and Tracy Barnes of the Compass Group. NAHMA contributors have primarily been Terry Ross, Mike Goodwin, Gwen Volk and Roxie Munn. Their contributions, in particular, went beyond the call of duty. Additional and helpful guidance was provided by Chris Hanback, Kathy Coughlin, Peter Burkett and Fred Wood. Invaluable assistance was also provided by Beverly Heegaard, who stayed the course of this work during its reconstruction, and Shiela Salmon, whose comments helped to loosen the knots.

Additional Copies and Information

See the last page of this book for information on how to purchase additional copies of this book

Other Publications

The Compass Group has published two other books of interest to housing professionals: "Shelter from the Storm: Successful Market Conversions of Regulated Housing" and "Managing Housing Credit Apartments, A Question and Answer Handbook." See the back of this book for more detailed information on these publications.

The Compass Group, LLC

The Compass Group is a consulting partnership that specializes in affordable housing policy, management and finance. Its two principal partners are:

Charles S. Wilkins, Jr.

cwilkins@compassgroup.net

&

Anker Heegaard

anker@compassgroup.net

NAHMA

The National Affordable Housing Management Association represents the interests of owners and managers of government-regulated housing. See the back of this book for more information on the services and mission of NAHMA, and how you can join.

Fair Housing

A Guidebook for Owners and Managers of Apartments

TABLE OF CONTENTS

Note: References are to Question Numbers

Table of Contents

Chapter Fifteen: **Disability-Related Requirements in Federally-Assisted Housing**

Chapter Sixteen: **Accessibility and Federally-Assisted Properties**

Chapter Seventeen: **Occupancy, Persons With Disabilities, and Federally-Assisted Housing**

Chapter Eighteen: **Fair Housing Marketing and Admissions Issues for Federally-Assisted Properties**

Chapter Nineteen: **Familial Status Issues in Federally-Assisted Housing**

Chapter Twenty: **"Mixed Population" Issues in Federally-Assisted Elderly Properties**

Appendices

Index

About Us and Our Publications

Table of Contents

Chapter One: Fair Housing Laws and Regulations

1   *What Is Fair Housing?*

Fair housing refers to the prohibition against discrimination in any activity relating to the sale or rental of dwellings, in the availability of financing or other real estate related transactions, or in the provision of housing-related services.

Regulations under the Fair Housing Act provide that:

> *"No person shall be subjected to discrimination because of race, color, religion, sex, handicap, familial status or national origin in the sale, rental or advertising of dwellings, in the provision of brokerage services or in the availability of residential real estate-related transactions."* [i]

Technically, only the Fair Housing Act (Title VIII of the Civil Rights Act of 1968, as amended by the Fair Housing Amendments Act of 1988) is a "fair housing" law. However, there are other federal, state and local laws that also prohibit discriminatory conduct in housing-related activities, although these non-discrimination laws sometimes have a broader application than housing. For purposes of this guidebook the term "fair housing" will refer to the entire collection of federal, state and local requirements governing non-discrimination in housing.

This guide addresses fair housing issues applicable to multifamily rental housing. Readers should be aware, however, that significant fair housing requirements apply to for-sale housing, real estate brokerage, and other areas of residential real estate practice.

For guidance on how fair housing laws apply to small properties, see question 3.

Additionally, for purposes of this guidebook, multifamily housing is defined as buildings with five or more rental units. Some laws apply to small rental housing properties of one to four units.

---

i.   24CFR, §100.5

2   Who Must Obey the Fair Housing Act?

- Persons engaged in the real estate profession (such as owners, managers, sellers or financiers) who have been involved in three or more sales or rentals in the prior 12 months.

- Owners of buildings that contain two or more dwelling units.

See question 15.

Housing providers should also determine whether applicable state and local laws may impose additional requirements beyond those of the Fair Housing Act.

3   I Have a Small Rental Property. Do the Federal Fair Housing Laws Apply to Me?

Concerning small properties, the following rules apply:

Note that the federal fair housing law discussed at right applies to the total number of units, not the actual occupancy. Additionally, state and local fair housing laws, as well as federal, state or local civil rights laws may apply. See question 15.

- The rental of single-family homes is exempt from federal fair housing laws, unless (1) the owner has an interest in more than three single-family homes, or (2) a broker or agent is in any way involved in the transaction. See the last two bullets on this page for exceptions.

- The owner of a property with fewer than five dwelling units is exempt *only if* the owner actually resides in one of the units. See the last two bullets on this page for exceptions.

- Owners of buildings with two or more rental units, where the owner is not a resident of one of the units, must adhere to all federal fair housing requirements.

- Owners of buildings with five or more rental units, regardless of the occupancy of the owner, must adhere to all federal fair housing requirements.

- Prohibitions against discriminatory advertising, statements and notices apply to all rental properties, regardless of the number of units. Therefore, even single-family rentals must abide by certain fair housing requirements.

- Any person engaged in three or more rental transactions in the last twelve months must abide by fair housing laws.

Exceptions for Small Properties

*HUD Administrative Law Judge, 02-98-0276-9, HUD v. Schmid

> *The owner of a duplex resides in the downstairs unit, and offers the upstairs unit for rent. A woman and her five-year-old child apply and are rejected by the owner who says, "I don't want any children here." While the owner of this small (and otherwise exempt) building is free to reject the woman and child on any grounds, including their familial status, the owner's verbal statement was discriminatory and is not exempt.*

4 Which Federal Laws and Regulations Govern Fair Housing for Apartments?

For greater detail on the Fair Housing Act, see questions 5 and 6.

Title VIII of the Civil Rights Act of 1968 (the "Fair Housing Act") provides protection from discriminatory housing practices based upon race, color, religion, and national origin. In 1974, sex was added to the list of protected classes. The Fair Housing Amendments Act, discussed below, added two additional protected classes and also provided for the award of monetary damages for discriminatory housing practices.

For greater detail on the Fair Housing Amendments Act, see question 6.

The Fair Housing Amendments Act of 1988 ("The Amendments Act") expanded the scope of protection under the Fair Housing Act to prohibit discrimination against persons with disabilities and against families with children. The Amendments Act also significantly enhanced HUD's ability to investigate complaints under, and enforce, the Fair Housing Act. This book uses the term 'Fair Housing Act' to refer to the protections against discrimination afforded by both the Civil Rights Act of 1968, and the Fair Housing Amendments Act of 1988.

For greater detail on the ADA, see question 13.

The Americans With Disabilities Act (the "ADA") requires accessibility for persons with disabilities, and prohibits discrimination against persons with disabilities, in employment, governmental activities and commercial activities.

For greater detail on Section 504, see questions 107 and 108, and Chapters 14 and 15.

Section 504 of The Rehabilitation Act of 1973 ("Section 504") requires accessibility to persons with disabilities, and prohibits discrimination against persons with disabilities, in housing and other programs that receive federal financial assistance.

Title VI of the Civil Rights Act of 1964 ("Title VI") prohibits discrimination on the basis of race, color or national origin in all HUD-assisted programs. Title VI covers all HUD housing programs except for its mortgage insurance and loan guarantee programs.

See question 15; also see question 107 for laws and regulations specifically affecting federally assisted properties.

Note that in addition to the Federal Fair Housing laws listed above, many states and localities have issued their own laws, some of which accord protection from discrimination to additional classes of people.

5   Who Is Protected by Federal Fair Housing Laws?

Protected Classes

With respect to rental housing, providers may not discriminate in any activity relating to the rental of dwellings, or in the provision of services or facilities, on the basis of:

- race;

- color;

- religion;

- sex;

- national origin;

- handicap or disability;[ii] or,

See question 6 and Chapter 7.

- "familial status" (generally, the presence of children under 18 in a household).

---

ii. The preferred term in this book is 'disability', however, some laws and regulations governing Fair Housing use the term 'handicap' and that term will be used in the context of those laws and regulations.

Note that many states and localities have issued their own laws, some of which accord protection from discrimination to additional classes of people. See question 15.

The above seven categories, known as the 'protected classes,' are the only groups explicitly protected by the federal fair housing laws.

In addition to the direct protection against discrimination afforded by membership in a protected class, applicants and tenants are protected from discrimination based on the protected status of their guests or associates.

Persons are Protected from Discrimination Based on their Guests

> Resident Alfred enjoys frequent visits from his mother, who has a mental disability. The owner of the property attempts to evict Alfred, fearing that his mother will cause some harm. Alfred is protected from eviction by the fair housing laws.[*] In addition to protection from eviction, Alfred is also protected from interference with his 'enjoyment of a dwelling.'[†]

   [*] 24 CFR §100.60(b)(5)
   [†] 24 CFR §100.400

Persons are Protected from Discrimination Based on their Guests

> Applicant Gerry is a white woman. She appears at the leasing office of an apartment property to submit a rental application accompanied by her friend Harry, an African American. Her rental application is declined. The property is liable for discrimination against Gerry if its refusal to rent to her is based on her association with Harry, even though the discrimination is not based on Gerry's race.

Exclusions and Exceptions

See question 59 for exemptions from familial status requirements under the Fair Housing Act.

There are a few specific exclusions to the protected classes listed at the beginning of this question:

- Although familial status is a protected class, certain properties reserved for seniors are exempt, and may deny applications based on the presence of children.

- Although religion is a protected class, housing provided by religious organizations for non-commercial purposes may give preference based on religion, unless membership in that religion is restricted by race, color or national origin.

See questions 91 through 96.

- Although drug addicts are protected, those currently using illegal, controlled substances are not. Additionally, anyone convicted of the illegal manufacture or distribution of a controlled substance is not protected.[iii]

See 103 for further information on mental illness as a disability.

- Although mental illness is protected, HUD's fair housing regulations make a specific exception for transvestism, which is not protected. Note however that a transvestite may have other mental disorders that would provide for protected status.

6   What Is the Fair Housing Amendments Act of 1988?

The Fair Housing Amendments Act of 1988 extended to persons with disabilities and to families with children the same protection from discrimination in housing which was provided in Title VIII of the Civil Rights Act of 1968 to individuals based on race, color, religion, sex and national origin.

Disability-Related Requirements

A disability is an impairment which substantially limits a major life activity. Persons who have a "record of" such an impairment, or are "regarded as" having such an impairment are also considered to have disabilities. The Fair Housing Act requires that rental housing providers permit residents with disabilities to make reasonable modifications to existing premises if necessary to enable them to take full advantage of rental housing opportunities. Housing providers must make reasonable accommodations in rules, policies, practices and services to accommodate the disabilities of residents and applicants.

Key Areas of Concern Related to Disability

With respect to persons with disabilities, housing providers and persons with disabilities have expressed the following key areas of concern:

See also question 26.

- How to respect the rights (or, accommodate the needs) of persons with disabilities in the applicant screening process;

---

iii. 24CFR, §100.10(a)(4)

- How to balance the obligation to provide accessibility against other obligations of the property, in the context of a limited budget; and

- How to balance the rights of persons with disabilities with the rights of other residents and applicants.

Require-ments Related to Familial Status

Familial status protections of the Fair Housing Act prohibit providers from discriminating against households with individuals who are under 18 years of age, pregnant women and households seeking custody of an individual under 18 years of age. In addition, providers may not:

- Limit the use of facilities or services by such households;

- Impose special charges for such households; or

- Inappropriately influence the household's choice of a dwelling unit.

Key Areas of Concern Related to Familial Status

With respect to families with children, housing providers and families with children have expressed the following key areas of concern:

- Occupancy limits for dwelling units which may serve to exclude families;

- The imposition of additional charges or fees on families; and

- The imposition of rules and regulations which limit families' full enjoyment of housing facilities.

See question 59 for definitions of these properties.

Note that there are a few apartment properties that are reserved exclusively for the elderly and as such are exempted from the prohibition against familial discrimination.

The Fair Housing Amendments Act[iv] also gave the Department of Housing and Urban Development the power to administer and enforce the Act including the power to make regulations that interpret and implement the Act.

---

iv. FHA regulations are found at 24 Code of Federal Regulations, Sections 100-105.

7   Who Is Responsible for Enforcing Fair Housing Laws?

Congress has charged HUD with the principal enforcement responsibilities under the law, including the development of regulations, initiation and investigation of complaints, conciliation between parties, and referral of complaints for judicial action.

See question 31 for further information on the referral of complaints to agencies of states or localities that have substantially equivalent laws.

States and localities may be authorized by HUD to assume some of these responsibilities if they adopt fair housing laws which are 'substantially equivalent' to the federal act. Under most circumstances, if a state or local law is substantially equivalent, a complaint filed with HUD may be referred for investigation to the state or local agency charged with enforcing the substantially equivalent law.

8   What Are Examples of Prohibited Conduct Under the Fair Housing Laws?

Prohibited conduct under the Fair Housing Act includes not only an outright refusal to rent or sell housing to a member of a protected class, but more subtle forms of discrimination in advertising, applicant screening, resident selection, occupancy requirements and eviction. While this book addresses only rental housing, housing providers should be aware that there are similar fair housing requirements for housing for sale.

Examples of Prohibited Rental Housing Practices

A number of practices are prohibited by the Fair Housing Act. These include, but are not limited to:

- Refusing to rent after a bona fide offer has been made, or to negotiate the rental of a dwelling, based on membership in a protected class;

- Establishing requirements for admission which operate to exclude protected groups;

See Chapter 5 for applicant screening and selection considerations.

- Using different lease or contract provisions to discriminate against a person with disabilities, a family with children or another protected class;

See Chapter 6 for occupancy issues.

- Employing any form of quota system to limit occupancy by protected individuals;

See questions 55 and 63 for examples of discriminatory conduct.

- Limiting the use of facilities or services by a protected individual, or providing a lower quality of service to such a person;

- Providing false or misleading information about a housing opportunity;

- Discouraging applications or inappropriately influencing the choice of a dwelling through 'steering', threats or intimidation; (steering is any attempt on the part of the leasing agent to direct an applicant to or away from a particular unit or area).

See questions 26, 37 and 38.

- Having advertising or on-site marketing activities that indicate any preference, limitation, or discrimination based on membership in a protected class;

See questions 101 and 102.

- Failing to provide equally effective communications to individuals with disabilities.

See questions 64, 76 and Chapters 9 and 11 generally.

- With respect to persons with disabilities, refusing to make reasonable changes in rules, policies, services or practices to permit full use and enjoyment of the housing by such persons;

See questions 72, 73, 69 and Chapters 9, 10 and 11 generally.

- Failing to allow reasonable modifications to dwellings and common areas to permit accessibility by persons with disabilities;

See question 69.

- In the case of new construction, constructing buildings and units that are inaccessible to persons with disabilities;

See questions 58 and 97.

- Employing different eviction standards for a member of a protected class, or in any way enforcing lease provisions based on membership in a protected class.

See questions 11 and 12.

- Taking any action against an employee of a real estate organization for refusing to violate fair housing laws, or refusing to hire an employee to a real estate organization based on membership in a protected class.

The above examples are not a definitive listing of the ways in which a housing provider can violate Fair Housing laws.

Unintended Discrimination

Discrimination complaints are based not only on intentional discrimination, but also on the perception of discrimination by the applicant or resident. Thus, even "good faith" actions may result in the filing of a discrimination complaint.

Example of 'Unintended Discrimination'

> *A leasing agent may feel that a family wants to be closer to the playground, which is in the back of the property. The family is only shown units in the back of the property and is not informed of the availability of other units closer to the front of the property. The agent may have done this with "good intentions;" the family however perceives that they are not offered the same options as other applicants and calls the local fair housing council to file a complaint. The leasing agent in this case should have shown the family a list of all available apartments for which they qualified; it is up to the applicant to decide which units are suitable, not the leasing agent.*

See question 64 for more on 'reasonable accommodation'.

Most housing providers are aware that intentional discrimination against protected classes is prohibited. In addition to intentional discrimination, acts with an unintended but discriminatory effect are also prohibited. For example, a policy that all rental payments must be made at the rental office without exception fails to consider that someone with a disability may not be able to physically come to the office but could instead mail their rent payments. If you do not reasonably accommodate the needs of the disabled, you could be faced with a discrimination complaint.

9   What Is "Disparate Impact"?

Disparate impact discrimination occurs when a housing provider implements an apparently neutral policy or procedure (i.e. one that on its face applies to all persons equally and is not overtly discriminatory) yet can be shown to have a disproportionately negative effect upon members of a protected class.

Example of Disparate Impact

* HUD v. George and Mary Ross; HUDALJ 01-92-0466-8

** Gilligan et al v. Jamco Development Corporation et al, case number 95-56290, US Court of Appeals, 9th Circuit, (a final resolution of this case is pending).

† Also see Achtenberg Memo dated Dec. 17, 1993.

In two cases, housing providers had a policy of refusing to accept as tenants persons who received Aid to Families with Dependent Children (AFDC). Source of income is not a protected class under the federal Fair Housing Act and therefore this policy did not, on its face, violate the Act. However, in the first case evidence was tendered to prove that the overwhelming percentage of AFDC recipients in the relevant County were women. The policy therefore had an indirect but palpable impact on women and as such the housing providers were held to have discriminated against women on the basis of their sex. In the second case** the court ruled that a prima facie case of discrimination under the Fair Housing Act was established against a housing provider that had a policy of not renting to any recipients of AFDC benefits. Since only families with children are entitled to receive AFDC it was alleged by the Plaintiffs that the policy had a disparate impact on that protected class (i.e. families with minor children).†*

Where there is a finding that an apparently neutral policy disproportionately affects members of a protected class, the housing provider must demonstrate that the policy has a solid business justification.

10 What Are the Consequences to Owners and Managers Who Violate Fair Housing Laws?

In general, anyone engaging in activities related to the rental of dwelling units who is found to have engaged in a prohibited practice can be subject to serious penalties of law. Managers should be concerned not just about a "finding" of discrimination but also about "filing" of discrimination complaints. Anyone in the chain of command can be sued, including the person alleged to have committed the act of discrimination and anyone responsible for the professional activities of that person including the property manager, the owner of the management company and the owner of the property.

It is important to note that housing owners and managers may be sued both for their direct actions as well as for the actions of their agents, under the principle that they have a "nondelegable duty" to assure that the conduct of their agents fully complies with the law. For example, if a property's managing agent violates the fair housing laws, both the managing agent and the property owner may be sued even though the property owner neither authorized nor knew of the agent's conduct.

11 What If My Employer Asks Me to Violate Fair Housing Laws?

It is unlawful to discharge or take any adverse action against an employee for refusing to participate in a discriminatory housing practice.

See also questions 2 and 10.

An employee cannot be required by an employer to take actions that are in violation of the law, or that would expose the employee to personal liability for housing discrimination.

12 Do Federal Fair Housing Laws Address Discrimination in Hiring Practices?

The federal fair housing laws do not address discrimination in hiring or employment, as these are practices prohibited by existing employment laws. However, it is a violation to "impose different standards or criteria for membership in a real estate sales or rental organization because of race, color, religion, sex, handicap, familial status or national origin."[v] The term 'membership' refers to associations or other non-employment based affiliations.

13 What Is the Americans With Disabilities Act?

The Americans With Disabilities Act extends protection to persons with disabilities, in the following contexts:

Employment (Title I)

Title I of the ADA requires employers with more than 15 employees to make reasonable accommodations and reasonable modifi-

---

v. 24CFR, §100.50(7)

cations for employees with disabilities, and applicants for employment with disabilities, so that they can perform essential job functions. Technically, this Title is not a fair housing issue, and so it is not covered in this Guidebook. However, many of the general principles regarding accessibility are relevant to Title I.

Activities of State and Local Governments (Title II)

Title II of the ADA prohibits discrimination against qualified individuals with disabilities in all programs, activities and services of public entities. It applies to all State and local governments and their departments and agencies. A state or local government must eliminate any eligibility criteria for participation in programs, activities and services that screen out or tend to screen out persons with disabilities (whether intentionally or not), unless it can establish that the requirements are necessary for the provision of the service program or activity. Included in this requirement is a requirement that a public entity must ensure that individuals with disabilities are not excluded from services, programs and activities because existing buildings are inaccessible.

Public Accommodations, Accessed by the General Public, but Operated by Private Entities (Title III)

A public accommodation is a private entity that owns, operates, leases, or leases to, a place open to the general public. Title III prohibits discrimination against persons with disabilities in the use and enjoyment of goods, services and facilities of any place of public accommodation. Places of public accommodation include a wide range of entities, such as restaurants, hotels, theaters, retail stores, museums, libraries and parks. It also includes, however, parts of private residential facilities to which members of the public are entitled to have access, for example rental offices. With respect to rental offices and other common areas (for example laundry rooms), as long as the rental office or common area is open to the public, it is subject to the ADA.

With respect to apartment properties, the ADA has the following general applicability:

Governmental Activities

The ADA's Title II covers 'activities of state and local government'. Some properties are owned by governmental entities, which would bring all of property operations under Title II. Properties that are bond-financed are discussed under State/local bond financing below.

State or local government programs that operate on property premises (such as Head Start, public school programs, Meals on

Wheels, etc.) will be subject to ADA Title II. Expert managers advise that the property and the sponsoring government agency should determine who will bear the responsibility for ADA compliance with respect to the program and the on-site environment in which it operates.

Business Locations

In general, rental housing units are not covered under Title III of the ADA; however, the property's rental office is covered (and thus must be made accessible). Thus, the ADA may require reasonable changes to structures, policies and procedures so that persons with disabilities can access the rental office and its business services. These modifications might include removing structural barriers or relocating offices to accessible locations, or adding technological aids such as intercoms or doorbells in parking areas.

See also question 23.

Businesses that operate on property premises (such as day care centers) may be subject to ADA Title III. The housing provider and the independent business should determine who will bear the responsibility for ADA compliance with respect to the business and the on-site environment in which it operates. Typically, these sorts of non-housing activities will be subject to written agreements with the third party service providers. For existing agreements, that do not discuss ADA compliance issues, there may be provisions stating who has the responsibility for maintenance of the premises, who is responsible for ensuring that the physical facility is in compliance with governmental requirements, and so forth. These existing provisions may give an indication of which party should bear the responsibility for any physical modifications necessary for ADA compliance.

There are two areas where expert opinion is divided as to whether or not the ADA applies:

Short-Term Furnished Rentals

Some apartment properties offer furnished apartments for stays of 30 days or more. Because hotel operations are covered under the ADA's Title III, and because the services offered by these apartment properties are in some ways comparable to those provided by hotels, expert opinion is divided as to whether these activities are covered by the ADA. Currently, the weight of opinion seems to be that stays of 30 days or more do not fall under the ADA "transient housing" definition, and thus the ADA does not cover this type of activity. Check with your attorney for an up-to-date expert opinion.

State / local Bond Financing

Some apartment properties were financed by taxable or tax-exempt bonds issued by state or local governments. Because the ADA's Title II covers activities of state and local governments, expert opinion is divided as to whether these properties are subject to the ADA. Currently, the weight of opinion seems to be that, unless the housing is actually owned or managed by state or local government, Title II of the ADA is not applicable. Again, check with your attorney for an up-to-date opinion.

Properties subject to Section 504 should refer to questions 111, 119 and 129.

The ADA may require physical modifications to a property to allow access. Properties or portions of properties that are subject to Title III of the ADA must make changes that are "readily achievable without too much difficulty or expense."

14   What Is the Architectural Barriers Act?

Publicly owned residential properties including properties that were financed wholly or partially with federal funds are subject to the provisions of the Architectural Barriers Act and regulations made under that Act. These regulations provide that residential structures shall be designed, constructed or altered to ensure that physically handicapped persons have access to and use of those structures. It is also provided that this requirement is satisfied by using the specifications contained in the Uniform Federal Accessibility Standards (UFAS).

15   Do States and Localities Have Fair Housing Laws?

Many states have enacted fair housing laws that are "substantially equivalent" to the federal Fair Housing Act. Some state laws go beyond the federal requirements.

Some state and local laws add new classes of applicants and residents who receive protection against discrimination. Such examples of additional protected classes may include:

- Source of income (e.g., recipients of public assistance)

- Marital status

- Sexual orientation

See Chapter 6.

Other state and local laws create firm standards in areas where federal laws are less specific, for example in the area of occupancy standards.

See question 7.

Know that state and local fair housing laws may exist and may apply to you. In addition, a large percentage of Fair Housing cases are processed at the state and local level.

16   Have There Been Recent Changes in Federal Fair Housing Law?

Fair housing law is constantly evolving. The original law is enacted in statute (laws passed by legislative bodies), and carried out in regulations. However, it is case law (court decisions) that provides much of the definition and interpretation. Because cases are constantly being brought and heard, any up-to-date understanding of fair housing must be based on recent court decisions.

The courts have been active on a few 'hot' issues. Discussions of these have been incorporated into this book. See the appropriate reference.

See questions 86 and 104.

- Chemical sensitivities.

See question 79.

- Companion animals for the mentally ill or mobility impaired.

See question 33.

- The status of 'testers'.

Of course, courts are actively hearing cases on most aspects of fair housing, including reasonable accommodation, advertising, and other requirements under the law. This guidebook endeavors to reflect the most recent decisions on these matters. However, because of the breadth of the court system, and the on-going nature of case law, please consult your attorney for more up-to-date information regarding fair housing.

Chapter Two: Basic Fair Housing Compliance for Apartments

17   How Do I Avoid Fair Housing Complaints?

See question 8, 'unintended discrimination.'

Avoiding fair housing complaints often means going beyond the level of technical compliance with fair housing requirements. Many complaints originate because an innocently intended action or remark is interpreted as discriminatory. Expert owners and managers recommend the following guidelines to help create an environment in which complaints are less likely to be generated.

Signal that the Property is Fair Housing Sensitive

When applicants visit the property for the first time, do they see accessible parking spaces? Are fair housing posters prominently displayed? Does the property sign have the Equal Housing Opportunity symbol and slogan? Are all housing applicants and residents greeted in a courteous and professional way? Note also that under the Fair Housing Act failure to display the Fair Housing Poster is considered to be evidence of a discriminatory housing practice in a complaint of discrimination.

Avoid Words that May Be Misunderstood

Certain terms used in advertising or leasing may have a discriminatory effect, by discouraging applications from persons who are members of a protected class. For example, many real estate professionals may use the word "exclusive" to describe a desirable community, but to a member of a protected class this same word may indicate an intention to "exclude people like me." In particular, advertisements, brochures, and rental applications should be reviewed carefully to make sure that they don't inadvertently create a perception of discriminatory intent. The entire basis of a racial discrimination case brought against a housing provider was that over a three-year period all its advertisements (billboards, newspaper advertisements and brochures) featured only White human models.[i] This was regarded by a number of fair housing advocacy groups as an expression of a preference for housing that racial group to the exclusion of other racial groups—an impermissible practice under the Fair Housing Act.

Give Consistent Answers

Management staff, especially front line staff, will repeatedly be asked the same very basic questions by a great many potential applicants: "Do you have any two bedroom apartments?;" "How much are your two bedroom apartments?;" "Can I look at a two

---

i.   Anthony Tyus et al v. Urban Search Management et al, US Court of Appeals for the Seventh Circuit, Nos. 95-3793 and 95-3932 bedroom apartment?" If all members of staff answer these questions the same way to every applicant each day, the property will remove one common cause of fair housing complaints: the giving of inconsistent or inaccurate information. At the beginning of each day, make sure all management staff know which apartments are available, at what prices, which residents have given notice of intent to vacate, and so forth.

Do Consistent Screening

See question 44 on the use of informally obtained information, and Chapter 5 for recommended practices and policies in applicant screening and selection.

A property may have a very experienced manager who has a very well-developed ability to interpret nuances of body language and subtle differences in tone of voice and to make judgments about a person's character based on such factors. This manager may believe that she can "just tell" which applicants to accept and which to decline, and that she can short-cut the normal resident screening and selection process. This type of "intuitive" screening should be discouraged. In the litigious environment in which housing providers currently operate, decisions to reject applications for housing will frequently be challenged and must be justified on the basis of discernible and objective facts. Trying to defend a decision to reject an application on the ground that the manager "had a feeling" that the applicant would not comply with the requirements of the lease is not going to find favor with a court of law. The professional and prudent approach therefore is to (a) follow the standard process with all applicants and (b) make decisions based on the facts and according to established criteria.

Training

Expert owners and managers advise making fair housing education a part of every employee's orientation process, and providing ongoing fair housing training and support. Maintain proof of fair housing training in each employee's personnel file. In the event that a fair housing complaint is filed against a property a court may give favorable consideration to the fact that employees at the property received fair housing training.

Fair Housing Policy

Experienced management companies develop—and display prominently—a clear policy statement that commits the company to provide equal housing opportunity. For example: "XYZ Apartments is Fully Committed to Equal Housing Opportunity." This is a simple example of the articulation of broad policy that demonstrates the moral and legal commitment to meet both the spirit and the letter of the law. If backed by real policy measures, the establishment of clearly understood principles will provide the framework for decisions which employees must make every day. Have each employee sign this policy statement, and place a copy in the personnel file

Many fair housing complaints arise from perceptions of staff insensitivity, and from careless staff remarks that inadvertently give the impression that the property is not concerned about fair housing. By developing the proper atmosphere at your property you will avoid most complaints. HUD has stated that, in evaluating discrimination complaints, the manner in which fair housing responsibilities are carried out, or the "pattern of behavior," will be heavily weighed.

18   What Are the Basics of Fair Housing Compliance?

Appearing below are some suggested steps that you may wish take in order to help your property's operations comply with the requirements of the Fair Housing Act, the Americans with Disabilities Act, or Section 504 of the Rehabilitation Act (if applicable):

- Review your existing policies to identify any potential for fair housing misunderstanding. HUD has stated that, for enforcement purposes, it will not only look at your actual standards and practices but at whether, as implemented, they limit housing opportunities for protected households. Although your present policies may be intended to be fair, all policies should be reviewed carefully to determine if there may be unintended adverse effects on protected classes of applicants or residents. For example, house rules that, in trying to protect the property or the rights of other residents, are unusually harsh on children may be viewed as unfair to families. Or, having applications and leases available only in written form may be viewed as discriminatory against persons with visual impairments.

- Collect and study regulatory information concerning applicable fair housing requirements.

See question 13.

- Determine the extent to which your operations are covered by provisions of the Americans With Disabilities Act (ADA).

See questions 108 and 110.

- Determine whether the property receives "federal financial assistance" and thus is subject to Section 504 of the Rehabilitation Act.

See Chapter 20.

- For federally assisted seniors properties: determine if each property falls within the mixed populations provisions of the 1992 Housing and Community Development Act and, if it does, decide whether you want to implement those provisions.

See question 15.

- Determine whether your operations are subject to state and local fair housing laws whose provisions may be more extensive than those in federal fair housing laws. For example many States have extended their protected classes beyond the provisions of the Fair Housing Act by prohibiting discrimination in housing on the basis of age, marital status, sexual orientation, ancestry or other criteria.

- Meet with a local disability-oriented organization with accessibility expertise (for example, a local Independent Living Center) to gain insight into the experiences and expectations of persons with disabilities and to better understand how to accommodate people with various disabilities.

See question 23.

- Perform an Accessibility Review for the property. This encompasses a "self-evaluation" of existing barriers to accessibility (structural and procedural), plus a "transition plan" setting forth the steps for completing any needed changes.

See question 28 for detail on familial status reviews, and Chapter 6 on occupancy standards.

- Perform a Familial Status Review to identify and eliminate any unintended adverse impacts that your property rules and regulations or occupancy standards may have on families with children. For example, you may find that your occupancy standards (governing assignment of unit types or sizes based on household size and composition) need to be changed because they unduly restrict opportunities for families with children to live at your property.

- Hold a series of meetings with key management staff to develop a framework for analyzing fair housing issues. At these meetings, assist management staff in making proper judgments about the range of fair housing decisions involved in advertising, resident selection, accessibility modifications and accommodations, and occupancy and eviction standards.

- Have your management staff attend training in fair housing compliance issues, particularly those employees who routinely interact with applicants or residents. Consider developing in-house training, if appropriate.

See question 39 for further information on the use of the non-discrimination statement, logo and slogan.

- Develop improved policies and procedures. For instance, your advertising and marketing plan should specify how you will use the disability nondiscrimination logo, statement and/or slogan. You should also address questions such as, how will persons with hearing or vision impairments communicate with you?

- Make needed physical and procedural modifications, so that mobility impaired persons can visit the property and submit rental applications.

See question 59.

- For seniors' properties: determine if each property meets the criteria for an exemption from the familial status provisions of the Fair Housing Act.

The above list is not exhaustive nor is it necessary that you undertake all of these recommendations. When you have completed those steps applicable to your property, you will be well on the way to a comprehensive compliance program. Be aware, however, that compliance is an ongoing process that requires your continuing attention.

19   What Does "Accessible" Mean Under the Fair Housing Act and the ADA?

Federally assisted properties should refer additionally to Chapter 16.

Regulations under the Fair Housing Act define "accessible" to mean that the public or common use areas of a building can be approached, entered and used by individuals with physical handicaps. Under the ADA the definition is a little wider: "Readily accessible to and usable by individuals with disabilities" means that a facility can be approached, entered and used by individuals with disabilities (including mobility, sensory and cognitive impairments) easily and conveniently. The ADA accessibility requirements therefore require that account be taken of other impairments besides physical handicaps.

20   What Are the Accessibility Requirements for New Construction, Under the Fair Housing Act?

See question 69 and Chapter 10 generally for further information on the accessibility requirements of the Fair Housing Act. Federally assisted properties should refer additionally to question 131.

Regulations under the Fair Housing Act[ii] require that covered multifamily dwellings constructed for first occupancy after March 13, 1991 must contain certain accessibility features; for example, at least one building entrance must be on an accessible route. In the case of dwellings constructed for first occupancy prior to March 13, 1991, the Fair Housing Act requires that residents be permitted to make "reasonable modifications" to their premises if this is necessary "to afford the handicapped person full enjoyment of the premises of a dwelling."[iii]

21   What are the Accessibility Requirements for New Construction, Under the ADA?

See question 13 for a discussion on the applicability of the ADA; see Chapter 10 for questions on physical modifications for accessibility.

The ADA[iv] requires that all newly constructed properties that are subject to Title II of the Act must be constructed in accordance with either the Americans With Disabilities Act Accessibility Guidelines (ADAAG) or the Uniform Federal Accessibility Standards (UFAS). Properties subject to Title III must follow ADAAG. New construction requirements apply to any facility first occupied after January 26, 1993. In addition, alterations that were begun after January 26, 1992 must be accessible to individuals with disabilities in accordance with ADAAG or UFAS to the maximum extent feasible. In the case of existing facilities, the ADA Title III requires that physical barriers to entering and using facilities must be removed when "readily achievable." "Readily achievable" means "easily accomplished and able to be carried out without much difficulty or expense."[v] If removal of physical barriers is not "readily achievable" alternative steps must be taken to provide accessibility. Title II, however, requires a public entity to

---

ii.   24 CFR Subtitle B, Chapter 1, Section 100.205
iii. 24 CFR, Section 100.203(a)
iv. 28 CFR, Section 35.151 and 28 CFR, Section 36.401
v.   ADA Title III, Section 36.304

make its programs accessible in all cases except where to do so would result in a fundamental alteration in the nature of the program or in undue financial and administrative burdens.

22 What Accessibility Requirements Apply to a Property That Is Subject to More Than One Law?

Generally, where a property is subject to the accessibility requirements of more than one law—for example the Fair Housing Act and the ADA—it should observe the more stringent standard. The more stringent standard would provide for greater accessibility. This also applies where a property is subject to any state or local requirements, which may go beyond federal requirements.

23 What Is an Accessibility Review?

Physical Accessibility Reviews are recommended for all properties that may be subject to accessibility requirements of the Fair Housing Act, the Architectural Barriers Act, Section 504 of the Rehabilitation Act or Title II and Title III of the ADA.

Experts recommend in particular that anyone acquiring a property completed for first occupancy after March 13, 1991, should conduct an accessibility review because the accessibility requirements of the Fair Housing Act apply to those properties. The accessibility review should comprise the following elements:

- Reviews to determine which federal accessibility requirements apply to the property. This should include the following:

See questions 107, 108 and 110.

- An analysis to determine whether accessibility requirements imposed by Section 504 of the Rehabilitation Act of 1973 apply to the property. If the property receives federal financial assistance, the Section 504 requirements will apply.

See question 14.

- A determination whether the property is subject to the requirements of the Architectural Barriers Act.

- A determination whether the requirements of Title II of the Americans With Disabilities Act apply. Properties owned by a state or local government entity are affected by this title of the ADA, requiring that all new buildings (i.e. completed for first occupancy after January 26, 1993) constructed by State or local governments be accessible to persons with disabilities and that pre-existing buildings must undertake structural changes to achieve accessibility by January 26, 1995.

- A determination whether the requirements of Title III of the Americans With Disabilities Act apply. Title III prohibits discrimination against persons with disabilities in places of public accommodation. Residential facilities are not considered places of public accommodation and are therefore not subject to Title III of the ADA and this applies also to amenities provided for the exclusive use of residents and their guests. However, rental offices and sales offices for residential housing are open to the public and as such are places of public accommodation and therefore they must comply with ADA accessibility requirements.

- In addition, all apartment properties are subject to the Fair Housing Act, which, in addition to the design and construction requirements for buildings constructed for first occupancy after March 1991, also requires all owners to allow residents with disabilities to make reasonable structural modifications to individual dwelling units and common areas as needed to provide or improve accessibility.

- Using the Uniform Federal Accessibility Standards (UFAS) Accessibility Checklist or similar instrument, inspect the exteriors and common areas of the property to determine if there are any physical barriers which prevent mobility-impaired persons from having full access.

- Determine if any of the units are accessible to wheelchair users, or can be modified to be accessible. "Accessible" includes an accessible route to the unit, plus interior accessibility features as well. Even if there is no current requirement to modify any units, it may prove useful to have developed a plan for use if and when a resident or applicant proposes such modifications in the future.

- An analysis of the physical characteristics of the property including both the exterior and interior, common areas and individual dwelling units, to determine whether there are structural barriers or impediments to accessibility for persons with handicaps and how the property must respond based upon the various laws and regulations that address accessibility.

See question 24 for more on reviewing policies and procedures that may serve as barriers to accessibility; see question 25 for more on transition plans.

- If barriers can be removed through nonstructural changes, such as reasonable accommodations in procedures and practices, the necessary changes should be implemented immediately. If structural modifications are required, a "transition plan" for accomplishing the modifications should be prepared.

24   What Is a Self-Evaluation?

Federally assisted properties should refer additionally to questions 108 and 110.

The self-evaluation is similar to an accessibility review. However, in addition to focusing on barriers to physical mobility, a self-evaluation is also an assessment of services, policies, procedures, rules and practices to see whether they facilitate or hinder accessibility. Although a self-evaluation is a good practice for any property, those that are subject to Section 504 were required to conduct a self-evaluation by July 11, 1989 and all relevant properties that have not yet undertaken this evaluation should do so. Properties that are subject to Title II of the ADA were also required to do self-evaluations by January 26, 1993. Self-evaluations may be useful to properties that are not legally required to undertake one as a means of identifying and correcting problems before they result in a fair housing complaint.

Organizations required to conduct these evaluations, which have more than fifty employees, must retain copies for at least three years. Smaller organizations were encouraged, but not required, to have kept these documents. A thorough self-evaluation involves the following steps:

- Evaluate current policies and practices to see whether they are reasonable, whether they truly afford equal housing opportunity, or instead have the unintended effect of limiting housing opportunities for certain types of households. To avoid unnecessary and costly legal challenges, housing standards and practices should also appear to be fair in addition to meeting the letter of the law.

See question 28.

- Conduct a Familial Status Review.

- Identify the policies and practices needed in order to accommodate applicants and residents with disabilities. Failure to implement such policies and practices can be costly if this failure amounts to a breach of the Fair Housing Act.

Failure to Reasonably Accommodate the Disabled Can Be Costly.

* Palmour & The Fair Housing Council of Greater Washington v. The Cathedral Avenue Cooperative.

> *The resident of a unit at a cooperative used a wheelchair because he had an illness that caused progressive deterioration of his neuromuscular system. His illness prevented him from traveling to an office and he therefore worked from home. He requested a reasonable accommodation to the property's policy that prohibited residents from working from their apartments. This request was refused. A lawsuit was filed against the property but the applicant died before the date of the trial. The case was, however, settled with the property agreeing, among other things, to pay the applicant's estate $180,000 and to institute a reasonable accommodation and reasonable modification policy for residents with disabilities.* *

- The self-evaluation will include a discussion of the number and mix of units that are accessible to wheelchair users, to persons with hearing impairments, and to persons with vision impairments.

See question 89.

- You should remove references to "independent living," and you should carefully review any references to disability conditions.

See question 84.

- Determine if any of the units have accessible fire alarm systems or other features for the vision- or hearing-impaired, or can be modified to include such features. Again, consideration should be given to developing a plan for future modifications.

- Consider reviewing all of the above with local disability organizations and individuals.

See question 25.

- Develop a Transition Plan.

25   What Is a Transition Plan?

If structural modifications are required, you should also prepare a transition plan. The following considerations should be addressed in the plan:

- The transition plan will discuss how the property will respond if there is a present (or future) need for additional units which are accessible to these populations. All properties should plan ahead for the time when a resident proposes to make accessibility modifications (under the Fair Housing Act) at his or her own expense. The property must permit these modifications but may impose reasonable requirements about the design of the modifications and how the work is done.

- A plan of action for accomplishing structural changes needed to provide accessibility to the rental office, and to any other common areas covered under the ADA.

See question 108.

- A plan of action for accomplishing structural changes currently required in order to provide accessibility to the apartments. For example, apartments must be made accessible immediately in properties subject to Section 504, to the extent needed by existing residents.

- The transition plan should include a schedule for implementation. Some modifications will be complex and will require significant architectural review. Other modifications may be costly, and require time because of resource constraints—both Section 504 and the ADA provide exceptions for particularly costly modifications.

- The transition plan should include, in appropriate detail, the construction or rehabilitation methods to be used to provide accessibility.

- The transition plan should discuss how funding will be sought, if present property resources are inadequate.

- The transition plan should identify the person who will be responsible for implementation of the plan.

- The transition plan should identify the persons or groups who assisted with the Accessibility Review. Experienced housing providers advise that this participative process is valuable in developing a high quality approach to accessibility. In most areas, local disability-oriented organizations (such as Independent Living Centers) are available to participate in the Accessibility Review.

26 How Can My Property Become Disability Aware?

Fair Housing has opened vast new opportunities to the several million Americans who have a disability. As a judge wrote in a 1990 legal decision against a Public Housing Authority:

"For over 200 years our Country has prospered under the principle that all men and women should have an equal opportunity to enjoy 'life, liberty and the pursuit of happiness.' There was a time when the disabled did not have the same opportunities and were relegated to a kind of second class status in employment, housing and transportation. That circumstance was caused more by the community's misinformation and thoughtlessness than by the individual's actual disabling condition. Much has been done to eliminate this situation but it would be simplistic to believe that problems do not remain. Public agencies must be especially vigilant to protect the disabled from all forms of discrimination—intentional as well as

benign discrimination caused by the public's perception of what is 'best' for the disabled." [vi]

Here are some general principles and practical suggestions to guide you in meeting fair housing obligations toward applicants with disabilities. These should not be viewed as requirements, but as guides to best practice.

Become a Disability-Aware Person

Your first step is to examine your personal attitudes toward various physical and mental impairments, and to strengthen your own awareness of persons with disabilities.

- In deciding how to treat a person with disabilities, think about how you would treat an AFDC recipient or Hispanic single parent or involuntarily displaced person. This is not a perfect approach, but it will get you started in the right direction. You will then regard the applicant as someone deserving of especially considerate treatment, and as someone who may have a history, or expectations, of being discriminated against.

- Evaluate your assumptions about how to treat persons with disabilities. Imagine that a wheelchair user visits your property, followed by an otherwise similar person who does not use a wheelchair. Would you treat these two people differently? How? As you study this guidebook, decide whether each example of different treatment is a good idea. Often, you will find that different treatment will not be welcomed by a person with disabilities. Further, different treatment will sometimes violate Fair Housing requirements.

- Set aside your personal opinions about disability conditions. You are a housing provider, not a medical expert. Your own opinions regarding disability conditions, no matter how well informed, are your worst enemies in your battle to avoid discrimination based on disability status. Your applicants and residents with disabilities are individuals, each with different needs and abilities. Treat them as individuals without making hasty judgments about what they can and cannot do.

---

vi. Cason v. Rochester Housing Authority; 748 F. Supp. 1002; 1990 US Dist.; Lexis 14229; FHFL 15, 643

• Set aside your personal opinions about the riskiness of accepting applicants with disabilities. Some housing providers may have the perception that persons with disabilities are high-risk applicants by comparison to persons without disabilities. If you share this attitude, we recommend that you discard it, because the facts do not support it (and because this attitude may lead you to take unprofessional and illegal actions in your job).

Become a Disability-Aware Property

There are a number of actions each property can take to create a disability aware atmosphere. Properties that take these actions are less likely to suffer fair housing complaints. It is just as important to appear disability-aware as it is to be disability-aware.

• Review all materials that are shared with applicants. Your property's Rental Application, your Resident Selection Plan, your newsletter, your advertisements, your brochures and the memos on your bulletin board can easily give the impression that you are not interested in housing persons with disabilities. Are you displaying the Fair Housing poster?

• Complete your self-evaluation and transition plan activities. For a typical property, this would include instituting procedural changes to accommodate persons with visual or hearing impairments, and structural changes to accommodate persons with mobility impairments.

• Pay special attention to unit availability questions. Large numbers of fair housing complaints arise when properties give different households different answers to the same question, especially the most frequently asked question: "Do you have any apartments available?" For properties with several staff members who deal with applicants, start each day with a briefing of exactly which apartments are available. For properties with waiting lists, develop a written explanation of how the waiting list works, and how long the wait is likely to be.

Develop Disability-Aware Application Procedures

Your application materials and your Resident Selection Plan need to be reviewed for disability awareness.

• Process each applicant as if he or she were fully able. Even if you are aware of a disability condition, ignore disability status right up to the point of accepting or declining the application. If a person with a disability can qualify without special treatment, so much the better. More importantly, you must not allow your personal ideas about disabilities to cause you to treat the applicant differently, at least not at this stage. (See the discussion below on declining applications).

Develop Disability-Aware Screening Procedures

Your procedures for resident selection should be examined to ensure that they focus only on lease compliance issues.

- Ask about lease compliance matters, not about lifestyle. As housing providers, you should care whether applicants can and will comply with the lease. Will they pay the rent on time? Will they respect the rights of other residents? Will they take reasonably good care of the apartment? Those are the things you should care about, not what medicine they take, how often they bathe, how they purchase and prepare their meals, or how they meet their transportation needs.

- Documentation, not guesswork. Much past discrimination against persons with disabilities has been caused by the public's often-incorrect assumptions about what these people could and could not do. Rely on each individual's prior rental history, not on your own ideas of what a particular individual can and cannot do.

- Follow normal screening practices consistently. If your policy is that neutral or favorable references from the current landlord and one prior landlord, assuming both are unrelated to the applicant, are sufficient to establish the applicant's ability and willingness to comply with the lease then follow this policy! If you have enough information to satisfy this criterion look no further; if you keep "digging," you run the risk of a discrimination complaint if the applicant turns out to have a disability and you ultimately refuse the application.

Fair Housing Requires Neutral Screening Criteria, Applied Consistently

* Milligan v. Lakeland Owner's Corp.; US District Court for New York.; FH-FL Reporter 16, 291, No, 96-CV-1091

A case of discrimination was brought against a co-op board by an applicant who suffered from a mental disability and whose application to sublet a unit at the co-op was refused by the board. Several reasons were offered for the board's refusal including that it did not want to participate in the Section 8 program. Because, however, the board had questioned the applicant about his medication and this was the first sublet request ever denied by the board, without ruling on the merits of the case the court held that a reasonable jury could find that the board's decision to deny the sublet was actually due to discrimination, despite the apparently neutral reasons they offered for their actions. Consequently the board's application to dismiss the case was denied and the court ordered that the case proceed to trial.

See question 89.

- We recommend that you remove "independent living" from your vocabulary. If you mention this phrase to five applicants with disabilities, you will get at least one fair housing complaint, no matter what you meant by the phrase, and no matter how well you explained it.

- Whether residents comply with the lease is your business; how they comply is their business. A resident who personally does housekeeping tasks, one whose grandchild comes over once a week to do housekeeping, and one who hires a chore service to do housekeeping are all the same to you as the housing provider, both for resident selection purposes and for lease enforcement purposes. If the housekeeping isn't being done at all, then you should be concerned.

- You can have special screening procedures for applicants who do not have a rental history. For example: find or ask the applicant to provide an objective, qualified third party who is familiar with the applicant, and ask that person the same types of questions you ask landlords (in other words, questions relating directly to lease compliance issues).

See question 9 for a discussion of disparate impact.

- You cannot have special screening procedures for applicants with disabilities. This also holds for applicants for one bedroom apartments, single person households, or other categories which may be viewed as intending to target a protected class. If applicants with disabilities apply disproportionately for one-bedroom apartments, screening procedures that apply only to applicants for such units would not be permissible because of the "disparate impact" such a policy would have on persons with disabilities—in other words, a set of special policies for one-bedroom or single applicants could be perceived as a way to indirectly discriminate against persons with disabilities.

Decline Applications in a Disability-Aware Manner

The point at which the housing provider indicates that the application for housing may not be approved is the point in the admissions process where applicants with disabilities are most likely to exercise their right to request a reasonable accommodation. Experienced housing providers suggest the following steps when declining an application from a person with disabilities:

• Before declining the application of a person with known disabilities, get a second opinion. You are most vulnerable to a discrimination charge when you are actually aware of a disability condition during the applicant selection process. Before declining the application, review your decision with someone whose judgment you trust.

• Before declining the application of a person with a known disability, offer an informal meeting. Prior to issuing a rejection letter, offer (in writing, with written response required) to meet with the applicant to discuss whether a reasonable accommodation would make the application acceptable. Your letter should explain the reasons why the application, as it presently stands, is unacceptable. Without this information applicants will not be able to address the issue of whether a reasonable accommodation would enable them to meet the admissions criteria.

• Whenever you decline an application, reach out to persons with disabilities. Your standard rejection letter should include something like this: "If you are a person with disabilities, and you feel that a reasonable accommodation by us would allow you to meet our admissions standards, contact us and we will hold a follow-up interview with you to discuss your application." Again, give the specific reasons for declining the application: reasonable accommodations cannot be discussed in a vacuum, rather, they must relate to some particular conduct, behavior or procedure. In the follow-up interview, ask the applicant to suggest reasonable accommodations. It is important to preserve the applicant's dignity and privacy during the "reasonable accommodation" discussion. The best approach is to allow the applicant to lead the discussion; you should discuss only information that the applicant volunteers.

Remember That Screening Has Its Limitations

In the rental housing business, we take a good deal of risk on all applicants, any of whom might turn out to be an undesirable resident no matter how good the application appears. We depend on the law of averages to keep us from having more than a few non-lease-compliant residents. A judge pointed this out to a Housing Authority, which had special "independent living" screening only for elderly and disabled applicants:

> "In renting to a non-handicapped person, the Authority takes a similar, and perhaps in some cases, a greater risk that some harm will come to the property or to other tenants. Yet such applicant's ability to live independently is never questioned, and they are not required to disclose their medical history. It would thus seem that the Authority is content to rely upon information of a less intrusive and personal nature to assess the threat posed by these non-handicapped tenants. Without any objective evidence to indicate otherwise, it appears that the difference in treatment of the handicapped stems from unsubstantiated prejudices and fears regarding those with mental and physical disabilities. This is precisely the sort of situation that the fair housing laws were designed to prohibit."[vii]

An Ounce of Prevention...

Once again: in fair housing it is just as important to avoid the appearance of discrimination as it is to avoid actual discrimina-

---

vii. Cason v. Rochester Housing Authority; 748 F. Supp. 1002; 1990 US Dist.; Lexis 14229; FHFL 15, 643 tion. If you have created a fair housing compliant atmosphere at your property, you are much less likely to suffer complaints, and you are much more likely to receive the benefit of the doubt if a complaint is actually filed.

27 How Should I Refer to Persons With Disabilities?

As a general rule, the term "disability" is preferable to "handicap." "Person with disabilities" is preferable to "handicapped person." "Wheelchair user" is preferable to "wheelchair-bound".

Experienced housing providers suggest that you ask the persons with whom you develop your self-evaluation and transition plan to comment on this question, because in some localities there may be a preference for different terminology.

In this book, because of legal context, the term "handicap" is sometimes used because that is the term used in the particular law or regulation being discussed.

28 What Is Included in a Familial Status Review?

See question 59 for qualifying properties.

Unless your property is a certain type of "seniors only" property the Fair Housing Act provisions against discrimination on the basis of familial status will apply to your property.

*   Examine any restrictions that are specifically geared towards either resident children or households that include minor children to see whether they are reasonably necessary either for the health and safety of the children or the protection of the property. If they are not, they should be removed.

*   Examine your occupancy standards (see below) for conformity to HUD regulations as well as any applicable local and/ or State laws.

*   Examine your advertising materials: do they suggest a preference (whether overtly or implicitly) for applicants without children?

See Chapter 7 and question 56 for further information on this issue.

- Consider whether all aspects of your property, internally and externally, are safe for children. If there are safety hazards at your property it is advisable that you take action to correct them since it is not permissible to discourage applicants with children from living at your property on the ground that it is unsafe for children.

See Chapter 6.

- Occupancy standards. This is a term that refers to your policy regarding the largest household ("maximum occupancy standard") or smallest household ("minimum occupancy standard") that can occupy a given unit type. For example your occupancy standard may provide that no more than four people can occupy a two-bedroom dwelling. Minimum occupancy standards are more commonly found in public or assisted housing where there is a shortage of available units.

See question 57.

- House rules. Your present house rules might (in violation of the Fair Housing Act) include rules that apply only to families with children. For example, based on the belief that households with children cause greater wear and tear within dwellings, your rules may wrongly require that such households must pay larger security deposits than childless households. This is not permissible as it amounts to discrimination on the basis of familial status under the Fair Housing Act. If you have house rules like this, you will want to modify or remove them to be compliant with the Fair Housing Act.

- Some experts recommend you remove all references to children from your lease, house rules, occupancy standards, and other property documents.

Chapter Three: Introduction to Fair Housing
                  Enforcement

29 Who Are the Parties to a Fair Housing Complaint?

The parties to a fair housing complaint are: (i) the aggrieved person; (ii) the complainant; and, (iii) the respondent.

- The *aggrieved person* is the person who actually experienced the discriminatory conduct and who provides the initial information for the filing of the complaint.

- The *complainant* is the person or entity in whose name the complaint is formally brought. In some instances the aggrieved person may also be the complainant, but HUD and fair housing organizations representing the aggrieved person may also be complainants.

- The *respondent* is the person or other entity accused in a complaint of a discriminatory housing practice. This may include the housing provider, the property manager and/or leasing agent.

30 Who May File a Fair Housing Complaint?

Complaints may be filed by anyone who believes he or she has received discriminatory treatment from a housing provider. The Fair Housing Act regulations refer to such persons as "aggrieved persons." This includes anyone, whether a member of a protected class or not, who has been injured in any way as a result of discriminatory conduct—even if this conduct was not directed towards them. The standard for determining whether a party has standing to sue or file a complaint is that the plaintiff must allege that: (1) he or she has suffered a "distinct and palpable" injury; and (2) that injury is "fairly traceable" to the defendant's discriminatory conduct.[i]

---

i. Havens Realty Corp. V Coleman, 455 US 363 (1982) at 376 (1) and (6); Sullivan v. Little Hunting Park, Inc., 396 U.S. 229 (1969) (5); Trafficante v. Metropolitan Life Insurance Co., 409 U.S. 205 (1972)(2)

Persons, Who Are Not Themselves Members of a Protected Class, May File a Fair Housing Complaint

* Simovits v. The Chanticleer Condominium Association, 933 F.Supp. 1394 (N.D. ILL 1996)(3)

† Gladstone Realtors v. Village of Bellwood, 441 US 91 (1979)(4)

‡ Sullivan v. Little Hunting Park Inc. 396 US 229 (1969)

> *Owners of a condominium successfully sued the condominium association for discrimination on the basis of familial status even though they had no minor children, because the association's unlawful policy of prohibiting sales of units to purchasers with minor children significantly hindered the owners in selling their own unit.* In another case it was held that white residents have standing under the Fair Housing Act to challenge racial discrimination directed against African-Americans in their neighborhood.† Similarly, the Supreme Court upheld the standing of a white plaintiff to sue who had been expelled from membership in a community recreational organization because he had rented property and assigned his membership rights to an African-American‡. So, the right to file a fair housing complaint extends beyond actual membership of a protected class*

See question 33 for further information on the role of testers in fair housing complaints.

Complaints may also be filed by fair housing advocates or other representatives of the aggrieved person. This includes "testers" employed by Fair Housing Enforcement Agencies on behalf of persons they believe were discriminated against.[ii] Additionally, courts have held that if testers are given false or misleading information they are also eligible to sue or file a complaint on their own behalf. The person or entity filing the complaint is referred to in the Fair Housing Act regulations as the "complainant."

31   What Is the Fair Housing Enforcement Process?

See also question 7.

The Fair Housing Act provides two alternatives for its enforcement:

- Civil actions may be instituted in district, state or federal courts by persons alleging violations of the Act; or

- Complaints of violations of the Act may be filed with HUD or with state or local fair housing enforcement agencies. These

---

ii.   Havens Realty Corp. V Coleman, 455 U.S. 363 (1982)

complaints may culminate in an administrative hearing of the complaint before an Administrative Law Judge.

Similarly, enforcement of the ADA and Section 504 of the Rehabilitation Act may also be achieved either by the filing of civil suits in the appropriate federal court or by administrative action by the agency responsible for administering the relevant law (the Department of Justice in the case of the ADA) or the relevant program under which the property operates (HUD in the case of Title II of the ADA and Section 504).

HUD's Administrative Procedure

The process begins with a *complaint*. Complaints filed with HUD under the Fair Housing Act must be filed within one year after the occurrence or termination of an alleged discriminatory housing practice. If the complaint is filed with HUD but there is a "substantially equivalent" state or local fair housing enforcement agency in the area where the acts complained of occurred, the complaint will be referred by HUD to that agency for investigation. (See "Referral" below).

The procedures described in this question are applicable only to enforcement of the Fair Housing Act. Enforcement of the ADA and Section 504 are covered more extensively in questions 32 and 109, respectively.

HUD or the state or local agency then *investigates* the complaint. The investigation may result in *conciliation* (a negotiated resolution), or in a *finding* (a determination by the enforcement agency). If the terms of the conciliation are not observed by the "*respondent*" the enforcement agency can turn the conciliation into a finding. The following flow chart shows the resolution process.

The Resolution Process

Action	By Whom	When
Complaint filed with HUD or equivalent agency	Aggrieved person	Within one year of the act of discrimination
Respondent notified of complaint	HUD or equivalent agency	Within ten days of filing of complaint
Answer to complaint filed	Respondent	Within ten days of notification of complaint

The Resolution Process

Action	By Whom	When
Commencement of investigation	HUD or equivalent agency	No time specified for HUD; equivalent agency must commence investigation within 30 days.
If no conciliation, then investigation completed by a finding of reasonable cause (charge issued) or no reasonable cause (charge dismissed)	Conciliation is handled by HUD or the equivalent agency. Findings are the reponsibility of the Assistant Secretary for Fair Housing.	Within 100 days of filing of complaint
Charge filed and served on respondent	Assistant Secretary for Fair Housing	Within three days of issuing charge.
Election of civil proceedings	Complainant, Respondent or Aggrieved Person	Within 20 days of service of charge
No election for civil trial, administrative hearing begins	Administrative Law Judge	Within 120 day of issuing charge.
Initial decision on case	Adminsitrative Law Judge	Within 60 days after completion of hearing
Petition for review of initial decision	Complainant, Respondent or Aggrieved Person	Within 15 days of initial decision
Final decision issued	HUD Secretary	Within 30 days of initial decision
Petition filed with Court of Appeal for review of final decision	Party adversely affected by decision	Within 30 days of final decision

Referral of Complaints

Complaints are handled by the appropriate enforcement agency. In many states, HUD is the appropriate enforcement agency. In other states with *"substantially equivalent"* fair housing laws, state and/or local agencies are responsible for handling enforcement. If there is an equivalent agency in the jurisdiction where the alleged discriminatory action took place, HUD is required to refer the complaint to that agency. Upon receipt of the complaint, the enforcing agency notifies the respondent by providing him or her with a copy of the complaint. Notification of complaints filed under the Fair Housing Act must be given to respondents within ten days of the filing of the complaint. If the "substantially equivalent" state or local agency fails to commence proceedings with respect to the complaint within 30 days from the date when the complaint was referred, HUD may revoke the referral and assume responsibility for investigating the complaint.

Investigation

The enforcing agency reviews the complaint, interviews the person who filed the complaint, and interviews the respondent. Typically, the investigator will review a variety of files and documents. The investigation sometimes also includes a visit to the property and may often include sending testers to the property.

See question 33 for further information on the use of testers and question 35 for more on questions that investigators may ask.

The Fair Housing Act states that investigations should be completed within 100 days of the filing of the complaint, but they often take longer. If the investigation is not completed in the 100-day period the enforcement agency must give written reasons to the complainant and respondent why they failed to do so.

Conciliation

HUD's enforcement regulations require the enforcement agency, after investigating the complaint, to attempt a negotiated resolution of the complaint. This negotiated resolution process is called *conciliation*. If the complaining party and the respondent are able to reach agreement on the terms of the conciliation, the enforcement process stops. HUD will terminate the conciliation process if a civil action has been filed with respect to the alleged discriminatory housing practice, and the trial in the action has commenced. HUD may periodically review compliance with the terms of the conciliation agreement. If HUD has a good reason to believe that the conciliation agreement has not been followed, HUD must refer the case to the Justice Department (Attorney General) and recommend that a civil action be brought against the respondent to enforce the terms of the conciliation agreement.

Findings and Appeal

If the complaint is not successfully conciliated, the enforcement agency issues one of two possible findings based on the evidence that has been collected during the course of the investigation:

- A *finding of reasonable cause to believe that a discriminatory housing practice has occurred or is about to occur* in which case the enforcement agency will issue "a charge" against the respondent. The charge will be heard by an Administrative Law Judge unless either the complainant, the aggrieved person on whose behalf the complaint was filed or the respondent elects to have the charge decided in a civil action.

- A *finding of no reasonable cause to believe that a discriminatory housing practice has occurred or is about to occur* in which case the complaint will be dismissed.

Findings of "Reasonable Cause" or "No Reasonable Cause" cannot be appealed by any of the parties to the proceedings.[iii]

The Court Process

Civil actions under the Fair Housing Act may also be brought by aggrieved persons in an appropriate district or state court. These actions must be brought not later than two years after the occurrence or termination of the alleged discriminatory housing practice. If a complaint about the discriminatory housing practice had been filed with HUD, the computation of this two-year period would exclude any time during which the complaint is pending with HUD. Many lawsuits (whether related to fair housing or not) are *settled* by the parties before or during trial. A trial, if pursued to completion, will result either in *dismissal* of the complaint or an *order* for such relief as may be appropriate against the respondent. Such an *order* may include the assessment of a financial penalty.

Potential Remedial Actions

Typically in conciliation agreements or when a court rules against the respondent, the respondent agrees, or is ordered, to modify any procedures or practices that are determined to be in violation of fair housing laws. The respondent may incur financial penalties as well, in the form of fines and/or payments of damages to the complaining party. Often, the respondent agrees or is ordered to reverse the action that led to the complaint (e.g., accepting rather than declining the household's application, terminating an eviction action, agreeing to, rather than refusing to, make a reasonable accommodation or modification).

---

iii. Marinoff V U.S. Department of Housing & Urban Development 892 F. Supp. 493; aff'd and adopted 78 F. 3d 64 (2nd Circuit 1996)

32 What Is the Enforcement Process for the Americans With Disabilities Act?

Federally assisted properties subject to Section 504 should refer to question 109 for the 504 enforcement process.

Remember, complaints of discriminatory housing practices may be brought under various laws, including the Fair Housing Act and the ADA. The procedures outlined in the previous question are applicable to complaints under the Fair Housing Act. The ADA has its own procedures, an outline of which appears below.

Complaint and Investigative Procedures for ADA Title II

Any individual who believes that he or she is a victim of discrimination prohibited by Title II may file a complaint. Individuals wishing to file Title II complaints may either file:

- An administrative complaint with an appropriate federal agency; or,

- A lawsuit in federal district court.

The following additional provisions apply to Title II complaints:

- Complaints must be filed within 180 days of the date of the alleged act(s) of discrimination.

- HUD is the "appropriate federal agency" for filing complaints involving programs, services and/or regulatory activities relating to State and local public housing. However, complaints may also be filed with the Department of Justice (DOJ), but that department will refer the complaint to the appropriate federal agency for handling.

- HUD processes Title II complaints under the same procedure as it processes complaints under Section 504.

- Cases may be referred for resolution to a mediation program sponsored by the DOJ.

- If the complaint does disclose non-compliance with the ADA, HUD will, in the first instance, try to obtain voluntary compliance by the housing provider. If this cannot be achieved, the law will be enforced either by the termination of federal funding following an administrative hearing or by a referral to the the Department of Justice ("DOJ") for judicial enforcement.

Complaint and Investigative Procedures for ADA Title III

Title III complaints may be filed either with:

- The Department of Justice; or,

- In a U.S. District Court

Complaints filed with DOJ will be investigated, with a view to determining whether or not there is an ADA violation. If the DOJ believes that there is a pattern or practice of discrimination, or if the complaint raises an issue of general public importance it may attempt to negotiate a settlement of the matter. If negotiations to settle the matter are unsuccessful then suit may be filed against the offending party in US District Court. The following provisions also apply to complaints under Title III:

- When private parties bring lawsuits to stop discrimination no monetary damages are available in such suits.

- In suits brought by the Attorney General monetary damages (not including punitive damages) and civil penalties may be awarded.

- Civil penalties may not exceed $50,000 for a first violation and $100,000 for any subsequent violation.

33   What Are "Testers"?

Testers are individuals who, without an intent to rent or purchase a home or apartment, pose as renters or purchasers for the purpose of collecting evidence of discriminatory practices.

Fair housing enforcement organizations sometimes employ testers as a way of determining whether an owner or manager is engaging in discriminatory conduct. For example, an applicant is denied housing and believes that the denial is discriminatory. The applicant may then complain to the local fair housing advocacy group, which may employ a paid "tester" with similar rental qualifications but who is not a member of the same protected class as the applicant. The tester will apply for housing at the property that denied admission to the original applicant. If the tester receives the same treatment or information as the original applicant, that is an indication that the housing manager's conduct was not based on the applicant's protected status; however, if the tester is treated more favorably than the original applicant, that is instead an indication that the housing manager may have violated fair housing non-discrimination requirements.

Another variation on the use of testers may involve two testers with similar rental qualifications being sent to the property. One tester will be a member of the same protected class as the original applicant while the other is not. Again, if both testers receive the same information and treatment this would tend to suggest that the original applicant had not been discriminated against. However, if the tester who is not a member of the relevant protected class receives more favorable treatment or information than the other tester this would support a conclusion that discriminatory conduct had occurred.

An example of the use of testers can be seen in a case of housing discrimination filed with HUD by the Fair Housing Council of Greater Washington..

An Example of the Use of Fair Housing "Testers"

See question 42 for a discussion on the importance of consistency in leasing practices.

> An apartment property was tested as part of a project by the Fair Housing Council of Greater Washington to assess the incidence of racial discrimination in apartment rental in Northern Virginia and not as a result of an actual complaint. In the first instance the Council sent a black tester to the property who was given information on only one available apartment style that rented for $775 per month. A white tester was then sent to the property and received information on two apartment types ranging from $705 to $775. There were also discrepancies in the availability dates on the units shown to each tester. On a subsequent visit to the property the black tester was told that no one-bedroom apartments were available until May 15 and was instead encouraged to rent a two-bedroom unit while the white tester was told of a one-bedroom availability upcoming on May 10 and was invited to place a deposit on that unit. This unequal treatment of the two testers led to the filing of the complaint with HUD. Resolution of the complaint is pending.

The Supreme Court has ruled that testing is often the only way to determine whether discrimination occurred. Additionally, courts have held that testers who are given false or misleading information are also eligible to sue on their own behalf.

A housing provider may also be ordered to pay damages to the organization that employed the testers. For example, the organization would be entitled to recover damages for economic losses stemming from the time and resources it devoted to investigating the complaint.

34   How Do I Respond to a Fair Housing Complaint?

Experienced housing providers give the following advice:

- *Designate a fair housing coordinator* – Have a central person in your organization who will be notified immediately if anyone in the organization receives a fair housing complaint.

- *Resolve it* – Many fair housing issues involve unclear areas of the law. Most fair housing issues involve expenses that are relatively small, by comparison to the costs of defending (or pursuing) a lawsuit. Accordingly, both parties typically have strong motivations to negotiate a solution quickly, rather than to pursue a lengthy legal process.

- *Seek expert advice* – Build business relationships with attorneys and other experts who are familiar with the range of fair housing issues you are likely to encounter. When a complaint occurs, consult your expert advisors before taking any other action.

- *Respond appropriately* – After seeking the advice of your experts, respond completely to requests for information.

- *Respond timely* – When an investigator requests information, respond promptly. More importantly, note and adhere to any deadlines imposed for responding or providing information. For example, answers to complaints under the Fair Housing Act must be filed within ten days of receiving notification of the complaint.

35   What Questions Do Investigators Ask?

Investigators can ask a wide variety of questions. Some of the more typical are:

- *Similar situations* – What information do you have about other applicants with similar characteristics to the rejected applicant? What were the results of their applications? For example, if the complaint was from a mobility-impaired applicant whose application was denied, the investigator will want to establish if there is a pattern of similar actions by the housing provider.

- *Resident profile* – Do other members of the relevant protected class live in the property? If no other members of that protected class reside at the property, then it is possible that there have been prior discriminatory acts. On the other hand, if there are a number of residents representing that particular protected class, then it is less likely that the housing provider discriminated in denying the application of the particular complainant.

- *Similar units* – If the complaint relates to choice of unit offered to the complainant, the investigator will want to know where similar units are located within the property. The investigator will want information pertaining to vacancies and rent readiness of similar units at the time of the alleged discrimination.

- *Similar households* – The locations of similar households within the property may establish if there has been a process of steering those households to specific locations within the property.

- *Policies and procedures* – The investigator will want to review your resident selection policy, your lease and house rules, your lease enforcement policy, and other policies that have to do with fair housing or with the action (or alleged action) that led to the complaint. Good policies are not by themselves enough to provide protection from charges. You may have to demonstrate that you have followed the policies. Good record keeping is critical. Other things being equal, the investigator is likely to respond favorably if management has good policies and procedures, good records indicating compliance with the policies and procedures, and good records documenting interactions with applicants and residents.

Chapter Four: Fair Housing Marketing and
                Advertising Requirements

36   Does the Fair Housing Act Impose Requirements on Marketing?

The goal of professional marketing is to reach the maximum number of potential customers in the most cost-effective way with the most effective messages. Professional apartment marketing must also be non-discriminatory. Under the Fair Housing Act it is illegal to:

> "make, print, or publish, or cause to be made, printed, or published any notice, statement, or advertisement with respect to the rental or sale of a dwelling that indicates any preference, limitation or discrimination because of race, color, religion, sex, handicap, familial status or national origin, or an intention to make any such preference, limitation or discrimination."[i]

Even if there is no evidence of discrimination in your admissions policies and practices, you could still be faced with a fair housing complaint based solely on the way in which your property is marketed. To avoid this possibility. You should:

See question 37.
• Be inclusive rather than exclusive in your marketing;

See question 38.
• Avoid 'red flag' words;

See question 39.
• Ensure proper use of the "Equal Housing Opportunity" logo, slogan and statement;

See question 40.
• Depict diverse individuals when using human models in your advertising; and,

See question 41.
• Display the Fair Housing Poster.

At the very least, review your entire marketing campaign to ensure that persons who are members of a protected class do not feel unwelcome.

---

i.   24 CFR Section 100.75(a)

There are no federal requirements, other than the general prohibition outlined above, that apply to advertising. At this point, HUD's advertising guidelines exist in two forms:

- The Code of Federal Regulations (24 CFR Part 109) contained guidelines on advertising and fair housing. This part of the Code was removed (effective May 1, 1996) in a Federal Register notice dated April 1, 1996.

- Memo from Roberta Achtenberg (then Assistant Secretary for Fair Housing and Equal Opportunity) dated January 9, 1995 and titled, "Guidance Regarding Advertisements under 804(c) of the Fair Housing Act."

The Fair Housing Poster is required, however, of all properties; see question 41. Federally regulated properties face additional requirements, addressed in Chapter 18.

Neither (the removed) Part 109 of the Code of Federal Regulations, nor the Achtenberg Memorandum are legally binding, and neither require any specific action regarding use of models, language, or the EHO logo. HUD refers to both documents as "guidance" and considers whether a housing provider has followed these guidelines in determining whether advertising is discriminatory. Courts of law, outside of HUD's jurisdiction, also consider whether this guidance has been followed in determining whether advertising is discriminatory.

37 What Are the Basic Fair Housing Considerations in Apartment Marketing?

See question 42 for leasing considerations.

Fair Housing Marketing should be inclusive rather than exclusive. Look at your complete marketing campaign and ask yourself these questions.

- Are we using a variety of media outlets that reach diverse groups in the community?

- Does our advertising campaign reach people who would want to live here and could afford the rent, regardless of their status as a member of a protected class? In practice, this generally means people who either live or work within a reasonable proximity of the property.

- Convey awareness of Fair Housing issues.

Before finalizing signs, brochures, flyers and advertisements, review design and content to determine if members of protected classes might take offense at something you might or might not say or imply. There are words and messages that are advisable to avoid in your marketing materials. Some subtle examples:

Examples of Discrimination in Advertising and Marketing

A property feels its competitive strength is in its fitness-related amenities and wants to market its exercise equipment, jogging trails, sauna and pool. It reasonably concludes that these amenities should be illustrated in the property's brochure. The result includes pictures of young adults running, swimming, jogging, and exercising happily. Although the models in the brochure are racially diverse, there are no children (families are a protected class), and no persons with disabilities (also protected). Some readers of the brochure will notice that certain classes of people are not represented, and may conclude that their absence is an intentional message that they are not welcome. The property should show that its fitness activities are available to all and in some manner accessible to all.

Another property finds that many of its residents attend the Catholic church across the street. The manager concludes that this proximity to the church has marketing value, and decides to give prominence to the church in the new brochure. The church is a backdrop in one of the photos, and the location of the property is billed as being, "across the street from the Catholic church." Because of the prominence given to the church, some readers might conclude that other faiths are not welcome (or as welcome) at the property. Discrimination on the basis of religion is prohibited under the Fair Housing Act and this property could face fair housing complaints.

Consistency

To the extent that your staff follow consistent procedures, give consistent answers, and present the property in consistent ways to all applicants, you are less likely to receive fair housing complaints. Perfect consistency is neither possible nor appropriate (after all, good leasing technique involves responding to each applicant's particular needs and interests), but reasonable consistency is achievable and advisable. It is recommended that non-leasing staff, such as maintenance or groundskeeping crews, either be equally well informed about the current operations of the property or be instructed to direct all questions to the appropriate leasing staff. Your best efforts at being consistent can be defeated if the maintenance technician incorrectly informs a prospective housing applicant that there are one-bedroom units available and the leasing staff correctly informs the applicant that no one-bedroom units are available.

38   Fair Housing Considerations for Advertising

Avoid "Red Flag" Words or Phrases

Managers always attempt to portray the property in ways that will appeal to prospective residents. Sometimes, managers choose wording that, although innocently intended, raises fair housing concerns. Here are some examples:

- *"An exclusive community"* – Meaning to convey that the property is desirable and preferred, uses a word ("exclusive") that literally means excluding those who are not wanted.

- *"Close to churches"* – Raising concerns that the property is not interested in renting to people who are not religiously observant, or to people whose religions don't involve "churches."

- *"Ideal for seniors"* – Raises concerns that the property isn't interested in renting to families with children. An exception would be for properties that are permitted to operate specifically as housing for seniors and that would then be marketed as such.

- *"For the active lifestyle"* – Intending to market fitness amenities, the property sends a different message to some persons with disabilities.

- *"Quiet, peaceful, restful community"* – This may raise concerns that the property is attempting to discourage applications from families with children.

- *"Latino neighborhood"* – This would raise concerns that the property is specifically for Latinos, to the exclusion of others.

Individual words descriptive of protected classes that may convey discriminatory intent are:

- Race specific references such as black, African-American, white, Hispanic, Asian or Asian-American;

- Color specific references such as white or black;

- Specific references to national origin such as Mexican-American or Russian;

- Specific references to religion such as Protestant or Christian; (Note however that advertisements that use the legal name of the property (e.g. Concord Catholic Home) or that advertise services on the property such as "provides Kosher meals" or use of certain non-secular terms like "Merry Christmas" are allowable.

- Indicators of gender are not permitted. For example, it would be inappropriate to advertise that an apartment is "perfect for a bachelor." However, words that are traditionally descriptive of apartment features, such as master-bedroom or mother-in-law suite, are allowable.

- A phrase such as "no wheelchairs" is not permitted; but terms like "walk-up," "jogging trails," or "great view" are. The general rule is that you may describe features of the apartments, but you should avoid referring to who would benefit from those features.

- References to resident characteristics such as adults, retired, singles or couples are not permitted as they may discourage families with children from applying. However, terms like "family room" are allowable.

Media Selection

Although it is important to ensure that your advertising doesn't contain any discriminatory statements or messages, it is also important to ensure that you communicate broadly and inclusively. Certain media outlets may be perceived as being associated with particular racial or ethnic groups. If you select media outlets that cater to specific segments of the population, you should have as part of your larger advertising campaign similar advertising that is directed to other groups and/or directed to a wider population. If you are uncertain whether the audience you will reach through a newspaper advertisement or radio commercial is sufficiently broad, ask for readership or listenership demographics before making your media selection. Your entire marketing campaign should be addressed towards and attractive to people who would want to live there and who are capable of affording the rent.

Media Selection Should be Broad and Inclusive

> *The Dunes Apartments is advertising solely in general-circulation media (consisting of the main local paper and the local apartment guide). It has experienced increased traffic and leases from the Russian immigrant community and based on this, it wants to do some targeted marketing to the Russian community. The Dunes may undertake this targeted marketing, but only if it also undertakes targeted marketing to other groups so that it's entire marketing approach is sufficiently broad and inclusive. To market exclusively to this community on a regular basis would demonstrate a preference for this group over others.*

Special Requirements for Federally Regulated Properties

If your property is required to prepare an Affirmative Fair Housing Marketing Plan (AFHMP) and the segment of the population that you are trying to reach is a heavily under-served population, the HUD approved plan may include marketing that is targeted to that specific group (to the exclusion of others).[ii] See question 157.

39 When and How Do You Use the EHO Logo, Statement or Slogan?

HUD guidelines require[iii] that all advertising for the sale, rental or financing (whether existing or planned new constructed) of residential housing contain an equal housing opportunity (EHO) logotype, statement or slogan.

EHO information should be included in all written or verbal advertisement including phone book ads, realtor signs, business

---

ii.   HUD Directive 8025.1, rev-2, 3-5, 3-8 and 3-12.

iii. The Guidelines "require" use of the logo as a best practice. When reviewing a case against a housing provider, the Department will consider whether its marketing activities are discriminatory, and the standard it will use in its consideration will be the extent to which those activities are consistent with HUD's Guidelines on advertising, see question 36.

cards, flyers, brochures, radio or television commercials, print advertisements (including newspapers and apartment shoppers guides) and the Internet.

Definitions and Examples

- The EHO Slogan reads: "Equal Housing Opportunity" or "EHO," depending on space available.

- The EHO Logo shows the graphic Fair Housing symbol:

EQUAL HOUSING
OPPORTUNITY

- The EHO Statement reads:

  "We are pledged to the letter and spirit of U.S. policy for the achievement of equal housing opportunity throughout the nation. We encourage and support an affirmative advertising and marketing program in which there are no barriers to obtaining housing because of race, color, religion, sex, handicap, familial status, or national origin."

See question 15.

You can change the language of the Statement to reflect additional protected classes in your area.

When to Use the EHO Slogan, Logo or Statement

In general, large ads, brochures and signs should use either the Statement or Logo, and smaller ads may use the Slogan. The size of the logo varies according to the size of the ad or sign, but it should be proportionally sized.

The HUD guidelines for the content and size of EHO Statements and Logos are as follows:

- Advertising of 4 column inches[iv] or less should include the Equal Housing Opportunity Slogan or a Statement that the housing advertised is available to all without regard to race, color, religion, sex, handicap, familial status or national ori-

---

iv. A "column inch" is the width of a standard newspaper column one inch long.

gin. Check to see if there are additional local protected classes.

- All other print advertising may include either an Equal Housing Opportunity Statement or an Equal Housing Opportunity Logo. Verbal advertising (voicemail recordings, radio commercials, etc.) should include the Statement.

- The site sign is advertising, and as such must include the Logo or Slogan.

Size and Placement of EHO Slogan, Logo or Statement

If the Statement is chosen, it should be clearly visible and in print size comparable to that used in the rest of the advertisement.

If the Logo is chosen, HUD provides the following size standards:

Size Standards for Use of the EHO Logo

Size of Ad	Size of Logo
½ page or larger	2" x 2"
⅛ page to ½ page	1" by 1"
4 column inches to ⅛ page	½" by ½"
Less than 4 column inches	Slogan not logo

If these sizes are not relevant (for example, for a small pamphlet, brochure or other advertisement), the EHO Logo should be of a size at least equal to other logotypes in the ad. If there are no other logos, the EHO Logo should be in bold display face that is clearly visible. If an EHO Statement is used instead, it should take up 3 to 5 percent of the ad.

Using the Slogan, Logo or Statement consistently may be instrumental in demonstrating to HUD or a court that your marketing campaign is not discriminatory. For this reason, experts recommend that you establish a company policy, or standard practice of using the EHO Slogan, Logo and Statement. Of course, these do not, by themselves, constitute a comprehensive fair housing marketing plan. In addition, as discussed above, your advertising campaign should make appropriate media selections, avoid 'red flag' wording, and if you use human models they should reflect appropriate diversity.

40   The Use of Human Models in Advertisements

The use of human models (generally, pictures or visual representations of people in any element of your marketing) can be a complex issue. Some housing providers have opted to discontinue the use of human models in marketing materials, while others seek legal guidance as a matter of practice.

See question 36.

The goal in proper use of human models is to ensure that you fairly represent different groups; thereby communicating that your property does not have a preference for one group over another.

When the courts and HUD receive a complaint based on advertising that is claimed to infer a preference for one group over another (protected) group they typically evaluate each individual advertisement in the advertising campaign, the overall advertising campaign for a particular property over a period of time, and the company's overall advertising campaign for all properties over a period of time. They will attempt to ascertain from this examination whether the campaign shows a "pattern" of discriminatory conduct. As stated in a legal case on the matter[v],

> *"The discriminatory character of an advertising campaign is often not self-evident, and the law does not automatically make every ad showing persons of only one race actionable. Only when enough ads have run to allow a pattern to emerge is a violation likely to become apparent."*

In evaluating whether advertising materials violate the Fair Housing Act, determine whether the ad suggests to an ordinary reader that a particular group is preferred or discouraged from the housing in question; would the ad discourage an ordinary reader of a particular (protected) group from answering it? These questions should be considered when you decide upon a particular format

---

v. *Tyus et al v. Urban Search Management*

for your advertising. There are a number of other considerations when you evaluate your overall advertising campaign:

- Are the human models in your ads fairly diverse or are they skewed to a particular group?

- Are the models in ads for your up-scale suburban property mainly white adults and the models in ads for your moderately priced urban property mostly minority families?

- Are you representing not only different races, but different age groups?

- Are you portraying families with children?

- Are people portrayed in equal social settings? It may not be perceived as an equal social setting if the residents are of one race and the service workers are of another.

How Extensive Should Diversity of Representation Be?

Managers need to take into consideration the demographic make-up of the geographic area in which the advertisement is to be placed and should be careful to ensure that the groups represented are reflective of that population and include members of protected classes.

Some state and local jurisdictions have additional laws on the type and placement of advertising. Become familiar with this information for all localities in which you market your properties.

41 What Is the Fair Housing Poster, and How Am I Required to Display It?

All multifamily rental properties must display the required Fair Housing poster[vi]. This poster states the basic requirements of the law, and informs the public about where they may file a complaint.

The poster must be "prominently displayed so as to be readily apparent to all persons seeking housing accommodations..."[vii] Generally, the poster is displayed in both the rental and leasing

---

vi. 24 CFR, Part 110
vii. 24 CFR Section 110.15

offices. The poster is available from regional and area offices of the U.S. Department of Housing and Urban Development.

The required poster is 11 by 14 inches, and appears below:

U.S. Department of Housing and Urban Development

**EQUAL HOUSING
OPPORTUNITY**

We Do Business in Accordance With the Federal Fair Housing Law

(The Fair Housing Amendments Act of 1988)

It is Illegal to Discriminate Against Any Person Because of Race, Color, Religion, Sex, Handicap, Familial Status, or National Origin

---

In the sale or rental of housing or residential lots

In advertising the sale or rental of housing

In the financing of housing

In the provision of real estate brokerage services

In the appraisal of housing

Blockbusting is also illegal

Anyone who feels he or she has been discriminated against may file a complaint of housing discrimination:
  1-800-669-9777 (Toll Free)
  1-800-927-9275 (TDD)

U.S. Department of Housing and Urban Development
Assistant Secretary for Fair Housing and Equal Opportunity
Washington, D.C. 20410

Previous editions are obsolete

form HUD-928.1A(8-93)

Chapter Five: Applicant Screening and Selection

42   Fair Housing Considerations for Apartment Leasing

There are two primary practices that should be followed to ensure compliance with the Fair Housing Act in your apartment leasing policies: consistency and accommodation.

Consistency

Consistent application of your leasing policies will minimize the risk that an applicant or resident will perceive illegal discrimination.

If a member of a protected class receives information that deters them from leasing an apartment at your property and this information is in fact incorrect, there may be a perception that the information was deliberately misleading in order to discourage the application.

In many instances inaccurate information is provided to applicants for discriminatory reasons—precisely the type of activity that the Fair Housing Act was intended to address. Inaccurate information is also given to applicants when a rental office is not operated in a professional or organized way; for example:

- *The office is disorganized and information is in disarray.* Pricing information is not clear, even to employees who are trying to provide the right information. As a consequence, different applicants receive different information.

- *Too many employees are involved in providing information.* Even with good systems and accessible information, when too many people are providing information, it is inevitable that information will not be consistent.

- *Don't overlook the role of your maintenance staff.* They should either be kept as regularly informed as your leasing staff or should be instructed to direct all inquiries concerning the leasing of apartments to the leasing staff.

See question 33 for more on testers, and 37 for additional information on the importance of consistency in leasing.

When a fair housing agency investigates a complaint by sending testers, and each tester receives different information on apartment availability, or different treatment in general, it is likely that a claim of discrimination will be filed with HUD, regardless of whether the discrimination was intended, or was the result of disorganized management operations.

Accommodation

You are obligated to make reasonable accommodations to enable applicants with disabilities to have equal opportunity to apply and be considered for leasing an apartment. You can't inquire into the nature or severity of a disability, but once an applicant has requested that you accommodate his or her disability, you do have the right to verify the existence of the disability and that the disability would be addressed effectively by the proposed reasonable accommodation.

Reasonable accommodations during the preliminary leasing process might include:

- Offering to read materials that normally are provided in written form (for visually impaired applicants);

- Offering to provide in written form materials that are normally provided orally (for hearing impaired applicants);

For other examples of accommodations, see Chapter 11.

- Allowing the applicant to take the application home and return it later (for applicants with disabilities that affect their ability to read, write or understand) even though your normal policy is that applicants have to complete the application during the initial interview.

The obligation to make reasonable accommodations exists throughout all stages of the leasing process, from the initial contact with an applicant to their continuing occupancy as a resident of your property.

See questions 64 and 65.

Expert managers advise communicating your commitment to accessibility in a way that encourages applicants and residents with disabilities to request the accommodations they need.

43   Fair Housing Considerations for Applicant Screening

Neutrality. Consistency. Reasonable Accommodation.

All aspects of your resident selection criteria should be geared towards assessing the likelihood that the applicant will (1) pay the rent on time and in full; and (2) adhere to the other terms of the lease. These generally include: respecting the rights of neighbors, avoiding undue wear and tear on the apartment, maintaining it in good condition and refraining from criminal activity. A manager may reject an applicant for either a history of prior non-payment or a history of prior lease violations as long as he or she does not discriminate on the basis of race, color, religion, sex, familial status, national origin, disability or locally protected classes, if any.

Neutrality

Make certain that your criteria are neutral and do not affect an applicant by virtue of membership in a protected class. Once you've ensured that your criteria are neutral, then take steps to ensure that they are applied consistently.

Consistency

Your screening process should use the same set of criteria for all applicants. These criteria should be applied consistently. By reviewing each application against the same criteria, all applicants receive equal consideration. If you do more thorough background checks on the housekeeping histories of families with children (vs. single applicants), your practices are discriminatory.

See question 9 for the definition of disparate impact.

However, special screening procedures may be permissible for certain categories of applicants who are not members of a protected class. For example, you may have additional screening for students, provided students do not disproportionately represent members of a protected class. While age is not a federally protected class, requiring home visits on elderly applicants might be viewed as discriminatory to persons with disabilities, since elderly persons have a higher rate of mobility impairments than the general population.

Expert managers have learned that certain practices are more likely to result in consistency, for example:

- *Have all screening done by one person.* This prevents inconsistencies that might occur as a result of different interpretations and applications of established criteria.

- *Use standard forms whenever possible.* Using standard forms will increase the likelihood that each applicant receives the same consideration. Further, used properly they will document the fairness of your own practices, should you ever need to prove this.

- *Use objective criteria whenever possible.* If you remove opinion and subjectivity, you are more likely to treat all applicants equally.

- *Follow written standards for processing applications.*

Reasonable Accommodation

Provide reasonable accommodations in screening. Make certain that your screening requirements, including the procedures for actually submitting an application, do not discriminate against persons with disabilities.

An Example of Reasonable Accommodation in Screening

> *Your screening criteria require applicants to have a history of timely rent payment. An applicant appears who has a rental history marked by frequent late rent payments. The applicant requests, as a reasonable accommodation, that you consider mitigating circumstances. This applicant previously lived in a place where rent had to be paid in person, at an office that was not accessible and therefore the applicant had to rely on another person to take the check to the rental office. Hence, it tended to be late. Your rent is to be paid at an office that is accessible (or you'll accept the check by mail) so this will no longer be a problem.*

Requiring Additional Information

In some cases, you may require additional information from an applicant to determine eligibility because the applicant may have an unconventional credit or rental history. In most cases, it is best to establish this procedure directly on your rental application. For instance, ask, "If you don't have at least X years rental history please describe where you have lived for the last X years and what, if any, financial arrangements you had while living there."

Generally, your screening criteria should allow for the pursuit of additional information by (1) specifically determining when additional information may be sought, (2) how it should be obtained, and (3) how it should be factored into the determination of eligibility. As with other aspects of screening, however, you must be certain that any requirements for additional information are applied consistently, and are neutral (i.e., do not have a specific impact on any member of a protected class). For example, you have a (written) screening policy that allows you to accept personal references in lieu of landlord references, *if* the applicant has insufficient rental history.

When your screening criteria stipulate that you should request additional information, make certain that these requirements are related to the issues of the individual applicant's likelihood of (1) paying the rent and (2) abiding by the lease terms. Make certain that requirements for additional information are not triggered merely because the applicant is a member of a protected class. Make certain that any additional requirements are applied consistently.

The Application Process

The purpose of the application process is to screen out unqualified applicants (i.e., those unlikely to abide by the terms of the lease and pay the rent). No aspect of your application process should have the effect of either discouraging a qualified applicant from pursuing the application or rejecting an applicant who is qualified.

The type of information requested during the applicant screening process must, of course, be consistent and neutral to membership in a protected class. Similarly, the application process must also be consistent and neutral. However, variations from your standard procedure (reasonable accommodations) may be required in order to accommodate a candidate with disabilities.

44 Can Informally Obtained Information Be Used in the Screening Process?

The short, definitive answer is NO. Many properties repeatedly run into this problem. It may seem like "common sense" for a manager to consider information obtained from informal sources in an attempt to more fully screen applicants. However, the use of any information not obtained through the normal screening process opens a hornet's nest of potential fair housing issues. Your screening process has to be designed so as to maximize your ability to get the truest and most complete information about the applicant, which is relevant to the application. One purpose of a well-designed screening process is to keep the decision making process fair and nondiscriminatory. Gossip or other inside information, no matter how reliable it seems, is most likely discriminatory because it is not obtained equally for all applicants. For example, a person who has resided in a community for some time would most likely have an informal reputation, which could be used against him or her, but a newcomer to the area would not.

Professional managers are very careful to ensure that only information obtained through the normal screening process is relied upon when deciding to accept or reject an application.

45 Can a History of Non-lease Compliant Behavior Be a Cause for Rejection (or Eviction) Even If the Conduct Is a Manifestation of a Disability?

Different considerations may apply depending on whether the case involves an application for housing or the continuation of an existing tenancy.

Prior Misconduct by an Applicant

In many cases it may be difficult, if not impossible, for a leasing agent to determine whether the prior misconduct of the applicant with a known disability (1) occurred because of the applicant's disability and, if it did (2) is something that is likely to continue and, if so (3) can be addressed through a reasonable accommodation by the property.

The prohibition against probing into the nature and extent of an applicant's disability makes it difficult to determine if prior violations are a product of a disability, and whether they are likely to recur.

Considerations in Rejecting An Applicant With a History of Disruptive Conduct

Also see question 90 for a discussion of "direct threat."

Suppose the applicant's previous lease was terminated because the applicant frequently engaged in disruptive behavior that interfered with the ability of other residents to quietly enjoy the property. This behavior may have resulted from the applicant's mental disability, but a leasing agent may not know this when reviewing the application.

In addition, the agent should be aware that accepting this application, despite the previous misconduct, might impose a responsibility on the housing provider to take steps to ensure that the applicant does not again interfere with the rights of other residents to quietly enjoyment of the property.

In these circumstances, if nothing more is known than that the applicant has a history of disruptive behavior, it should be safe to reject the application on the ground that all the information that can be legitimately obtained strongly suggests that the applicant will not observe the requirements of the lease.

On the other hand, suppose the applicant voluntarily discloses information about the circumstances surrounding the misconduct, revealing for example (1) the existence of a disability, (2) that the medication he was taking at the time was not effective in controlling the disruptive behavior; and (3) that he has now switched medications and there are no more behavioral problems. Furthermore, he produces credible written medical evidence that confirms these facts. To reject the applicant because of the prior misconduct in those circumstances could conceivably lead to a charge of discrimination on the basis of disability.

HUD regulated properties should also see question 150.

Some experts recommend notifying applicants in the rejection notice of their right to request a reasonable accommodation (though this is not required under the Fair Housing Act). If an applicant then requests an accommodation, he or she will likely reveal the details of the situation.

Misconduct by an Existing Occupant	The case of misconduct by an existing occupant with a known disability is more clear-cut. There are several legal decisions stating that if the lease non-compliance is due to the resident's disability, there is a duty to try to accommodate the disability before taking eviction action. The housing provider is required to take steps to accommodate the non-compliant behavior, as soon as it is known to be a manifestation of the resident's disability.

46 May an Owner Deny Occupancy to a Member of a Protected Class Based Upon the Fact That No One in the Household Is of "Legal Age"?

If an applicant is not of legal age to enter into a binding contract (such as a Lease Agreement), occupancy may be refused on that basis, regardless of the applicant's status as a member of a protected class. "Age" is not a protected class under the Fair Housing Act (though it is under some state's fair housing laws).

Providers must be aware of, and consistently adhere to, the precise provisions of applicable state or local law as regards age limitations for engaging in certain types of activity. In some localities housing may be refused on the basis of the applicant's age, without any qualification. In others, there may be significant qualifications; for instance, a person under "legal age" who is married, who is enlisted in the Armed Forces, or who has obtained a court order declaring him or her to be an "emancipated individual" may be able to enter into a legally binding contract, despite being "under age."

Consistent adherence to state or local laws or customs with respect to contracts for the rental of housing would not be assumed to be in violation of the Fair Housing Act or federal regulations.

47 Fair Housing Considerations for the Use of Criminal Background Checks

See question 43 for general applicant screening considerations. Federally regulated properties should also see question 161 for additional considerations when conducting criminal background checks.

If you are using, or considering using, criminal background checks as part of your resident screening procedures, expert managers recommend that these checks be applied consistently to all applicants at a property. They caution against applying the checks selectively, even if you suspect that a particular applicant has a checkered past, or as an additional screening criteria. Note, however, that some managers recommend an alternative strategy. They advocate placing a question on your application that asks whether the applicant or other adult household member has any criminal convictions. Considerations to include in the use of background checks are:

- Managers must get written consent from an applicant before undertaking a criminal background check. Even where such checks are required (for example in public housing) the applicant must give his or her signed consent for this information to be released.

- If you run criminal background checks, you should do so on all adult members of each household. Otherwise, a household might list the member without such a record as the head of household.

- Be extremely careful about using criminal background checks at only some properties in your portfolio. The level of existing criminal activity at a particular property or in a particular neighborhood may be a reasonable justification. However, if you perform criminal background checks at a single property due to the level of crime there, be sure that all other properties in your portfolio with an equivalent level of crime also use the same background checks.

- Use criminal background checks as a part of your screening process only after you have established clear procedures for their use. Apply them consistently to all applicants.

- Use written standards when reviewing the results of criminal background checks. The type of crime and how long ago it was committed may be taken into consideration in your decision making process.

- Written screening criteria for criminal background checks should focus on the terms of your lease and whether the applicant's criminal history would cause a reasonable person to doubt the applicant will adhere to the lease. For example, convictions of most violent crimes, especially if committed recently, would lead you to reject based on a lease clause that prohibits any activity that interferes with the peaceful enjoyment of the premises by other residents. Similarly, drug-related convictions would raise the issue of observance of a lease clause prohibiting drug-related activity. Expert managers advise that any rejection for past criminal behavior should be related to the lease terms, and these decisions are more likely to be upheld by the courts.

- If you can't make a reasonable connection between the offense and the requirements for residing at your property, then you should probably not reject. For example, there is no logical connection between having been convicted of driving under the influence of alcohol and being unable or unwilling to abide by the terms of a residential lease. To reject an applicant because of such a conviction could lead to a charge of illegal discrimination if the applicant is a member of a protected class. The goal always is to avoid the perception that the reason given for rejection is really based on membership of a protected class rather than the past criminal conviction.

- Owners and managers should not assume that courts will uphold rejection decisions that are based on information on arrests and pending charges.

- Consistency of rejections is also important. Make certain that you do not reject one applicant for a criminal record, and then fail to reject another applicant with a similar record. Keep a log of rejections, and review each one against your own history of rejections.

48 How Should Applicants Without Rental/Credit Histories Be Processed?

The purpose of investigating an applicant's rental and credit history is to provide you with some indication of the applicant's ability to (1) pay the rent in full and on time, and (2) adhere to the other terms of the lease. These include respecting the rights of the neighbors, avoiding undue wear and tear on the apartment and refraining from criminal activity. Some members of protected classes may not have a traditional rental history. Examples could be an individual who was hospitalized because of chronic mental illness or someone who has been in a residential drug/alcohol rehabilitation facility. If your application form asks a question about gaps in a rental history and asks what the housing arrangements were during that time you should have enough additional information to assess and process the application

Other means of assessing an application where information is not consistently available might include considering employment history or references, the applicant's involvement in civic activities, or statements from neutral, credible professionals who are knowledgeable about the applicant.

Experience has shown that higher risks of lease violations are posed by:

- Applicants who have never had primary responsibility for their housing, and

- Applicants whose current and prior housing situation is different from your apartment environment.

With those applicants there is greater uncertainty in predicting whether the applicant will abide by all the terms of the lease. When assessing an application, housing providers may take into account the differences between the applicant's previous housing history and the rental environment offered by your property.

Chapter Six: Occupancy Standards

Copyright, 2000 NAHMA and Compass Group

49   Owner's Right To Set Occupancy Limits

Federally assisted properties should also refer to Chapter 17 for questions that address the occupancy requirements of these properties.

Property managers and owners may set reasonable limits on the number of persons that may occupy a rental dwelling covered by the Fair Housing Act. Nothing contained in the Act limits the applicability of any reasonable local, state or federal restrictions regarding the maximum number of occupants permitted to occupy a dwelling.[i] The question of what constitutes a "reasonable" maximum occupancy standard is, however, one on which tenant advocates and housing providers have not yet reached consensus.   This is a complex and rapidly evolving area of fair housing practice. Because the imposition of maximum occupancy standards often has the effect of excluding families of a certain size from renting dwellings, housing providers are advised to obtain the advice of counsel regarding decisions on such standards in order to reduce the likelihood that these standards will be found to be discriminatory.

See question 55 for additional information on the relationship between occupancy standards and discrimination on the basis of familial status.

Owners and managers may adopt reasonable occupancy requirements for each unit-type based upon factors such as the size and number of sleeping areas, and the overall size of the dwelling relative to household size. Such requirements must be applied to all households and may not unreasonably limit or exclude opportunities to obtain rental housing by families with children. Because families with children are most likely to be adversely affected by the imposition of occupancy standards, challenges to those standards usually arise from claims of discrimination on the basis of familial status. Many of these challenges stem from restrictive maximum occupancy standards that have the effect of excluding families with children from the property. It may be held in such cases that the occupancy standard is not reasonable and is in reality a device to discriminate against families with children.

See Attachment B.

A March 20, 1991 Memorandum from HUD's General Counsel (known generally as the Keating Memorandum) contains the most widely accepted guidance on acceptable occupancy standards. HUD indicated in that Memorandum that, in general, a standard of two persons per bedroom may be considered reasonable, depending upon the size of the dwelling and the number

---

i.   42 USC 3607 Section 807 (1)

and type of rooms it contains, and taking into account a number of additional factors. On December 18, 1998 HUD adopted this Memo[ii] as its official policy for use in resolving fair housing complaints in which occupancy standards are called unreasonable and therefore discriminatory. Housing providers should note, however, that in many areas, state and local agencies handle fair housing enforcement, and these agencies are not required to follow HUD's policy on occupancy standards. In these cases, following the Keating Memorandum guideline may not render an occupancy standard immune from challenge on the ground that it discriminates against families with children.

Many apartment units are of modest size, with relatively small sleeping areas, and do not include dens. For these units, a maximum occupancy standard of two persons per bedroom should satisfy the Fair Housing Act test of "reasonableness" and would be consistent with HUD guidelines and practices. For some of these units, a more restrictive occupancy standard might be appropriate, based on other relevant property-specific conditions (for instance, health and safety issues that are affected by the property's infrastructure such as the capacity of utility systems and considerations of the residents' comfort based on the size of recreational facilities, adequacy of parking, and other factors). For units that are larger, have larger sleeping areas, or include dens, a less restrictive standard might be appropriate.

Experienced housing providers advise that, to reduce the likelihood of a challenge on the ground of familial status discrimination, occupancy standards should refer to the number of persons permitted to occupy a dwelling, not to the number of adults versus children.

50   Occupancy Guidelines

The following questions should help you to establish the appropriate occupancy standards for your property:

*   Do any state, county or city laws regulate occupancy standards?

---

ii.   *Federal Register,* December 18, 1998, at 63 FR 70256-70257

- What are the building codes for your state, county and city?

- What are the laws established by your state, county or city health department regarding occupancy standards, if any?

When you have this information, you should be able to develop a chart with the apartment sizes your property has, with assignments of the maximum number of occupants for each apartment type. Review this with your legal counsel before adopting it as your policy.

51   Owner's Occupancy Limits vs. Local Law

Some states and localities have adopted various codes that govern the maximum number of persons who may occupy a dwelling unit.

In general, a housing provider's occupancy standards should not permit *greater* occupancy than the local codes, as this would place the property in violation of the local code. You may, however, provide for *lower* levels of occupancy than the local codes, but in doing so there may be a greater risk of having the standard declared "unreasonable" by a court, should it be challenged. Courts consider a variety of factors in deciding whether or not an occupancy standard is reasonable, including a comparison between the owner's standard and the standard set by any applicable law or code. If the owner's standard is more restrictive then it may be more difficult to prove that that standard is reasonable and therefore not discriminatory towards families with children.

An Example of Occupancy Standards and Discrimination on the Basis of Familial Status

* HUD v Ineichen
HUDALJ 05-93-0143-1

> *In one case* a property owner adopted more restrictive occupancy standards than the applicable local and state laws. He refused to rent his three-bedroom townhouse to a married couple and their four children on the ground that he would not allow more than four people to occupy the unit. Despite the fact that he subsequently rented the unit to a married couple and their two children (suggesting that he was neither "anti-family" nor "anti-children") the judge held that this occupancy policy was unreasonable and was discriminatory in that it denied a rental unit based on familial status and also applied differential terms and conditions based on familial status. The judge also noted that the existence of more liberal local or state occupancy laws would tend to undermine an argument that a landlord's more restrictive occupancy standards are in fact reasonable. This suggests that if a landlord intends to adopt a more restrictive occupancy standard he or she will need to provide very compelling evidence to justify it.*

See question 49.

It is likely that a maximum occupancy standard that conforms to the HUD Keating Memorandum would not be successfully challenged. However, make certain that your standard is appropriate to your own property.

Each lease agreement should specify the maximum number of occupants permitted in the particular unit so that if the number is exceeded after the commencement of the lease, appropriate eviction or relocation action can be taken.

Consistency in the application of your occupancy standards is also critical. Once developed and instituted, any uneven application of the standard could expose your property to charges of discrimination by the persons who are adversely affected.

52 Is There a National Occupancy Standard?

No. The closest thing to a National Occupancy Standard is HUD's Keating Memorandum. As stressed before, these are guidelines, not standards, and adherence to them is entirely discretionary.

Individual states have also passed legislation governing occupancy standards, but these apply only to the particular state.

Chapter Seven: Familial Status Definitions and
                   Requirements

---

53   What Does "Familial Status" mean?

The term "familial status" refers to the condition of being part of a household that includes a child or children, actual or anticipated. Discrimination on the basis of "familial status" means discriminating against applicants or residents, on the ground that the household of which they are a part includes or will include a child or children. The prohibition against this type of discrimination was instituted in the Fair Housing Amendments Act of 1988 primarily to curtail the widespread problem of owners either refusing to rent their property to families with children or restricting families with children in the use and enjoyment of facilities at the property.

54   Who Is Protected Under The Familial Status Provisions of the Fair Housing Amendments Act?

The categories of households that are protected are:

• Households including one or more persons under the age of 18 who live with a parent or other adult who has custody of them or has been designated by the parent to have custody of them;

• Pregnant women;

• Foster families;

• Persons in the process of adopting an individual who is under the age of 18; and

• Households in the process of securing legal custody of an individual who is under the age of 18.

See questions 59 and 184. Certain housing specially designated for "older persons" is excluded from the familial status non-discrimination provisions of the Act, but the exemption is narrow.

55   Examples of Familial Status Discrimination

Illegal discrimination based on familial status may take the form of:

- Refusing to rent, sell, show, or finance a dwelling unit to a household with children, a pregnant woman, or a household that anticipates obtaining custody of a child.

- Requiring families with children to meet additional requirements or pay additional fees not required of others.

- Imposing any conditions or restrictions on the use of a dwelling or housing-related facility, applicable only to families with children.

- Making facilities unavailable to families with children.

- Making, printing or publishing or causing to be made printed or published any notice, statement or advertisement with respect to the sale or rental of a dwelling that indicates preference, limitation or discrimination based on familial status.

- Creating unfair barriers to occupancy by families with children.

- Restricting families with children to certain buildings or to certain units within a building.

The following are examples of conduct that is prohibited by the Fair Housing Amendments Act:

- A landlord tells Ms. Jones that there are no vacant units, when there are such units, because Ms. Jones has children.

- A property is advertised for rent stating "mature couple/ mature person" preferred.

- A landlord suggests that Ms. Jones may not be happy living in a property because so few families with children live there.

- A landlord asks Ms. Jones to pay a greater security deposit or a higher monthly rent than is asked of a resident who does not have children (or who has fewer children than Ms. Jones).

- A landlord limits the use of facilities such as swimming pools to adults only (rather than allowing children to use the pools with proper supervision which is a reasonable rule).

- Ms. Jones' housing choices are restricted to a certain section of a property or to certain units (even though other units for which she qualifies are also available) because that is where other families with children live.

- A landlord of a high-rise property refuses to rent to Ms. Jones because the landlord feels the children may not be safe there.

- An owner refuses to rent her property to a family with a child because the property has a swimming pool and she's concerned about liability.

- An owner refuses to rent his property to a family with a child because the property has lead-based paint.

- An owner requires families with children to sign waivers of liability that are not required of others.

See questions 49 and 50.

In general, policies or practices (including overly restrictive occupancy standards) that unfairly limit the opportunities for families with children to rent a dwelling unit or to have full enjoyment of facilities or services available to other residents are violations of the Fair Housing Amendments Act.

See Chapter 6 for a discussion of "Occupancy Standards."

It is clear that intentional discrimination against protected classes is prohibited. However, an action taken in good faith may result in a finding of discrimination if it has an unintended discriminatory effect. A common example of this is when a seemingly neutral maximum occupancy standard has the effect of excluding families with children. In fact many allegations of discrimination on the basis of familial status arise from a refusal to rent because the owner has deemed the applicant's family to be too large for the size of the dwelling unit.

56 Can I Refuse To Rent My Property to a Household With Children on the Ground that Some Aspect of the Property's Condition Makes it Unsafe for Children?

See question 59 for exemptions for elderly properties.

No. Unless your property is exempted from the provision against discrimination on the basis of familial status (i.e., is an "elderly property"); you cannot exclude households on the basis of familial status. You will need to immediately correct the deficiencies or conditions at your property that make it unsafe for children.

The decision whether to live in a high-rise building, near a busy street, far from play areas, etc. is for the family to make, not the housing provider. HUD's Counsel has said[i] that under some circumstances property owners may tell prospective residents about perceived hazards at the property without breaching the Fair Housing Act; however, such information must not be misleading or discouraging and must not have the effect of steering families away from the property. In other words, the provider may inform parents of possible dangers but must make it clear that the family will not be excluded nor will the terms, privileges or conditions respecting their occupancy of the dwelling be affected because of those dangers.

In one case[*] a landlord refused to rent an apartment to a woman who was six months pregnant because it was suspected that the apartment contained lead-based paint. Because of the suspected presence of this paint it was the landlord's policy not to rent to families with children under 6 years old. The applicant complained that she was discriminated against on the basis of familial status. The court ruled that such discrimination had occurred since health and economic considerations (it was estimated that it would cost the landlord between $26,400 and $60,000 to de-lead the property)— were not exceptions to the rule against discrimination on the basis of familial status. In another case of discrimination on the basis of familial status the Administrative Law Judge wrote "...nothing in the Fair Housing Act permits the owner of rental property to determine that his property per se presents unacceptable risks to the health, safety and welfare of children. That decision is for the prospective tenant/parent to make."[†] In other words there is no "unsafe for children" exemption to the Fair Housing Act's familial status discrimination prohibitions.

[*]   HUD v DiBari HUDALJ 01-90-0511-1
[†]   HUD v Schmid HUDALJ 02-98-0276-8

i.   Directive Number GME-0010 "Fair Housing Act Enforcement: Safety issues as defenses to familial status discrimination"

57 Can I Impose Rules Limiting the Use by Children of Certain Facilities at My Property?

Yes, if the limitations relate to the health and safety of children and are reasonable. Examples of restrictions that apply only to children, that have been allowed by HUD, include:

- Prohibiting children under 18 from using a swimming pool unless accompanied by a parent.[ii]

- Excluding children from a utility building containing water pumps, shutoff valves and electrical units unless accompanied by a parent.[iii]

- Prohibiting children under 14 from using a pool or clubhouse without an adult and prohibiting children between 14 and 18 from using the billiard room without a parent.[iv]

Generally, in order for restrictions or prohibitions to be considered acceptable and non-discriminatory, the perceived danger must be real, and the rules must be a reasonable means to provide for the health and safety of both the facilities and residents.

An example of a rule that HUD has deemed impermissible (because there was no justifiable health and safety reason for it) is a rule restricting children from using swimming pools at certain hours.[v]

58 Are There Additional or Special Requirements for Terminating the Lease of a Household With Children?

Generally, no. Households with children are required to observe all the obligations of the lease to the same extent as childless households. Failure to do so will entitle the landlord to terminate the lease in accordance with the relevant provisions. For example, if the behavior of an occupant's child or children is such that

---

ii. Fernandes v Kastes Case No. 04-89-0350-1
iii. HUD v Gugliemi, Fair Housing-Fair Lending (P-H) 25,004 at 25076
iv. HUD v Murphy, Fair Housing-Fair Lending (P-H) 25002 at 25053
v.   Directive Number GME-0012 "Use of Recreational Facilities by Children"

it interferes with the quiet enjoyment of other residents, the lease can be terminated for that reason because, "[w]hile the Act protects families with children from discrimination, it does not afford them a license to act unreasonably or irresponsibly."[vi]

In the event that a charge of discrimination on the basis of familial status is made, it would be wise to have documented the instances of misconduct and complaints about it from other residents, and to have given the resident written warning(s).

Of course, lease provisions must be neutral to the presence of children; instituting requirements that are more likely to result in violations by (and consequences to) families with children could be found to be discriminatory.

59 Familial Status Exemptions for Elderly Properties

The Fair Housing Act provides that certain properties for older persons can exclude children from residency without being liable for discrimination on the basis of familial status. However, expert owners and managers advise exercising caution in excluding children from elderly properties because:

- Many properties' legal documents prohibit excluding children (federally-insured mortgage loans generally contain such a provision and properties subject to these provisions may not exclude families with children, regardless of whether they otherwise meet the exemptions in the Fair Housing Act).

- Sometimes, elderly households wish to add grandchildren to their households. A no-children policy would prohibit this.

Owners and managers of properties designed and operated for older persons may exclude families with children in accordance with general exemptions specified in the Fair Housing Act. These include:

- *62 or Over* – Housing intended for, and occupied solely by, persons 62 and over is exempt from the Fair Housing Act's prohibitions against discrimination on the basis of familial

---

vi. HUD v Ludwig 05-93-1324-1, per William C. Cregar, *Administrative Law Judge* status.[vii] A property qualifies as "62 or over" housing if *all* occupants of the household, who became residents after September 12, 1988, are 62 years old or older.

- *55 or Over* – Housing intended and operated for households comprised of at least one person 55 years of age or older, per unit,[viii] is exempt. In order to qualify, at least 80% of the units must be so occupied. See below for additional discussion.

- *State and Federal Elderly Housing Programs* – Housing operated under a federal or state housing program that the Secretary of HUD has determined is specifically designed and operated to assist elderly persons.[ix]

Note however, that HUD has a policy of refusing to designate any HUD-assisted or HUD-insured property as exempt from the Fair Housing Act's familial status provisions.[x] Therefore, families with children may not be expressly excluded from any federal housing program. In practice though, all applicants to federal housing programs must meet standard eligibility criteria. In some federal elderly housing programs, because of minimum age requirements for occupancy, this has the effect of excluding families with children.

"Significant Facilities and Services Designated for the Elderly"

As originally written, the Fair Housing Act required properties that sought the 55 or over exemption to "provide significant facilities and services designated for the elderly." The Housing for Older Persons Act of 1995 amended the Fair Housing Act, and removed this requirement.[xi]

The Policies and Procedures Requirement

Language requiring policies and procedures consistent with the operation of elderly housing were removed from the HUD Fair Housing regulations and supplanted by identical requirements under the Housing for Older Persons Act (HOPA) of 1995. The HOPA policies and procedures requirement has been reaffirmed in one legal case, and the original factors covering the policies

---

vii. 24 CFR, Section 100.303
viii. 24 CFR Section 100.304 (Section 807(b)(2)(c) as amended by the Housing for Older Persons Act of 1995 (42 U.S.C. Section 3607(b)(2)(C).)
ix. 24 CFR, Section 100.302
x. HUD Handbook 4350.3 CHG 24 2-5(e)
xi. Federal Register 61-FR-14378, April 1, 1996

and procedures requirement are still relevant in establishing the property's intention to provide housing for persons aged 55 and older.[xii] For this reason these factors should not be ignored, even though they have not been placed into the (amended) regulations implementing the Fair Housing Act. They are:

- The housing facility's written rules and regulations;

- The manner in which the housing is described to prospective residents;

- The nature of advertising;

- Age verification procedures;

- Lease provisions;

- The actual practices of the management in enforcing the relevant rules and regulations.

**Documen-
tation and
Age Verifi-
cation for
Properties
Claiming the
55 or Over
Exemption**

Whenever a household is excluded from residency on the ground that it includes a minor child, a complaint of discrimination on the basis of familial status may be made. The housing provider must then prove that the 80% requirement was satisfied when the refusal to rent occurred. Housing providers, therefore, should maintain accurate and current files containing copies of residents' driver's licenses, birth certificates or other identity documents that verify their ages. When residents vacate the premises, the impact on the 80% requirement must also be assessed.

The pitfalls of not maintaining such documentation were demonstrated in one case where a housing provider claimed the 55 and over exemption as a defense to a charge of discrimination on the basis of familial status.[xiii] The Administrative Law Judge who heard the case ruled that the evidence presented to support the claim was insufficient.

Accurate records of all residents' ages should be maintained because this will also provide evidence that there has been a consistent policy of limiting residence to persons 55 years of age and older. In the case referred to above, the failure to consistently

---

xii. Simovits v The Chanticleer Condominium Association 933 F. Supp. 1394 (N.D. ILL 1996)
xiii. HUD v Tems HUD ALJ 04-91-0064-1 & HUD ALJ 04-91-0066-1

document the ages of residents also weighed heavily against the claim that the property was intended for occupancy by those aged 55 years or older.

In order to establish and maintain housing for older persons status, it is important that the lease or other agreement governing occupancy stipulate that minor children are not permitted to reside at the property. Further, it may be advisable to provide that if residents decide to have a child reside with them, they will move out from the property. HUD has even allowed what was referred to as a "pregnancy" clause in a lease i.e., a clause stating that if a female resident becomes pregnant, the resident will vacate the dwelling by the time the child is born.[xiv]

Providers who wish to claim exempt status for their properties on the ground that they are providing housing for the elderly are advised to seek advice from professionals who are well acquainted with the requirements of the Fair Housing Act.

---

xiv. Directive Number GME-0006 "Exemptions for Housing for Older Persons"

Chapter Eight: Fair Housing and Persons With Disabilities

60 Which Fair Housing Laws Protect Persons With Disabilities?

See question 61 for definitions, and question 63 for examples of prohibited practices.

Title VIII of The Civil Rights Act of 1968, as Amended in 1988 ("The Fair Housing Act") - The Fair Housing Act applies to all apartment properties except for certain small properties. An "individual with handicap," or with a "record of" such an impairment, or who is "regarded as" having such an impairment, is protected by the Fair Housing Act from discriminatory housing practices.

See question 13.

Americans With Disabilities Act ("ADA") - Title III of the ADA prohibits discrimination on the basis of disability at business locations; for apartments, Title III generally requires that the rental office and other on-site business locations used by the public be accessible. Title II of the ADA which prohibits discrimination on the basis of disability in all programs, activities and services of public entities, applies to public housing.

See questions 108 and 110, and Chapters 14 and 15.

Section 504 of the Rehabilitation Act of 1973 ("Section 504") - Section 504 imposes additional requirements on properties receiving "federal financial assistance"

61 What Is the Fair Housing Act Definition of Handicap or Disability?

"Individual with Handicap"

Under the Fair Housing Act, an "individual with handicap" is defined as:

> *"Any person who has a physical or mental impairment that substantially limits one or more major life activities; has a record of such an impairment; or is regarded as having such an impairment."*

A number of further definitions are required in order to interpret the basic definition given above:

"Physical Impairment"

The term "physical impairment" is defined as:

> *"Any physiological disorder or condition, cosmetic disfigurement, or anatomical loss affecting any of the major body sys-*

tems (the regulations contain a complete list).[i] This category includes persons testing HIV positive, whether or not they are asymptomatic of AIDS."

"Mental Impairment"

The term "mental impairment" is defined as:

"Any mental or psychological disorder." Examples of mental impairment include: mental retardation, organic brain syndrome, emotional or mental illness, specific learning disabilities, autism, epilepsy and cerebral palsy. The 'mental impairment' category includes alcoholics and recovering drug addicts."

"Major Life Activities"

The term "major life activities" is defined as:

"Functions such as caring for one's self, performing manual tasks, walking, seeing, hearing, speaking, breathing, learning and working."

"Record of"

The term "record of" means that the person has a history of having a covered impairment, even if the person is not currently impaired, and even if the history is incorrect.

"Regarded as"

The term "regarded as" having an impairment means having an impairment that does not substantially limit a major life activity but that is perceived by a housing provider or others as doing so. The perception of the provider is a key element. For example:

- A person with a disfiguring birthmark, or severe burns, may be regarded as disabled even though the condition does not limit the ability to perform basic life activities.

- A person may be misclassified as retarded despite the fact that he or she is fully capable of performing basic life activities.

- A person may be regarded as disabled because he or she is receiving medical treatment for an impairment (despite the fact that the impairment which is being treated is not severe enough to meet the "major life activities" test).

---

i. 24 CFR, Section 100.201

- A person might be capable of all major life activities, but the housing provider might (incorrectly) respond as if the person were impaired.

- A housing provider might (incorrectly) assume the existence of a covered impairment, when the individual may not be impaired at all.

- A housing provider might (incorrectly) deny housing to an individual because of myths, fears, and stereotypes associated with disabilities, even though the individual's physical or mental condition did not meet the Fair Housing Act definition of "disability."

The "record of" and "regarded as" provisions of the definition are included in order to protect persons who are treated as being disabled, regardless of their actual disability condition or lack thereof.

See question 22 for further information on the appropriate standard to follow when a property is subject to more than one law.

Some states and localities have enacted laws providing additional protections to persons with disabilities. In some instances, the definition of "disability" incorporated into these state and local laws may differ from the federal definitions.

62   What Is the ADA Definition of Disability?

Providers of assisted housing should also refer to questions 117, 118, 120, and 121 for various program definitions of disability.

The ADA protects three categories of individuals with disabilities:

- Individuals who have a physical or mental impairment that substantially limits one or more major life activities;

- Individuals who have a record of a physical or mental impairment that substantially limits one or more of the individual's major life activities; and,

- Individuals who are regarded as having such an impairment, whether they have the impairment or not.

The first category of persons covered by the definition of an individual with a disability is restricted to those with "physical or mental impairment." Physical impairments include:

"Physical Impairment"

- Physiological disorders or conditions;

- Cosmetic disfigurement; or,

- Anatomical loss (Affecting one or more of the following body systems; neurological; musculoskeletal; special sense organs (which would include speech organs that are not respiratory such as vocal cords, soft palate, tongue, etc.); respiratory, including speech organs; cardiovascular; reproductive; digestive; genito-urinary; hemic and lymphatic; skin; endocrine.)

Specific examples of physical impairments include orthopedic, visual, speech, and hearing impairments, cerebral palsy, epilepsy, muscular dystrophy, multiple sclerosis, cancer, heart disease, diabetes, HIV disease (symptomatic or asymptomatic), tuberculosis, drug addiction, and alcoholism.

"Mental Impairment"

Mental impairments include mental or psychological disorders, such as mental retardation, organic brain syndrome, emotional or mental illness, and specific learning disabilities.

"Regarded as"

The ADA also protects certain persons who are regarded by a public entity as having a physical or mental impairment that substantially limits a major life activity, whether or not that person actually has an impairment. Three typical situations are covered by this category:

- An individual who has a physical or mental impairment that does not substantially limit major life activities, but who is treated as if the impairment does substantially limit a major life activity;

- An individual who has a physical or mental impairment that substantially limits major life activities only as a result of the attitudes of others towards the impairment; and

- An individual who has no impairments but who is treated by a public entity as having an impairment that substantially limits a major life activity.

Covered Disabilities

In its regulations implementing Titles II and III of the ADA, the Department of Justice discusses the definition of disability and how it is to be interpreted. While the following statements are not necessarily applicable to the Fair Housing Act or Section 504, they are indicative of the evolving views of the legal community regarding disability rights:

- HIV disease is covered, whether symptomatic (AIDS) or asymptomatic (HIV positive, AIDS Related Complex).

- Contagious disease is included under "physical or mental impairments."[ii]

"Substantially Limits"

To constitute a "disability," a condition must substantially limit a major life activity. Major life activities include such activities as caring for one's self, performing manual tasks, walking, seeing, hearing, speaking, breathing, learning, and working. There is no absolute standard for determining when an impairment is a substantial limitation.

"Substantially limits" means:

"... the individual's important life activities are restricted as to the conditions, manner, or duration under which they can be performed in comparison to most people. A person with a minor, trivial impairment, such as a simple infected finger, is not impaired in a major life activity. A person who can walk for 10 miles continuously is not substantially limited in walking merely because, on the eleventh mile, he or she begins to experience pain, because most people would not be able to walk eleven miles without experiencing some discomfort."

"... temporary impairments, such as a broken leg, are not commonly regarded as disabilities, and only in rare circumstances would the degree of the limitation and its expected duration be substantial... The question of whether a temporary impairment is a disability must be resolved on a case-by-case basis, taking into consideration both the duration (or expected duration) of the impairment and the extent to which

---

ii. This arose from the Supreme Court decision in School Board of Nassau County v. Arline. 480 U.S. 273, (1987) *it actually limits a major life activity of the affected individual."*

".... a person with hearing loss is substantially limited in the major life activity of hearing, even though the loss may be improved through the use of a hearing aid. Likewise, persons with impairments, such as epilepsy or diabetes, that substantially limit a major life activity, are covered under the... definition of disability, even if the effects of the impairment are controlled by medication."

Not Covered Are...

Simple physical characteristics or disadvantages attributable to environmental, cultural, or economic factors are not considered impairments by the ADA. Examples would be physical characteristics such as blue eyes or black hair or other disadvantages such as an inferior education, a prison record or being poor. However, a person who has these characteristics and also has a physical or mental impairment may be considered as having a disability for purposes of the (ADA) based on the impairment.

See question 92 for a discussion on housing admission issues and drug use.

The phrase "physical or mental impairment" does not include homosexuality or bisexuality. Drug addiction, however, is an impairment under the ADA. The decision to deny housing can be made on the basis that an addict is engaged in the current and illegal use of drugs. An individual who no longer takes controlled substances is protected.

The following conditions are specifically excluded from the definition of "disability:" transvestism, transsexualism, pedophilia, exhibitionism, voyeurism, gender identity disorders not resulting from physical impairments, other sexual behavior disorders, compulsive gambling, kleptomania, pyromania, and psychoactive substance use disorders resulting from current illegal use of drugs.

See also question 104.

The Department of Justice refused to state definitively that environmental illness, also known as "multiple chemical sensitivity," and allergy to cigarette smoke are disabilities, because only in some individuals will the effect be severe enough to meet the def-

inition of disability. Whether multiple chemical sensitivity constitutes a disability within the meaning of the ADA must be
determined on a case by case basis. However, housing providers
should be aware that a large number of complaints are being
received from persons suffering from multiple chemical sensitivity; thus, there is the possibility that a judge may rule that these
persons are covered by the ADA, and perhaps by the Fair Housing Act and Section 504 as well.

63 What Does The Fair Housing Act Require Regarding Persons With Disabilities?

**Prohibited
Actions**

The following actions are prohibited with respect to rental housing:

- Discrimination in the rental of a dwelling because of a handicap or disability of the renter or of a household member or
person associated with the renter.

- Discrimination in the terms or conditions of rental or in the
provisions of services or facilities because of a handicap or
disability of the renter.

- Inquiries to determine whether a person seeking to rent a
dwelling unit is handicapped or disabled.

**Allowable
Actions**

However, the following types of inquiries are permissible so long
as such inquiries are made of all applicants:

- An inquiry to determine eligibility based on a handicap or
disability, for some federally assisted housing programs.

- An inquiry to determine ability to meet the terms of the lease.

- An inquiry to determine whether an applicant is qualified for
a priority available to persons with disabilities.

- An inquiry to determine whether any member of the applicant's household engages in the current illegal use of a controlled substance, or has been convicted of illegal
manufacture or distribution of a controlled substance.

**Allow
Reasonable
Modifications**

Under the Fair Housing Act owners must permit reasonable modifications to dwelling units and common areas, at the expense of a

person with disabilities, if necessary to permit the person full use and enjoyment of a dwelling.

Make Reasonable Accommodations

Owners must make reasonable accommodations in rules, policies, practices or services when necessary to afford a person with a disability equal opportunity to enjoy a dwelling, including public and common areas.

Chapter Nine:	Accommodations in Policies and Practices

64   Reasonable Accommodation

The Fair Housing Act imposes an obligation on housing providers to make reasonable accommodations in rules, policies, practices and services in order to enable persons with disabilities to have equal opportunity to use and enjoy a dwelling unit, including public and common use areas.   Title III of the ADA requires private entities that maintain facilities open to the general public to make reasonable accommodations in policies, practices and procedures when such accommodations may be necessary to allow access to any goods, services or facilities.

Professional housing managers recommend that all properties have a written "Reasonable Accommodations Policy."

Reasonable accommodations for vision-impaired persons might include such changes as oral presentation (including audio tape recording) of material normally presented in written form, or the presentation of written materials in large print or Braille.

Reasonable accommodations for hearing-impaired persons might include written presentation of material ordinarily presented orally, provision of such material through an interpreter, or the provision of closed-captioning to televisions located in common areas.

Federally-assisted properties should also refer to question 125 for more on 'assistive devices.'

Under the Fair Housing Act, housing providers are not required to provide individually prescribed items (such as service animals, hearing aids, or reading machines) or personal items (such as telecommunications equipment in the resident's unit, eyeglasses, wheelchair, or a personal reader or interpreter). Note that properties affected by Section 504 are required to provide certain 'assistive devices.'

Allowing a person with disabilities to use an assistive device, special alarm or auxiliary aid would be considered reasonable. For instance, a building that prohibits pets would, as a reasonable accommodation, allow a vision-impaired resident to keep a seeing-eye dog.

See question 42 for
Fair Housing
considerations in the
leasing process.

Reasonable accommodation should also be applied to resident selection criteria:

An Example of Reasonable Accommodation

> *An applicant has a history of behavior that, if displayed by a resident, would violate the lease. The housing provider declines the application for this reason, and the applicant requests a meeting. At the meeting, the applicant presents evidence that she has a mental impairment which causes the behavior, that control of the behavior requires medication and supportive services, and that she has arranged for, and is now receiving, the needed medication and supportive services. The housing provider's resident selection policy provides that these types of mitigating circumstances are not taken into account when there is a history of non-lease-compliant conduct; in this example, it would be a reasonable accommodation to consider the mitigating circumstances. The housing provider would be permitted to verify any information provided as mitigating circumstances, and would make the decision to accept or reject based on the facts and circumstances.*

65 How Do You Determine Whether a Request for Accommodation Is "Reasonable"?

See questions 26,
77, 87, and 88.

In general, an applicant requiring a reasonable accommodation must first make such a request. Housing providers should not make assumptions about the specific needs of an applicant with disabilities, and should instead rely on the applicant's request to initiate the process.[i] Of course, your screening practices should not serve to discourage persons with disabilities from applying to your property, and should encourage applicants and residents to make requests for reasonable accommodations when they feel it would enable them "an equal opportunity to use and enjoy the dwelling."

---

i.   Generally, housing providers may rely upon the applicant or resident to initiate the accommodation process by making a request. However, some courts have imposed a higher standard on housing providers requiring landlords to identify and implement a suitable reasonable accommodation, even when the tenant does not propose one. See Cobble Hill Apartments Co. v. McLaughlin 1999 WL 788517 (Mass. App. Div. June 23, 1999).

In order to determine whether a requested accommodation should be given, the following must first be determined:

See question 61.

- That the tenant/applicant suffers from a disability as defined in the Fair Housing Act;

- That the housing provider or manager knows of the handicap or should reasonably be expected to know of it; and

- That accommodation of the handicap "may be necessary" to afford the tenant/applicant an equal opportunity to use and enjoy the dwelling.

Case law provides guidance on the factors that one should look at in deciding whether a requested accommodation is or is not reasonable. The following statements from court decisions provide some insight into the standards currently being applied by the courts:

"An accommodation is considered appropriate when it enables the disabled tenant to enjoy the premises to the same degree as that of a similarly-situated non-disabled tenant. In determining what is reasonable accommodation for Complainant, I will consider the following factors: 1) the overall size of the housing provider, including the number of residents, number and type of facilities involved, and the size of the budget; 2) the type of facilities involved, including the composition and structure of the residences; and 3) the nature and cost of accommodation needed." [ii]

"We believe that in enacting the anti-discrimination provisions of the FHAA, Congress relied on the standard of reasonable accommodation developed under Section 504 of the Rehabilitation Act of 1973, codified at 29 U.S.C. Section 794. The legislative history of section (sic) 42 U.S.C. Section 3604 (f)

---

ii. HUDALJ 05-93-0517-1 U.S. V. California Mobile Home Park Management Co. 29 F.3d 1413 (9th Circuit 1994) *plainly indicates that its drafters intended to draw on case law developed under section 504… Thus, Cadman Towers can be required to incur reasonable costs to accommodate Shapiro's handicap, provided such accommodations do not pose an undue hardship or a substantial burden."[iii]*

"The requirement of reasonable accommodation does not entail an obligation to do everything humanly possible to accommodate a disabled person; cost (to the defendant) and benefit (to the plaintiff) merit consideration as well… Similarly the concept of necessity requires at a minimum the showing that the desired accommodation will affirmatively enhance a disabled plaintiff's quality of life by ameliorating the effects of the disability."[iv]

66 Can I Refuse a Request for an Accommodation on the Grounds that It Will Set a "Damaging Precedent" for the Granting of Future Requests for Accommodation?

Case law has shown that requests for accommodation are sometimes refused by housing providers because they fear that if they grant one request they will be faced with numerous requests of a similar nature in the future, which they will have to grant because they granted the first one. In other words, a potentially "damaging precedent" will be set by agreeing to the first accommodation requested. The attitude of the courts, however, is that each request for accommodation must be assessed in light of the circumstances that exist at the property at the time the request is made. For example, existing circumstances may permit the granting of the first, second and third requests for an assigned parking space. However, when the fourth such request is made the prop-

iii. Shapiro v. Cadman Towers; Docket No. 94-6053 US Court of Appeals 2nd Circuit
iv. Bronk and Jay v. Ineichen; US Court of Appeals 7th Circuit No. 94-2882

erty no longer has the physical space to provide an assigned parking space. The fact that the three previous requests were granted would not oblige the property to grant the fourth.

67 Can a Request for Accommodation be Refused on the Grounds that It Will Precipitate Similar, Additional Requests that in the Aggregate Are Not Affordable (and Therefore in the Aggregate Pose a Potential, Unreasonable Burden on the Property)?

See question 79.

Happy Acres Apartments serves a tenant population of seniors and the disabled. Resident Gerty has a disabling mental condition and wants to be allowed to have a dog as a 'companion' animal. While the property manager wouldn't object to a single dog, he fears that accommodating Gerty will precipitate numerous similar requests, which will have to be treated consistently. The manager fears that accommodating all of these requests will create an unreasonable burden on the property. Can the property reject a request for a single accommodation, based on its expectation of the aggregate impact of the accommodations?

This question was addressed in a case decided by a HUD Administrative Law Judge[v] who had to consider whether a refusal to grant a reserved parking space to a disabled resident was justified on the grounds that similar requests from other disabled residents would also have to be accommodated, potentially resulting in non-disabled residents being deprived of parking spaces altogether. The finding was, however, that at the time the request was made there was no shortage of available parking at the relevant property and the cost of assigning the resident a permanent parking space was limited to the cost of affixing a sign to the space. It was therefore ruled that the requested accommodation should have been given. In other cases before HUD, judges have found the fact that granting a single accommodation would create a "domino effect" and lead to an avalanche of similar requests was not a sufficient reason to refuse the accommodation. Each request for accommodation must be assessed in light of the circumstances

---

v.   HUD v Dedham Housing Authority; HUD ALJ 01-90-0424-1

prevailing at the time of the request and not on speculation about what may transpire in the future if the accommodation is granted. Therefore, if the refusal of the accommodation is based on costs of future similar accommodations this refusal will not be justified. In short, the reasonableness of a specific request must be considered on its own merits in light of current factors.

68 Does the Fair Housing Act Require Me to Provide Support Services to Applicants and Residents?

See question 64.

No. However, housing providers must furnish various types of reasonable accommodations to persons with disabilities.

Chapter Ten: Physical Modifications for Accessibility

Copyright, 2000 NAHMA and Compass Group

69   Accessibility Requirements for New Construction

**Fair Housing
Act**

Properties built after March 13, 1991, including dwelling units and non-housing facilities such as roads, walks and common areas, must be designed and constructed to meet specific design and construction standards acceptable under the Fair Housing Act.

See below as well as question 133 for information on requirements that apply to federally-assisted properties; see question 22 for a discussion on the applicable accessibility standard where a property is subject to more than one law.

The new construction requirements for properties that consist of buildings with an elevator and four or more units are:

- At least one building entrance must be on an accessible route;

- The public and common use areas must be readily accessible to and usable by persons with disabilities;

- All doors must be sufficiently wide to allow entry by wheelchairs;

- There must be an accessible route into and through dwelling units;

- Light switches, electrical outlets, thermostats and other environmental controls must be in accessible locations; ·

- There must be reinforcements in bathroom walls to allow later installation of grab bars; and,

- The kitchen and bathrooms must be so designed that individuals in wheelchairs can maneuver within those areas.

For buildings that have four or more units but have no elevator the standards listed above apply only to ground floor units.

HUD has published "Fair Housing Accessibility Guidelines" to facilitate compliance with the accessibility requirements of the Act. The primary standard used in the Guidelines is the American National Standards Institute ("ANSI") standard. While the Guidelines are neither "performance standards" nor "minimum requirements," compliance with the Guidelines "shall be a basis for a determination that there is no reasonable cause to believe that a discriminatory housing practice...has occurred or is about to occur in connection with complaints filed with the Department relating to covered multifamily dwellings." [i] The Guidelines are not, however, the exclusive standard for compliance with the Fair Housing Act's accessibility requirements.

In general, the Fair Housing Act requires all newly-constructed premises to contain basic features of "adaptable" design (i.e. easily modifiable to be accessible). "Adaptable" is a less demanding standard than "accessible." For example, an adaptable unit will contain framing to facilitate the future installation of grab bars; an accessible unit will actually contain the grab bars. For elevator properties, all units must be adaptable. For walk-up properties, only units on the ground floor must be adaptable.

See question 109.

Areas such as mechanical rooms, which by their nature are not intended to be open to residents or members of the public, need not be adaptable or accessible to the physically disabled members of those groups.

New apartment properties that receive federal financial assistance, and are thus subject to Section 504, must also meet the Section 504 accessibility standards.

The Americans With Disabilities Act

Title II of the ADA provides a choice of two standards for new construction and alterations. You can choose either:

- The Uniform Federal Accessibility Standards ("UFAS"), or

- The Americans with Disabilities Act Accessibility Guidelines for Buildings and Facilities ("ADAAG"). If the ADAAG standard is chosen, you are not entitled to the elevator exemption (which permits certain buildings under three stories or under 3,000 square feet per floor to be constructed without an elevator). In addition, you must also comply with the Fair Housing Act, including the design and construction requirements applicable to covered multifamily dwellings constructed for first occupancy after March 13, 1991.

Title III of the ADA does not provide a choice; it requires that you use the ADAAG standard.

---

i. Appendix III to Ch.I, Subchapter A –Preamble to Fair Housing Accessibility Guidelines. 24 CFR Ch.I, Subch.A.,App.II

70   Do Modifications Have to Comply With the American National Standards Institute ("ANSI") Standards?

Federally-assisted properties should see questions 134, 135 and 136 for a discussion on accessibility requirements that are triggered by various types of alterations.

If a rehabilitation project that is significant enough to trigger accessibility requirements is planned, all components of the modifications generally should conform with ANSI, or with another substantially equivalent standard acceptable under HUD's Fair Housing Accessibility regulations. Providers who are considering substantial rehabilitation should consult with qualified professionals concerning these standards.

For other properties (and for substantial rehabilitation properties once the major renovation is completed), case-by-case modifications must be appropriate to the needs of specific applicants or residents. It will usually be appropriate for each component of such modifications to comply with ANSI or an acceptable equivalent standard. For example, if a resident's disability can be accommodated by installation of grab bars in a bathroom, the housing provider is under no obligation to allow other modifications in the bathroom; however, the grab bars should be installed to ANSI specifications or acceptable equivalent, unless the standard approach would not be effective in removing the resident's barriers to occupancy.

In general, there is a presumption in favor of the applicant's or resident's own assessment of his or her needs. Housing providers who feel that the modifications requested by a resident or applicant are beyond what is needed bear the burden of proving this.

71   Accessibility Requirements for Rehabilitation

Fair Housing Act

See question 73 for further information on reasonable modifications.

There are no accessibility requirements under the Fair Housing Act associated with renovations. In other words, if an existing multifamily building were undergoing renovations, there is no requirement that any of the dwelling units or common areas be retrofitted. However, an applicant or tenant with disabilities must be allowed, at their expense, to make reasonable modifications when necessary to have full enjoyment of the premises.

The Americans With Disabilities Act

Alterations to properties subject to Title II are required to provide accessibility to persons with disabilities to the maximum extent feasible and in accordance with UFAS or ADAAG standards. Those subject to Title III should use the ADAAG standard. See question 69.

72 Accessibility Requirements for Existing Housing

The Fair Housing Act

In general, the Fair Housing Act requires:

See questions 64 and 76.

- Reasonable accommodations in policies and procedures, to facilitate accessibility for applicants and residents with disabilities.

See question 73.

- That the housing provider allow applicants and residents with disabilities to make, at their own expense, reasonable modifications to dwelling units and common areas.

Title II of the ADA

See question 69 for a discussion on these standards.

Title II of the ADA requires public entities to make their programs, services or activities readily accessible to individuals with disabilities unless this would result in a fundamental alteration in the nature of the program, service or activity or in undue financial and administrative burdens. Alterations that are undertaken to provide accessibility must be in accordance with either UFAS or ADAAG standards.

Title III of the ADA

See question 13.

In general, Title III of the ADA requires that the rental office (and other on-site business locations such as laundry rooms and community rooms that are used by the public) be accessible.

73 The Fair Housing Act Accessibility Modification Requirements

Under the Fair Housing Act, housing providers must allow accessibility modifications to be made at the expense of the person with disabilities.

The Fair Housing Act regulations allow the housing provider to require restoration of the premises to their former condition following termination of residency, where it is reasonable to do so. Generally, it would be unreasonable to require such restoration where the modifications will not interfere with the next tenant's use and enjoyment of the dwelling. However, experienced housing providers do not agree on whether or not to require restoration following termination of residency. You should consider the following before making a decision whether or not to require restoration of a unit. Your decision can then be based on what is most reasonable for your particular situation.

- Requiring restoration by removal of accessibility modifications will result in a lower supply of accessible units.

- Because the regulations allow the housing provider to condition approval of the modifications on assurances of the quality of workmanship, it should be possible in most instances to have the modifications performed in a way that will be acceptable on a long-term basis.

- Modifications that do not detract from the future marketability of the unit should be permitted to remain.

- Some modifications, such as lowered kitchen cabinets or grab bars in the bathroom around the toilet and shower/bath, could make the unit less marketable.

74   Reasonable Modification

Federally assisted properties should also refer to question 119.

A reasonable modification is an alteration to the physical characteristics of a dwelling unit or to the common areas of a building, requested by an applicant or resident, to allow accessibility by a member of the household.

Depending upon cost and available alternatives, a reasonable modification may include such things as installation of a ramp into a building, the lowering of the unit entry threshold, or the installation of grab bars in a bathroom.

See questions 123, 127, 128 and 137.

In conventional apartments, reasonable modifications are generally undertaken at the expense of the person with disabilities. However, housing providers who are subject to Section 504 (recipients of federal financial assistance) and/or Title II of the ADA (state and local government activities) generally must provide and pay for reasonable modifications unless to do so would result in "undue financial or administrative hardship."

In the absence of compelling evidence to the contrary, housing providers are advised to accept the applicant's or resident's own assessment of what is needed in order to allow accessibility.

Experienced housing providers advise that often there will be multiple methods for providing accessibility, and that the various methods may vary widely in cost. Sometimes, it is possible to provide accessibility through a relatively cost-effective procedural accommodation, instead of a relatively costly structural modification.

75   Accessible Route

Regulations under the Fair Housing Act[ii] define an "accessible route" as:

> "A continuous unobstructed path connecting accessible elements and spaces in a building or within a site that can be negotiated by a person with a severe disability using a wheelchair and that is also safe for and usable by people with other disabilities."

The Americans with Disabilities Act Accessibility Guidelines for Buildings and Facilities ("ADAAG") defines an accessible route as

> "A continuous unobstructed path connecting all accessible elements and spaces of a building or facility. Interior accessible routes may include corridors, floors, ramps, elevators, lifts, and clear floor spaces at fixtures. Exterior accessible routes may include parking access aisles, curb ramps, crosswalks at vehicular ways, walks, ramps and lifts."

ADAAG requires that, in the case of new construction:

* There must be at least one accessible route within the boundary of the site from public transportation stops, accessible parking spaces, passenger loading zones, and public streets or sidewalks to an accessible entrance.

---

ii.   24 CFR, Section 100.201

- That there must be at least one accessible route connecting accessible buildings, accessible facilities, accessible elements and accessible spaces that are on the same site.

- That at least one accessible route shall connect accessible building or facility entrances with all accessible spaces and elements and with all accessible dwelling units within the building or facility.

- That an accessible route must connect at least one accessible entrance of each accessible dwelling unit with the exterior and interior spaces and facilities that serve the accessible dwelling unit.

- That the surfaces of accessible routes and accessible rooms in newly-constructed or altered buildings and facilities be stable, firm, and slip-resistant. If carpet or carpet tile is used on a ground or floor surface it must be securely attached and have a firm cushion, pad or backing or no cushion or pad. Pile thickness cannot exceed ½ inch.

Interior accessible routes may include corridors, floors, ramps, elevators, lifts, and clear floor space at fixtures. Exterior accessible routes may include parking access aisles, curb ramps, crosswalks at vehicular ways, walks, ramps, and lifts.

The accessible route on a site or within a building or facility must be designed to provide slip-resistant locomotion for both level and inclined travel by persons with disabilities. Wheelchair users are also affected by the rolling resistance of the surface of the floor. In addition, cross slopes on walks and ground or floor surfaces can cause difficulty in propelling a wheelchair in a straight line. Wheelchairs are propelled most easily on surfaces that are hard, stable and regular. Materials such as gravel, wood chips, wet clay or sand, often used for outdoor walkways, are neither firm nor stable, nor can they generally be considered slip-resistant. A cobblestone surface is also irregular and significantly impedes wheelchair movement. Thus, walks surfaced in these materials could not constitute an accessible route.

These Regulations require that all new construction must have at least one building entrance on an accessible route, "unless it is impractical to do so because of terrain or unusual characteristics of the site." [iii] However, HUD's Accessibility Guidelines provide that all new multifamily properties with elevators should be designed and constructed to provide at least one accessible entrance on an accessible route, regardless of terrain or unusual characteristics of the site. HUD's rationale for not exempting elevator properties from the accessibility requirements due to "site impracticality" is the belief that "the type of site work that is performed in connection with the construction of a high rise elevator building generally results in a finished grade that would make the building accessible". [iv] Housing providers should note that, at least for existing housing, there is no requirement that every building be accessible. Thus, overall accessibility can be provided via those units that are located on accessible routes.

Sometimes, due to terrain constraints or building design, no units are located on an accessible route. For example, lack of an accessible route could arise where the slope from the parking area to the building is so steep that an accessible route cannot be provided cost-effectively. It might also arise where the building design is such that no units are at ground level (for instance, when entering the building, residents have to walk up or down steps in order to reach their units).

If there are no units on accessible routes, the property will not be able to serve wheelchair users, but will be able to serve other persons with disabilities (such as persons with hearing or vision impairments and persons with various mobility impairments that do not require the constant use of a wheelchair). Accordingly, the common areas should be made accessible to the disabled populations that the property can serve.

---

iii. 24 CFR Subtitle B, Ch. I (4-1-99 Edition) Section 100.205
iv. Appendix III to Ch.I, Subchapter A – Preamble to Fair Housing Accessibility Guidelines. 24 CFR Ch.I, Subch. A., App. II

Chapter Eleven: Frequently Requested Procedural Accommodations and Structural Modifications

76 How Do I Decide Whether To Modify Procedures or Structures, to Accommodate Applicants and Residents With Disabilities?

The term "reasonable accommodation" refers to a procedural change to accomplish accessibility. The term "reasonable modification" denotes a structural change to facilitate accessibility.

Fair housing issues tend to be complex. They also tend not to be susceptible to rigid, standardized solutions. Accordingly, providers will want to develop their own analytical framework for evaluating individual circumstances. Keeping in mind certain basic understandings should help both in establishing policy, and in applying the policy to different situations over time.

Do First Things First

When a property faces the task of achieving accessibility compliance, often the sheer volume of tasks can seem overwhelming. Experienced owners and managers advise prioritizing these tasks.

See questions 23 and 24 for guidance on accessibility reviews and self-evaluations.

• First, perform a physical accessibility review and self-evaluation of the property, its policies and procedures.

• Then, remove barriers and/or adopt methods that enhance accessibility. Make nonstructural changes in programs first. Next, make the common areas accessible. The next priority is structural modifications for existing residents. Modifications for the visually and hearing impaired should follow, as soon as practicable.

Review Basic Requirements for Screening

Applicants with disabilities sometimes request accommodations to admissions and screening procedures, for example a vision-impaired applicant may request that the lease be read aloud.

However, housing providers are not required to waive reasonable, basic requirements for admission of applicants who are members of protected classes. Basic requirements for admission may include the submission of evidence supporting:

• The timely payment of rent and utilities.

• The maintenance of the dwelling in decent, safe and sanitary physical condition.

- That the applicant has not interfered with other residents' enjoyment of the housing.

- That the applicant has not engaged in any criminal activity (or any criminal activity of a nature that would raise the possibility of non-compliance with lease provisions and house rules).

See questions 43 and 88.

Factors such as the likelihood that an applicant will cause excessive wear and tear in a dwelling may also be included, so long as they are reasonable and are applied to all residents equally. A "no excessive wear and tear requirement" cannot, however, be used to exclude the use of wheelchairs or strollers or to discriminate against applicants who intend to use such equipment.

Be Consistent

When reviewing applications for housing, ask each applicant for the same information essential to determining basic eligibility.

Lease Compliance Is the Bottom Line

The test of eligibility of applicants must be their ability to meet the terms of the lease, not a subjective judgment about *how* they will do so. For example, a housing provider may not reject an applicant simply because the applicant does not "appear" capable of maintaining a unit.

77 Professionally Managing Requests for Accommodation or Modification

As a manager, you will be dealing with individuals with disabilities who are eligible for a variety of procedural accommodations and structural modifications. It is the responsibility of the individual to make such requests for accommodations or modifications; it is not your responsibility to offer them. In fact, you should not inquire whether an individual has a disability and may need an accommodation. However, when an individual makes a request, it is your responsibility to deal with it in a timely and appropriate manner.

Expert managers recommend instituting certain practices to ensure fair and proper treatment of all requests for accommodation. Written procedures that describe how to process each request are extremely useful. These should include clear policies on acceptable modifications, methods for verifying disabilities, criteria for accepting and rejecting contractors who make modifications, and on restoration requirements.

Consider implementing a method of documenting accommodations and structural modifications requests (by keeping a logbook for example) that includes information on the date and time when the request was made, the nature of the request, the identity of the person making it and the disposition of the request. Recordkeeping will demonstrate the fairness and professionalism of your management practices in the event of a discrimination charge.

If the request is of a routine nature—such as a request for a reserved, accessible parking space—you should be able to provide an answer within a relatively short time. A more complicated request, where you may need to seek a legal opinion or confer with upper management, may require more time. If the resident has some idea of when to expect a reply, they will be more inclined to think that the request is being taken seriously.

Written policies and procedures are valuable:

- They make it easier for staff to deal equally and fairly with all requests.

- Routine requests, such as for an assigned parking spot, can be quickly processed, following established procedures.

- Complicated requests, particularly those requiring consultation with others, can be handled efficiently, reducing wasted time and mistakes.

- Documentation provides a record of the number and type of requests and their resolutions. This is particularly important when a resident claims that his request was not fairly dealt with or makes repeated or more demanding requests as you will be able to rely on written records to justify your decision on the request.

If at all possible, you should attempt to avoid responding to a request with an outright "no." Most people would be satisfied with an accommodation that takes their needs into consideration and is a reasonable compromise even if it is not what they specifically requested.

78   Reserved Parking Space

For mobility-impaired individuals, the parking arrangements at a property may have a direct impact on their "equal opportunity to use and enjoy their dwelling units." For this reason, requests for reserved parking spaces are probably the most frequently requested procedural accommodations faced by managers.

Such requests are generally for a parking space in close proximity to the resident's dwelling and permanently assigned to the resident. Once you have verified the existence of the disability and have established a link between the nature of the disability and the need for an assigned parking space you should identify an appropriate space and designate it for that particular individual. Once the space is assigned to an individual it should remain with that individual for as long as the disabling condition lasts. Some unacceptable (but common) reasons for attempting to deny an assigned space include:

- Refusal on the ground that it would cause too radical a departure from the existing policies and procedures governing assignment of parking spaces. This is unacceptable even if there is a waiting list for parking and the policy is to assign an available space to the person at the head of the waiting list.

See questions 66 and 67.

- Fear that granting one request will unleash a "floodgate" of similar requests that the property must agree to, with the result that it no longer has any meaningful policy on the matter.

See question 62.

If parking is assigned to accommodate a disability it may be a good idea to ask the resident for re-verification of the disability annually because some disabilities are not permanent.

In response to a request for an assigned parking space you should not ask an individual to use an existing accessible space obtained originally for the use of the leasing office in order to meet either ADA or Section 504 requirements because spaces near the leasing office are regarded as meeting accessibility requirements for the public and not for specific residents.

If you are managing a property that has a high demand for limited, reserved parking you may have to institute a waiting list.

This situation is most likely to occur in a high-rise property serving seniors, where many residents could legitimately request reserved spaces. It is recommended that if there are competing requests from residents who all have a disability that justifies a reserved parking space being assigned that priority be determined solely with reference to the date when the request was received. Further, expert managers recommend date stamping all such requests.

Managers are not competent to determine whether, for example, a resident who suffers from rheumatoid arthritis is more mobility impaired than one suffering from multiple sclerosis and therefore more in need of reserved parking. Furthermore the Fair Housing Act neither authorizes nor requires that such a determination be made. Rather than engaging in a guessing game about which disabilities and impairments are more serious, the prudent course is to assign parking on a first-come-first-served basis.

The purpose and litmus test of a reasonable accommodation (including a reserved, accessible parking space) is that it afford the resident "equal opportunity to use and enjoy the dwelling unit." Consequently, a resident's visitors can also reserve a parking space, to the extent that their need for the parking is related to the resident's need for an accomodation. Therefore, it would be reasonable to reserve a space for use by a caregiver or aide who must pick-up and drop-off the resident on a regular basis. On the other hand, it would not be necessary to reserve a space only for use by friends of a disabled resident.

Guests, including visiting caregivers, do not always require accommodation. In one case,[i] an appeals court held that parking fees charged to a visiting caregiver need not be waived,

> "It is not unusual for any working person to incur parking expenses at their place of employment. The fact that some of these people may work with handicapped individuals does not require that their parking fees be waived."

---

i. US v. California Mobile Home Park; U.S. Court of Appeals for the Ninth Circuit; No. 95-55599

79   Companion Animals

Persons suffering from mental illness or disabilities that severely limit mobility are increasingly making requests that pet policies accommodate their need for a companion animal. They seek this accommodation as a way of addressing the isolation and loneliness that may result from certain disabilities. For this reason, allowing the companion animal is seen by some (including courts of law if the evidence of the benefit provided by the animal is sufficiently strong) to be a reasonable accommodation. In other words, the view is taken that the 'service' provided by the animal is companionship, rather than sight, as in the case of seeing-eye dogs.

See questions 66 and 67 for a discussion on relying on "damaging precedent" in refusing a request for an accommodation.

However, while a request to have a seeing-eye dog is a straightforward reasonable accommodation issue, the issue of "companion" animals is less clear. In a number of cases, property managers have refused requests from residents and housing applicants that they be allowed to keep companion animals. Some managers have expressed concern that they will be unable to enforce "no pets" policies if residents simply need to claim a need for companionship in order to be entitled to this accommodation. If a resident requests an accommodation for a companion animal, here are some points to consider:

- Seek professional third-party verification of the resident's disability. Further, request that the third-party establish a link between the resident's disability, and the need for the service (companionship) provided by the animal. Some firms have developed standard forms for this purpose. Although you may desire something concrete from a qualified medical professional such as a psychiatrist, know that courts have supported (in one case) a letter from a social worker stating no more than, "...*the cat is clearly important to Mr. X's well-being and overall health.*"[ii]

- If the nature of the property or disability is such that a dog cannot conveniently be accommodated suggest a cat instead.

---

ii.   HUDALJ 09-93-1753-8; Secretary US Dept. of Housing & Urban Development v. River Gardens Apartments , et al.

- You may not have to agree to more than one animal.

- A request for a more exotic animal, such as a snake, is more problematic. You may be able to deny a request to keep a snake citing other residents' right to "quiet enjoyment" of the premises.

- Make use of an addendum to the lease covering requirements for the care of the animal, and enforce the terms of the addendum should it become necessary to do so.

- You should not require that a deposit be paid as a condition of allowing the resident to keep a companion or service animal because the animal is a reasonable accommodation to the resident's disability. However, other provisions of your pet rules may be enforceable (i.e. vaccinations, restrictions on the type of animal (no rodents, for instance), and a requirement to clean up after the animal.

80   Help In Filling Out the Application

Expert managers differ on the matter of assisting applicants with disabilities in completing the rental application form. Some hold that it is not advisable for management to fill out any form for individual applicants, because if a dispute arose over information included on the form, the applicant could argue that what they said was not accurately written on the application. Other experts hold that the applicant still must sign the form, and in so doing is assuming responsibility for its content.

In either case, a refusal to accommodate a disabled applicant who needs assistance in filling out the application form may be viewed as discriminatory. If an applicant requests assistance in completing the rental application or paperwork, inquire whether he or she has someone who can assist them with this task.

81   Accommodating Laundry Facilities for the Disabled

An individual with disabilities may be unable to access the laundry room and may want to install a washer and dryer in the unit. You may wish to agree to this request if this can be done in a reasonable manner and does not conflict with the provisions of any local codes, necessitate expensive electrical rewiring or create a disturbance to other residents.

See questions 86 and 104.

An individual with chemical sensitivities may also request laundry facilities in their unit. The same considerations should apply.

82   Help With Mail

An individual with a disability may be unable to reach the mailbox assigned to their apartment or may be unable to use the key to open it. Whenever possible, you should try to accommodate residents with disabilities by assigning a more accessible mailbox. Other accommodations may include having the resident designate another resident as being authorized to collect mail on the resident's behalf.[iii] If either of these methods is chosen it is recommended that you obtain the resident's written authorization for this procedure to be followed. This authorization should be placed on the resident's file. The Post Office also facilitates what are called "hardship extensions" whereby, for example, a person can request and obtain "door delivery" service.[iv]

83   Accommodations to Waiting List Policies

Some federally-assisted properties commonly use waiting lists to handle the high demand for their affordable apartments. Properties governed by HUD Handbook 4350.3 should refer to it for guidance on the proper handling of waiting lists and accessible units.[v]

Non-assisted, conventional apartments are less likely to have either accessible units or waiting lists.

---

iii. Domestic Mail Manual (DMM) 042.2.0 permits delivery of mail to an addressee's agent—someone designated by the disabled customer to receive mail on his/her behalf.

iv. DMM 042.9.2 and 10.2 permit a change in the method of delivery, if the existing method presents an extreme physical hardship to the customer.

v. 4350.3, 27, 2-30(b)(1)

84   Visual Fire Alarms

Visual fire alarms afford the hearing impaired a way to be warned of a fire. It is advisable to inform all residents generally about the availability of these devices and to install them in individual dwellings on request. Even where a resident has a known hearing impairment you should not suggest that he or she install one of these devices; you should merely respond promptly to a request for its installation. You should note also that you cannot require hearing impaired persons to absolve the property from liability in the event of a fire or similar event as a condition of living at the property.

85   Help With Trash Removal

An individual with a disability may be unable to walk to a dumpster or be unable to lift a trash bag into a dumpster and may ask that the dumpster be relocated or access to it reconfigured. Consider whether accommodating this request is the best way to meet the resident's needs. If it is not practical or reasonable to move the dumpster, you may propose some alternatives:

- Provide a cart or wagon to the resident for easier transporting of the trash.

- Place a trash can next to the dumpster so that the resident (and if necessary, small children at the property) can properly dispose of trash without having to lift it into the dumpster. Have maintenance empty this trash into the dumpster as often as necessary.

86   Accommodating Chemical or Environmental Sensitivities

See also question 104 for additional discussion on accommodating chemical sensitivities.

HUD has determined that Multiple Chemical Sensitivity Disorder ("MCS") and Environmental Illness ("EI") can, if sufficiently severe, constitute disabilities under the Fair Housing Act.[vi] Therefore individuals suffering from these conditions may request

---

vi. MCS Disorder and Environmental Illness as Handicaps – Directive Number: GME-0009 reasonable accommodations from their housing providers. Before considering a request for an accommodation, housing providers may seek independent, third party verification of the disability and of the applicability of the request to the disability.

HUD has defined MCS as a condition that causes a person to have severe hypersensitive reactions to a number of different common substances and EI to refer to a condition that causes a person to have any type of severe allergic reaction to one or more substances.[vii] Ordinary allergies must be distinguished from MCS and EI as, generally speaking, ordinary allergies are not considered a disability because in most cases they do not limit a major life activity.

The area of chemical or environmental sensitivities is a growing and challenging area for managers. There are many chemicals in use in the daily operation of a multifamily property. Some residents may assert that they are sensitive to one or more of these substances, and that they consequently suffer from physical or mental symptoms, ranging from depression to rashes. When residents assert that they have either of these latter conditions and request accommodations on that basis they should provide some form of written verification to substantiate the existence of the condition.

Typical requests for accommodation and modifications could be:

- To give advance warning that pest control or other maintenance work is scheduled to be undertaken;

- The use of "environmentally correct" pesticides or paint within their unit; or

- More frequent cleaning and/or replacement of filters in air conditioning or heating ducts.

See questions 66 and 67 for guidance on "damaging precendent."

Because of the pervasiveness of chemicals in all areas, a person with chemical sensitivities may make repeated requests for accommodation. However, residents with disabilities are not restricted in the number of requests for accommodation they may make and requests cannot be refused on the ground that, in the

---

vii. Ibid

housing manager's opinion, the person has already made too many. In the case of properties that are subject to Section 504 a requested reasonable accommodation may, however, be refused on the ground that making it would constitute undue financial and administrative burdens. In the case of other properties that are subject only to the Fair Housing Act reasonable accommodation requests may be refused if, considering all the circumstances of the case, the requested accommodation is not "reasonable."

An Example of An "Unreasonable" Request for Accommodation

The plaintiff, who suffered from multiple chemical sensitivity, requested of her landlords (1) that the carpet in her apartment be removed and not replaced; (2) that the apartment be cleaned with specified products; (3) that the ductwork in the apartment be cleaned; (4) that they refrain from painting the unit before she moved in; (5) that the adjoining tenant use Lysol instead of Pine Sol to clean her floors; and, (6) that the adjoining tenant cover her registers with aluminum foil when she did her cleaning. The landlords and adjoining tenant complied with all of these requests but the plaintiff was still affected by fumes from the adjoining tenant's cleaning activities. The plaintiff therefore requested her landlords to evict the adjoining tenant, which they refused to do. The plaintiff vacated the premises and sued the landlords for housing discrimination on the ground that they failed to reasonably accommodate her handicap. The District Court ruled that "such an accommodation [evicting the adjoining tenant] is not required by either federal or state housing discrimination laws, particularly in light of the fact that [the adjoining tenant] was the prior tenant and that her greatest fault appears to be the habit of keeping her premises meticulously clean." On appeal this decision was upheld by the Court of Appeals, which reiterated the ruling in another case[*] that "The requirement of reasonable accommodation does not entail an obligation to do everything humanly possible to accommodate a disabled person;" consequently, it did not require that the adjoining tenant and her children be deprived of their residence.[†]

[*]   Bronk V Ineichen, 54 F. 3d 425, 429 (7th Cir. 1995)
[†]   Temple V Gunsalus et al, U.S. Court of Appeals 6th Circuit, 97 F. 3d 1452;

Also refer to question 104 for more discussion on Multiple Chemical Sensitivity.

Note also that, as with other types of disabilities, persons who suffer from MCS or EI are not relieved of the responsibility to observe all the provisions of their leases. Therefore they must take whatever steps are necessary to ensure, for example, that their unit does not become infested with vermin, rodents or insects if the lease has a clause requiring that the dwelling be kept in good and habitable condition. If the resident cannot tolerate the use of any available pest control products he or she will have to devise other methods of dealing with this problem.

Chapter Twelve: Admissions and Eviction Issues for Persons With Disabilities

87   General Inquiries Concerning Disabilities

In general, housing providers may not ask an applicant, resident, guest or associate of an applicant/resident whether he or she has a disability, or about the severity of a disability.[i] Experienced housing providers recommend verifying eligibility for occupancy not disability.

Typically, the most a housing provider needs to know is whether an applicant or resident has a disability (for example, in order to decide whether an applicant or resident is entitled to a reasonable accommodation). The housing provider should inquire into the nature of the disability *only to the extent necessary* to determine the reasonableness of a particular accommodation or modification. The provider does not need to know what the specific disability is, the medical diagnosis, the details of the treatment plan, or the likely future course of the disease or disability. Accordingly, administrative processes should be designed to prevent the inadvertent receipt of such unnecessary and unwanted information.

See questions 42 and 43.

Applicants with disabilities should be asked the same questions as other applicants. Ask about their ability to meet residency requirements, such as whether they will be able to pay the rent, comply with the terms of the lease and comply with other pertinent rules and regulations. Housing providers may ask all applicants:

*   Whether the applicant can meet the requirements of tenancy.

*   Whether the applicant qualifies for a dwelling unit designed for persons with physical disabilities.

*   If the property has a priority for admission which is available to persons with disabilities, whether any member of the applicant's household qualifies for such a priority.

*   Whether any member of the applicant's household is engaged in the current illegal use of a controlled substance.

---

i. If, however, the existence of a disability is a prime determinant of eligibility, an inquiry is permissible. This situation occurs primarily in federally assisted housing; see Chapter 15, particularly questions 120 and 121.

- Whether any member of the applicant's household has been convicted of illegal manufacture or distribution of a controlled substance.

88 Applicant Screening and Resident Selection for Persons With Disabilities

Policies and practices must be applied consistently. Because many fair housing complaints arise from a perception of different treatment, a housing provider whose policies are applied consistently will receive far fewer complaints than a provider with more elaborate policies that are applied inconsistently.

The decision to accept or decline an application for residency must be based on the applicant's demonstrated ability and willingness to meet the terms of the lease. Lease terms typically include: non-interference with others, timely payment of rent, proper care of the dwelling, not engaging in criminal activity, and adherence to reasonable rules and regulations. If information obtained during the application process and examination of screening materials, taken as a whole, do not support a conclusion that the terms of the lease will be complied with, the applicant may be rejected.

Applicants who are rejected may have disability conditions of which the housing provider is unaware. In its standard rejection letter, a housing provider may offer rejected applicants the opportunity to request a reasonable accommodation that would enable the applicant to meet the terms of the lease. For example, if an applicant's disruptive behavior is related to his or her failure to medicate, it may be a reasonable accommodation to accept the applicant if he or she can arrange for a live-in or visiting aide who would administer medication as needed.[ii]

See questions 64 and 65.

Accordingly, housing providers that employ such a technique typically include language such as this in each rejection letter: "If you are a person with disabilities, and the reason your application is being denied is related to your disability, you may contact us not

---

ii. *Blalock vs. Amityville Senior Development Corporation*, No. 99-CV-5447 later than (date, time) to discuss whether a reasonable accommodation by us would make your application acceptable."

If the discussion with the applicant identifies a possible accommodation, the housing provider may require verification of the information and must then determine whether the accommodation is sufficient to overcome the reason for rejection.

89 "Independent Living"

Housing providers may *not* make the ability to "live independently" a requirement for admission.

In a major case[iii] involving a large public housing authority the court ruled that the inability to live independently is not, in and of itself, a basis for denial of an application for rental housing by a person with disabilities.

The housing provider's decision to accept or deny an application must be based solely on the applicant's ability and willingness to comply with the terms of the lease. An applicant with disabilities may be able to achieve lease compliance, with the assistance of a third party, such as a live-in aide, a relative or a contract service provider.

90 "Direct Threat"

Under the Fair Housing Act, housing providers are not required to rent dwelling units to anyone "whose tenancy would constitute a direct threat to the health and safety" of others or whose tenancy would result in substantial physical damage to the property of others.[iv] A determination that an applicant would pose such a threat would necessarily be based upon the documented past history of the person. It would not be permissible to decline an application based on the housing provider's judgment that the applicant might display threatening behavior in the future despite there being no record of such behavior in the past.

---

iii. Cason v. Rochester Housing Authority 748F. Supp. 1002; 1990 U.S. Dist. Lexis 14229; FHFL 15643.

iv. FHA Regulations – 24 CFR Subtitle B Ch. 1 Section 100.202(d)

The "direct threat" provision affirms HUD's traditional stance that all applicants must meet reasonable basic admissions requirements. A record of behavior that would violate the lease is sufficient grounds to deny an application, even if the behavior is related to a protected disability condition.

See question 64.

However, if a reasonable accommodation for a person with disabilities would remove the "direct threat," the housing provider would be required to provide the accommodation, and it would not be lawful to decline the application based on the "direct threat" provision.

The ADA also provides that an individual may be excluded from participation in services, facilities, privileges and accommodations if that individual poses a direct threat to the health or safety of others.

The Department of Justice regulations implementing Titles II and III of the ADA state the following concerning "direct threat:"

- *"A direct threat is a significant risk to the health or safety of others that cannot be eliminated by a modification of policies, practices or procedures, or by the provision of auxiliary aids or services."*

- A determination of direct threat may not be based on generalizations or stereotypes about the effects of a particular disability; it *"must be based on an individualized assessment, based on reasonable judgment that relies on current medical evidence or on the best available objective evidence, to determine: the nature, duration and severity of the risk; the probability that the potential injury will actually occur; and whether reasonable modifications of policies, practices or procedures will mitigate the risk."*

While these ADA regulations are not necessarily directly applicable to the Fair Housing Act, they are indicative of the evolving views of the legal community regarding disability rights.

In practice, housing providers are not likely to list "direct threat" as grounds for declining an application. Rather, they will simply cite the specific behavior as grounds for denial. The "direct threat" language serves mainly to establish that the provider cannot be required to waive reasonable basic admissions requirements with respect to persons with disabilities.

91 Denial or Eviction Based on Drug Addiction or Alcoholism

Neither alcoholism nor drug addiction are lawful grounds for denial of housing. However:

See questions 92, 93, 94 and 95 for additional discussion; federally assisted properties should also see question 122.

- An applicant who is engaged in the current illegal use of a controlled substance may be denied housing on that basis.

- Discrimination is prohibited against an individual who is currently participating in a supervised rehabilitation program and is not engaging in current illegal use of drugs.

See also question 97.

- Subject to what appears below, a resident who violates the lease may be evicted, even if the violation is a manifestation of a disability condition.

- Subject to what appears below, if an applicant has a history of behavior that, if displayed by a resident, would be a lease violation, the applicant may be denied housing, even if the behavior is a manifestation of a disability condition.

In the last two examples, however, if the behavior is a manifestation of a disability condition, the applicant or resident with disabilities must be given an opportunity to demonstrate that a reasonable accommodation by the housing provider (including the consideration of mitigating circumstances) would address the non-lease-compliant behavior.

See question 44.

Persons with addictions, persons who have a "record of" addiction, and persons who are "regarded as" having addictions, are protected under the Fair Housing Act. Housing providers therefore must apply the same screening and selection criteria to addicts or suspected addicts that are applied to all other applicants or residents. Special screening procedures that are used only with respect to suspected drug users would violate the Fair Housing Act.

92 Admissions Requirements and Drug Use

It is permissible to have a basic admissions requirement that no household member be engaged in the current illegal use of drugs.

Experienced housing providers recommend that each applicant household be asked whether any of its members are engaged in the current illegal use of drugs in the written application form, and that this requirement be included in the property's resident selection plan.[v] As with all other resident selection criteria, it is important that this requirement be administered and enforced consistently.

Some properties, particularly those that have experienced significant problems with drug-related criminal activity, may desire to develop a resident selection plan that rejects applicants for specific types of conduct that are suggestive of the current illegal use of drugs and thus are grounds for denial of housing. Housing providers are strongly advised to seek legal guidance in this regard, as this is a rapidly evolving area of fair housing law. Examples might include discovery of controlled substances in a dwelling unit occupied by any member of the household, conviction of any household member for any drug related crime, and recent arrest of any household member for any drug-related crime. Housing providers are advised to check carefully any applicable state or local laws, plus applicable case law in this very volatile and controversial area of fair housing practice.

93 Inquiries Regarding "Current Illegal Use of Drugs"

Although it is permissible to inquire concerning "current illegal use" of drugs, it may not be prudent to inquire concerning a period as long ago as five years, which some would consider to extend beyond the meaning of the word "current."

Under Section 36.104 of Title III of the ADA "current illegal use of drugs" is defined as "illegal use of drugs that occurred recently enough to justify a reasonable belief that a person's drug use is current or that continuing use is a real and ongoing problem."

---

v. Experienced housing providers recommend the use of written resident selection plans by all multifamily rental properties, even though such plans typically are required only in federally assisted housing.

94 Can Evidence of Successful Drug Rehabilitation Be Required?

No, not even if there is direct evidence of the past illegal use of a controlled substance.

A direct inquiry of this nature runs the risk of being regarded as an inquiry into the nature or severity of a disability, and the Fair Housing Act contains broad prohibitions against this type of inquiry.

If an applicant lists a drug rehabilitation center as his or her current or previous address this would not be a justifiable reason for declining the application. In addition it would not be permissible to inquire whether the applicant had successfully completed rehabilitation. It would, however, be permissible to send to the rehabilitation center a questionnaire regarding the applicant's ability and willingness to comply with the terms of the property's lease. This questionnaire should be modeled on the verification materials that the property sends to the landlords of applicants who live or lived in standard rental housing.

95 Denial on the Grounds of "Current Illegal Use of Drugs"

See also questions 26 and 88 for additional considerations regarding rejection letters.

The process of denying an application on this basis is straightforward: an applicant who is engaged in current illegal use of drugs would be sent a standard rejection letter, stating that the application was being denied because the housing provider has evidence that the applicant is engaged in the current illegal use of a controlled substance. These are lawful and proper grounds for rejection. If your property is federally assisted the standard rejection letter must give the applicant an opportunity for an informal meeting to discuss the rejection.[vi] Note that a person engaged in the current illegal use of drugs is not protected under the Fair Housing Act.

---

vi. HUD Occupancy Handbook 4350.3, 2-30(c)(2) and Public Housing Handbook 7465.1, 4-4(2)(c).

However, there are several important procedural requirements governing how the housing provider makes the determination of current illegal use.

See question 94.

The information indicating current illegal use must have been obtained via the housing provider's standard application and screening procedures. Providers are specifically permitted to inquire of all applicants whether any member of the applicant household is a current illegal user of a controlled substance. Also, evidence indicating current illegal use may be encountered during the provider's standard applicant screening procedures (for example, landlord references and criminal records).

The information should be sufficiently convincing to justify the conclusion that a member of the applicant's household is engaged in the current illegal use of drugs. A recent conviction (or, state law permitting, arrest) for illegal drug use should be sufficient. Other forms of evidence may also be effective (for instance, statements from qualified professionals knowledgeable of the applicant, and credible statements from other third parties such as landlords).

Some experienced housing providers consider a history of illegal use of controlled substances to be sufficient evidence to deny housing based on current illegal use. In denying such an application, the housing provider must give the applicant an opportunity to introduce evidence of rehabilitation (for example, successful completion of a legitimate drug rehabilitation program), or other evidence sufficient to rebut the evidence of current, illegal use. To be acceptable, the applicant's evidence must be verifiable, as with any condition of eligibility, preferably via written verification from a qualified, neutral third party.

Drug addiction, like alcohol addiction, is an affliction that has a long recovery period, and that has a high recovery failure rate. Like alcohol addiction, drug addiction generally requires total abstinence in order to control the addiction. Drug-related activity is also extremely destabilizing when it occurs in apartment properties. Providers should take these facts into account when deciding drug-related issues with respect to applicants for housing.

Federally assisted properties should also ee question 122.

Experienced housing providers advise that applicants and residents who are currently using illegal drugs are likely to display other behaviors that violate the lease. Accordingly, drug users are most commonly denied occupancy not on the basis of their drug use *per se* but on the basis of other non-lease-compliant behavior that is less difficult to prove.

96 Denial on the Grounds of Drug-Related Criminal Activity

Because engaging in drug-related criminal activity would violate the lease, it is lawful to deny an application on the grounds that the applicant has a prior history of having engaged in drug-related criminal activity.

See question 47.

This is a legitimate ground for denial, even if the behavior is claimed to be disability-related.

97 Eviction of Persons With Disabilities

See question 91.

Persons with disabilities, like all other residents, may be evicted for failure to comply with the terms of the lease, rules and regulations of the property. However, as with initial occupancy, you are required to make reasonable accommodations to the extent necessary to allow the resident to have an equal opportunity to comply with the terms of the lease. In other words if the lease violations are a consequence of the resident's disability, the housing provider must make reasonable accommodations if these would enable the resident to comply with the lease terms.

Chapter Thirteen: Fair Housing Issues for Specific Disabilities

98   Is Disease a Disability?

Regarding HIV and AIDS, see question 106; see questions 61 and 62 for the definition of disability.

Under both the Americans With Disabilities Act (ADA) and the Fair Housing Act a person with a handicap (Fair Housing Act terminology) or disability (ADA terminology) is defined as having a physical or mental impairment which substantially limits one or more major life activities; having a record of such impairment or being regarded as having such an impairment. Various diseases are specified as examples of mental or physical impairments, for example cerebral palsy, muscular dystrophy, multiple sclerosis, diabetes, heart disease, etcetera. However, a disease in itself is not a disability or handicap. The disease becomes a disability or handicap under the Acts when it causes "physical or mental impairment which significantly limits one or more of a person's major life activities."

99   Wheelchair Users

Accessibility of the Office

See question 69 for FHA accessibility requirements; see questions 72 and 73 for the accessibility requirements of properties whose construction pre-dated the Fair Housing Act and ADA.

Wheelchair users want to be able to conduct business at the rental office, regardless of whether the property has any residential units that are wheelchair-accessible. For properties constructed after March, 1991 the Fair Housing Act requires that the entire property, including the rental office, be accessible to disabled persons including wheelchair users. For properties constructed prior to March, 1991 it should be noted that the rental office is considered a place of public accommodation under Title III of the Americans with Disabilities Act (ADA) and as such must be accessible to persons with handicaps, including wheelchair users.

Accessible Route

See questions 69 and 75.

Wheelchair users sometimes request modifications to provide an accessible route. The simplest example of a way in which a route may be made accessible is the installation of ramps so that curbs and front stoops do not prevent accessibility. Wheelchair users may request improvements to sidewalks, or additional, new sections of sidewalk.

Accessible Parking

Spaces must be at least 96 inches wide and must be located on the shortest accessible route to an accessible entrance. Accessible parking spaces must be designated as reserved by signage showing the symbol of accessibility.

Entry Threshold

If the existing entry threshold does not facilitate entry by persons with disabilities or wheelchair users, possible solutions include lowering the threshold, or providing a small ramp on both sides of the threshold.

Public Toilet Facilities

If public toilet facilities are provided at a rental office, then these facilities must be accessible. Note that allowing a single member of the public to use your restroom will subject it to accessibility requirements. Note also that if you plan to label a non-accessible bathroom as reserved "for employees only" you may violate laws designed to protect persons with disabilities from employment discrimination.

Accessibility requires that toilet stalls must be on an accessible route and in addition must comply with ADA Accessibility Guidelines (ADAAG) as regards the size and arrangement of toilet stalls, the type of doors used, the amount of clear floor space, the type of flush controls and other features. ADAAG provides that "Unisex" or single-user restrooms are permissible in alterations to existing facilities if it is not technically feasible to construct multiple single-sex facilities.

Wheelchair Damage

Wheelchairs may cause damage to walls and doors. The costs of repainting or repair may not be passed onto a resident or visitor using a wheelchair. Unless the damage is excessive when compared with the normal wear and tear caused by a wheelchair this expense will have to be included in routine maintenance expense.

100 Other Mobility Impairments

An accessible route is essential for wheelchair users. However, properties that lack an accessible route should still be able to serve persons with other mobility impairments not requiring the use of a wheelchair (for example, persons who use walkers or canes).

101 Vision Impairments

Persons with little or no usable vision depend upon environmental cues, including ambient sounds, edges and other physical elements that can be sensed by a cane, and texture changes underfoot, for safe and independent travel. Some people with impaired vision can also use color contrast as a navigational aid.

Cane Detectors

Many people with severe impairments of vision use a cane to aid mobility. To further assist such persons you may consider installing cane detectors. A cane detector is a barrier placed on an accessible route to prevent a person with visual impairment from walking into an obstacle. A visually impaired person approaching an overhanging obstacle (such as a set of stairs) would detect the ground-level barrier with his cane and follow the barrier around the object to the point of clear passage.

Communication

Public accommodations are required[i] to take steps necessary to ensure that no individual with a disability is excluded, denied services, segregated or otherwise treated differently than other individuals because of the absence of auxiliary aids and services, unless the provision of those aids or services would fundamentally alter the nature of the services, facilities or accommodations or would result in an undue burden. The Preamble to those regulations states,

> "Implicit in this duty to provide auxiliary aids and services is the underlying obligation of a public accommodation to communicate effectively with its customers... who have disabilities affecting hearing, vision or speech."

See question 151 for further information on communicating with hearing or vision-impaired persons in federally assisted properties.

There is therefore a requirement under Title III to provide effective means of communication. A common procedural accommodation is to provide materials orally instead of in writing. For example, the housing provider could have someone read the lease (and could audiotape this reading, for re-use in the future) and house rules. Some persons with vision impairments may request materials in Braille; however, advocates for persons with disabilities report that only some vision-impaired persons are literate in Braille. Remember, however, that the auxiliary aid requirement is a flexible one that allows the public accommodation to choose from a variety of alternatives as long as the result is effective communication. Therefore materials in Braille need not be provided if

---

i. 28 Code of Federal Regulations, Section 36.303 (ADA Title III Regulations) they can conveniently be read or communicated orally to the individual.

Title II of the ADA (applicable to public entities) requires that when an auxiliary aid or service is required, the public entity must provide an opportunity for individuals with disabilities to request the auxiliary aids and services of their choice and must give primary consideration to the choice expressed by the individual.[ii] "Primary consideration" means that the public entity must honor the individual's choice, unless it can demonstrate that another equally effective means of communication is available, or that use of the means chosen would result in a fundamental alteration in the service, program, or activity or in undue financial and administrative burdens.

102 Hearing Impairments

Materials Normally Delivered Verbally

A common procedural accommodation is to provide materials that are normally provided in a verbal presentation, in written form. For example, instead of a verbal presentation while touring the model unit, a hearing-impaired applicant is provided a written summary of features and benefits.

Sign Language Interpretation

Unless one of the housing provider's staff members is trained in sign language there will probably be a significant cost attached to providing sign language translation services for hearing impaired applicants or residents, especially considering that other methods of communication are possible—for example written communication.

Telecommunications Device for the Deaf (TDD)

Installation of text telephones is required under certain conditions in new construction and alterations of buildings and facilities covered by ADA. If a total number of four or more public pay telephones (including both interior and exterior phones) is provided at a site, and at least one is in an interior location, then at least one interior public text telephone is required.

Audible Alarms

Audible emergency signals must have an intensity and frequency that can attract the attention of individuals who have partial hearing loss.

ii. 28 CFR, Section 35.160

Visual Fire Alarms

A visual alarm provides persons with hearing loss the same warning delivered to hearing persons by an audible alarm. Visual alarms are flashing lights used as fire alarm signals. The terms visual alarm signal, visible signal device and visible signaling appliance are used relatively interchangeably within the fire protection community.

See question 84.

Persons with hearing impairments sometimes request the installation of visual fire alarms. This could be as simple as a battery powered smoke detector with a visual alarm, or the request could be to install a visual alarm that is compatible with the building's fire alarm system.

103 Chronic Mental Illness, In General

Myth of Violence

There is a persistent myth that the mentally ill pose a physical danger to their neighbors. However, research demonstrates that persons with chronic mental illness are *less* likely to engage in violent conduct than persons without chronic mental illness. According to the National Alliance for the Mentally Ill, people who have a mental illness are more often the victims rather than the perpetrators of violence.

See question 90 for further discussion on excluding applicants or residents because they pose a direct threat to the health and safety of others.

Remember, however, that you can terminate an existing tenancy or refuse an application for housing if there is evidence that the resident's or applicant's presence at the property poses or will pose a threat to the health and safety of other residents, which cannot be removed or minimized by any reasonable accommodation that the housing provider may furnish.[iii]

Failure to medicate

Many mental illnesses are well controlled by medication. However, a lapse in medication can result in conduct that violates the lease. Should this occur professional managers recommend meeting with the resident and his or her mental health care provider (if there is one) to discuss how the resident's behavior violates the requirements of the lease and to establish what steps the resident must take to become and stay lease compliant. The results of this meeting should be put in writing and a copy given to the resident and care provider. If there are continued documented lease viola-

---

iii. 24 CFR, Section 100.203(d)

tions then you may consider taking steps towards terminating the tenancy.

104 Multiple Chemical Sensitivity

Is Multiple Chemical Sensitivity a Disability?

Both HUD and the Department of Justice have taken the position that Multiple Chemical Sensitivity ("MCS") may constitute handicaps or disabilities under the Fair Housing Act or ADA respectively. However, a determination whether an individual who suffers from MCS is handicapped or disabled within the meaning of those enactments depends on whether the disease is sufficiently severe to substantially limit one or more major life activities. However, housing providers are not equipped to make decisions on whether in a particular case the symptoms of MCS are severe enough to qualify as a handicap or disability. Therefore once a resident produces credible evidence that he or she suffers from MCS and requests an accommodation on that basis the same consideration should be given to the request as would be given to requests for accommodation from other residents with disabilities.

See questions 62 and 86 for further information on accommodating chemical and environmental sensitivities.

Requests for Accommodation frequently made by people with Multiple Chemical Sensitivity include:

Pest Control

Persons with MCS sometimes request that pest control chemicals not be used in their apartments. Expert managers advise that it would be reasonable to agree to this request. However, some alternative method of ensuring that the dwelling does not become infested with pests must be devised. If there is pest infestation in the apartment, the housing provider, the resident, and the pest control professional should work together to find an acceptable pest control method.

Duct Cleaning

In older apartments, residents sometimes request to have the HVAC ducts cleaned on a more frequent basis than the routine HVAC inspections that the property conducts.

Carpet Cleaning

Residents sometimes request that management shampoo the carpets as a disability accommodation.

See question 64 on reasonable accommodation; federally-assisted properties should refer to question 126 on "burdens."

In determining how to respond to the above requests, determine first if the requested accommodation is necessary to afford the resident 'equal opportunity to use and enjoy the dwelling unit." Second, determine if the accommodation is reasonable. Properties subject to Section 504 should determine instead if the accommodation would impose an "undue administrative or financial burden."

105 Asthma

Asthma is a health condition involving an excessive immune system reaction that causes inflammation of the bronchial tubes. Inflammation leads to partial or full closure of the tubes, resulting in difficulty in breathing or inability to breathe. Asthma is gaining recognition as a leading health and environmental issue for children. For reasons that researchers have not been able to identify definitively, asthma affects disproportionate numbers of low income and minority children.

Asthma begins with *sensitization*, in which a person becomes highly sensitive to one or more allergens. Subsequently, asthma attacks occur when the sensitized person is exposed to a large concentration of an allergen. Allergens mentioned by researchers as likely major causes of childhood asthma include cockroaches, dust mites, mold, and animal dander. Researchers also believe that stress and environmental tobacco smoke may contribute to, or perhaps can cause, asthma attacks. Persons with asthma are less likely to suffer asthma attacks if their homes are relatively free of allergens.

Is Asthma a Disability?

Yes. Symptoms may vary from individual to individual, but generally requests for accommodation should be considered once there is evidence that the resident suffers from this condition.

Requests for Accommodation frequently made by persons with Asthma:

See questions 86 and 104.

• *Pest Control* - Residents with asthma sometimes request that pest control chemicals not be used in their apartments. As with similar requests from persons suffering from MCS it may often be reasonable to agree to this request.

- *Apartment Location* - Some residents request transfer to a ground floor apartment, or to an apartment nearer to the elevator, to reduce walking distances. If this request is related to the resident's mobility or other impairment to which a qualified professional has attested, it should be granted when an appropriate unit becomes available. You should not, however, displace an existing tenant in order to accommodate this request.

106 HIV/AIDS

See question 98 for further information on diseases covered by the ADA.

Human Immunodeficiency Virus (HIV) is specifically mentioned in the Fair Housing Act as an example of a physical impairment. However, persons with AIDS, and persons who are HIV-positive, are considered persons with disabilities under the Fair Housing Act only when their disease substantially limits one or more major life activities. Note however, that under the ADA, HIV need not be symptomatic in order to be regarded as a physical or mental impairment. Note also that people with asymptomatic HIV may nevertheless be regarded by members of the public as having a physical impairment and are therefore entitled to the protections given to the physically disabled by the Fair Housing Act.

Chapter Fourteen: Fair Housing Requirements Affecting Federally Assisted Properties

107 Are There Additional Requirements that Affect Federally Assisted Apartments?

Some federally assisted properties are subject to additional requirements. These include:

Section 504

Also see questions 108, 110, and Chapter 15.

Section 504 of the Rehabilitation Act of 1973 requires recipients of federal financial assistance not to discriminate against "otherwise qualified individuals with handicaps" in their programs which may include services (like counseling), activities (like senior citizen outings) or housing.

1992 Act

Also see question 112.

The Housing and Community Development Act of 1992[i] ("1992 Act"). Title VI of this Act allows owners of certain Section 8 properties designed primarily for occupancy by elderly families to elect to give a preference in admission to the elderly and, thereby, limit the number of nonelderly, disabled individuals.

Title VI

See question 14.

Title VI of the Civil Rights Act of 1964 prohibits discrimination on the basis of race, color or national origin in all HUD-assisted programs[ii] Title VI covers all HUD housing programs except for its mortgage insurance and loan guarantee programs.

Architectural Barriers Act

The Architectural Barriers Act of 1968 requires certain federal and federally funded buildings and other facilities to be designed, constructed or altered in accordance with standards that ensure accessibility to, and use by, physically handicapped people.

Age Discrimination Act

The Age Discrimination Act of 1975[iii] prohibits discrimination on the basis of age in programs receiving federal financial assistance. This Act, however, permits federally assisted programs and activities and recipients of federal funds to continue to use certain age distinctions if it is a factor necessary to the "normal operation or statutory objective of a program or activity."

Title II of the Americans With Disabilities Act

Title II of the Americans With Disabilities Act applies to activities of state and local governments. See question 13.

---

i.   24 CFR, Part 30 and Part 35
ii. 24 CFR, Part 1.
iii. 24 CFR, 146.13

The following is a brief summary of specific federal housing assistance programs and fair housing considerations they face in addition to the Fair Housing Act:

Rural Housing Service

The Rural Housing Service of the Department of Agriculture ("RHS") provides mortgage financing and/or rent subsidies to properties serving rural areas. In general, RHS properties are subject to fair housing requirements under the same laws that govern fair housing for HUD-assisted properties (also see question 113).

Public Housing

Public housing is subject to Section 504 and Title II of the ADA. See question 114.

Low Income Housing Tax Credit

See question 115.

In 1996, the IRS revised its Form 8823, the Low-Income Housing Credit Agencies Report of Noncompliance, to include the following paragraph, "the failure of Low-Income Housing Credit properties to comply with the requirements of the Fair Housing Act will result in the denial of the low income housing tax credit on a per-unit basis". This means that in addition to other penalties for non-compliance with the Fair Housing Act, Housing Credit properties risk the the loss of credits. Also note that Housing Credit properties do not appear to be subject to 504 regulations. Of course, other federal financing on a Housing Credit property may trigger 504 requirements.

HOME

HOME (The Home Investment Partnerships Program) is a federal program and is therefore subject to Section 504.

Section 8

Section 8 project based assistance is subject to Section 504. Additionally, those who rent to recipients of tenant-based Section 8 subsidy should review question 110.

Community Development Block Grant (CDBG)

Section 109 of the Housing and Community Development Act ("HCD") of 1974, Title 1, prohibits discrimination on the basis of race, color, national origin, disability, age, religion and sex within Community Development Block Grant (CDBG) programs or activities. In addition, CDBG is a federal program and is therefore subject to the requirements of Section 504.

108 What Is "Section 504"?

Summary

Section 504 is a provision of the Rehabilitation Act of 1973, as amended, which prohibits discrimination against an "otherwise

See also question 117. Chapter 15 contains additional information on the requirements of Section 504.

qualified individual with handicaps" by "recipients of federal financial assistance." The Section 504 definition of "individual with handicaps" is essentially identical to the Fair Housing Act's definition of "person with disability" The terms "recipients" and "federal financial assistance" are discussed further in question 110. This guidebook will use the term "housing providers" when referring to "recipients."

The Section 504 Regulations

On June 2, 1988, HUD published final regulations[iv] implementing the anti-discrimination provisions of the 1973 statute, as they relate to federally assisted housing. The regulation was intended to ensure that otherwise qualified persons with handicaps receive:

• Equal opportunity to participate in programs and services;

• Equal opportunity to gain the same benefits as other persons;

• No denial of rights to dwellings;

• No unnecessary differences in services;

• Provision of assistance in the most integrated setting that is appropriate; and

• The opportunity to serve on planning and advisory boards.

"Otherwise Qualified"

Section 504 requires the applicant to be "otherwise qualified" (that is, able to meet the requirements for the federal program benefits). This reaffirms HUD's position that all applicants for housing must meet basic screening criteria set out by management in addition to HUD eligibility requirements. An individual who cannot meet all program requirements is not a qualified individual, and his or her application may be declined on that basis, regardless of disability. However, housing providers should note that if a "reasonable accommodation" would allow the applicant to meet the housing program eligibility requirements, the housing provider must make the reasonable accommodation, and the applicant is entitled to the protections of Section 504. Providers are advised to establish clear written guidelines for determining and offering appropriate reasonable accommodations for applicants and residents.

See question 64 for an in-depth discussion of reasonable accommodation.

---

iv. Section 504 Regulations are found at 24 CFR, Parts 8 and 9.

**Program
Accessibility**

Section 504 regulations require subject properties to be "readily accessible to and usable by" persons with disabilities. Housing providers must ensure that persons with visual, speaking or hearing impairments can effectively communicate as necessary for their effective participation in the program. In addition, persons with mobility impairments must not be prevented from entering or using premises by virtue of the physical inaccessibility of the property. Reasonable modifications (i.e. structural changes) or reasonable policy accommodations (non structural changes) may be required, at the housing provider's expense, to make the property "barrier free."

**Fundamental
Alteration**

Housing providers are not required to make such physical or policy modifications if to do so would result in a fundamental alteration of the program. See question 123.

**Undue
Burdens**

Similarly, housing providers are not required to make accommodations or modifications if to do so would impose undue financial and administrative burdens on the housing provider. See questions 126, 127 and 128.

**Self-Evalu-
ation**

Properties covered by Section 504 were required to perform a self-evaluation of the property and its operations by July 11, 1989, and to modify policies or practices not in compliance with Section 504. Subsequently, properties must make reasonable accommodations in policies and procedures to enable persons with disabilities to occupy and make full use of dwellings and facilities. See question 24.

**Transition
Plan**

If physical modifications are needed to provide accessibility, a transition plan was required to ensure that common areas (including leasing and management offices), programs and facilities become accessible, and to establish a plan for providing accessible dwelling units. See question 25.

Any necessary structural changes that the plan identified as being necessary to make facilities accessible were to be completed by July 11, 1991.

**"Substantial
Alterations"
and "Other
Alterations"**

When ongoing maintenance, repair and replacement activities at a property meet the definition of "alterations," accessibility requirements apply (i.e. barriers to accessibility must be removed). These accessibility requirements mandate or strongly encourage housing providers to make a specified number of dwelling units accessible immediately. These accessibility requirements for individual units within a property apply until five percent of the units are accessible to persons with mobility impairments.

See also questions 137 and 138.

For substantial alterations only, up to an additional two percent of the units must be accessible to persons with visual or hearing impairments.

Reasonable Modifications

For all affected properties, providers must make reasonable, case-by-case, modifications to units, as needed to accommodate persons with disabilities, subject to certain exceptions. See question 74.

Enforcement

HUD's Office of Fair Housing and Equal Opportunity is responsible for monitoring Section 504 compliance and investigating complaints. Conciliation among parties is encouraged, but HUD may also seek other relief, including termination of federal financial assistance. See question 109.

Technical Assistance

HUD's Office of Fair Housing and Equal Opportunity staff provide Section 504 technical assistance to recipients of HUD financial assistance and to consumers of HUD services.

109 What Is the Enforcement Process for Section 504 of the Rehabilitation Act?

Complaint and Investigative Procedures for Section 504 of the Rehabilitation Act

Complaints under Section 504 may be filed by persons who believe that they have been discriminated against, or by their authorized representatives. Complaints may be filed either with:

- HUD; or

- In a US District Court

Complaints that are filed with HUD must be filed within 180 days of the alleged act of discrimination. HUD's procedure for handling complaints (which also applies to complaints under Title II of the ADA) is as follows:

1   The housing provider will be notified of the complaint within 10 days of receipt by HUD and will have 30 days from notification to respond to the complaint.

2   The complaint will be investigated and HUD will attempt to resolve the matter informally. Informal resolutions may result in a written "Voluntary Compliance Agreement" signed by the housing provider and HUD.

3   If the matter is not informally resolved, within 180 days of receipt of the complaint, HUD will notify the complainant and housing provider of the results of the investigation. This will be comprised in a "Letter of Findings" that will conclude that there was either compliance or noncompliance with the requirements of the law. This is referred to as a "preliminary finding."

4   Preliminary findings may be reviewed at the request of either the complainant or the housing provider. Such requests must be made within 30 days of receipt of the Letter of Findings.

5   A review of the findings will be concluded within 60 days of the request for review and will either sustain or modify the preliminary findings.

6   If neither party requests a review of the findings HUD will send the housing provider a formal written determination of compliance or noncompliance.

7   If there is a determination of noncompliance the housing provider has 10 days from receipt of the determination to come into voluntary compliance.

If the housing provider does not come into voluntary compliance federal financial assistance may be suspended, terminated or discontinued or the matter may be referred to the Department of Justice with a recommendation that legal proceedings be brought against the housing provider.

110 What Is "Federal Financial Assistance"?

Section 504 covers properties receiving "federal financial assistance," including "market rate" properties that receive some federal assistance. Examples of properties that must comply with Section 504 even though they may appear not to be "subsidized" include:

- Properties financed under HUD's Community Development Block Grant (CDBG) or Home Investment Partnerships (HOME) programs.

- Properties with a project-based Section 8 subsidy contract covering some or all of the units.

Section 504 applies to properties subsidized by HUD under the following programs:

- Section 236

- Section 221(d)(3) BMIR

- Section 8, Rental Assistance Payment (RAP) and Rent Supplement (see below)

- Section 202 and Section 811

- Other programs listed in Appendix A to the regulations;

There are some special cases involving Section 8 that deserve additional comment:

- Properties receiving Project Based Section 8 assistance are subject to Section 504. For example:

  - New Construction,

  - Substantial Rehabilitation,

  - State Agency Set-Aside,

  - RHS Home Set-Aside,

  - Moderate Rehabilitation,

  - Loan Management Set-Aside, and

  - Property Disposition Set-Aside

See Chapter 15.
- If a property has partial Project Based Section 8 subsidy, the Section 504 accessibility requirements cover the entire property's procedures and common areas, and HUD takes the position that all units -- including the unassisted units -- are covered by the Section 504 dwelling unit accessibility requirements.

- Properties that receive Resident Based Section 8 subsidies on behalf of residents are not "recipients of federal financial assistance" under the Section 504 regulations. However, housing providers should carefully read their contracts with the housing authority. The entity that provides the voucher (usually the public housing authority) is a "recipient," is therefore subject to Section 504, and must require participating owners to enter into HUD approved contracts which include assurances of nondiscrimination.

FHA Mortgage Insurance does not, by itself, trigger Section 504 requirements.

111 How Do the Fair Housing Act, ADA, and Section 504 Differ?

The following chart illustrates the major differences between these nondiscrimination laws:

Differences in Nondiscrimination Laws

Issue	FHA	ADA	504
Covers federally-assisted properties	Yes	Portions[*]	Yes
Covers all properties	Yes	Portions	No
Covers employment practices	No	Portions	Yes
Protects families with children	Yes	No	No
In-unit accessibility modifications are paid for by person with disabilities	Yes	n/a	Rarely
In-unit accessibility modifications are paid for by the housing provider	No	n/a	Usually

[*] The ADA does not apply to apply to apartment units except in those cases where the project is owned or financed by a state or municipality or in transient housing where the rentals are short term. It does, however, apply to places of business that are open to the public such as laundry rooms and offices.

See question 13 for a discussion of the limited applicability of ADA Title II to apartment properties, and a brief discussion of employment-related issues.

In the preceding chart, the ADA column refers to the ADA requirements shared by all apartment properties: Title I's employment requirements and Title III's requirements for accessibility of the rental office and other public places of business within the property.

The major additional requirement imposed by Section 504 beyond the requirements of the Fair Housing Act and ADA is that the housing provider must undertake and pay for accessibility modifications up to the point of undue financial and administrative burdens being created. Title II of the ADA (state and local government activities) imposes a similar requirement

Of course, under the Fair Housing Act, all housing providers continue to be responsible for ensuring non-discrimination based on race, color, religion, sex, national origin, familial status and disability.

This guidebook addresses rental housing issues only. Accordingly, this guidebook does not cover the Section 504 or ADA provisions regarding employment.

112 What Does "Mixed Populations" Mean?

See Chapter 20.

"Mixed populations" is a phrase used to describe the housing of elderly residents and non-elderly residents with disabilities, in properties originally designed and developed for occupancy primarily by the elderly. A large number of nonelderly persons with disabilities were admitted over the years. As a result, the elderly (i.e., those 62 years of age or older), for whom such housing had originally been built, were being admitted less frequently.

See question 107.

On October 28, 1992, Congress passed the Housing and Community Development Act of 1992 ("1992 Act"). Title VI of this Act allows owners of certain Section 8 properties to elect to give a preference in admission to the elderly. However, an owner's right to accord a preference to the elderly is subject to the requirement that a specified number of dwelling units at the property be set-aside for persons with disabilities who are under the age of 50. The final regulations were published on December 12, 1994.

113 How Does the Rural Housing Service Implement Fair Housing Act and Section 504 Requirements?

Like HUD, the U.S. Department of Agriculture's Rural Housing Service (RHS), formerly known as the Farmers Home Administration, has incorporated the Fair Housing Act and Section 504 into its regulatory requirements, as set out primarily in the Multi-Family Management Handbook 1930-C, which is used by all Agency staff, borrowers and managers.

Unlike HUD's 4350.3 Occupancy Handbook, the RHS 1930-C contains no detailed explanation of the purpose of Section 504 or Fair Housing Act. Nonetheless, the requirements are incorporated into the procedures for admission and occupancy of RHS properties, in many instances using actual wording from the Fair Housing Act.

Like HUD, RHS is committed to non-discrimination. RHS has a separate Equal Opportunity Office and a Civil Rights Coordinator in each state for review of compliance and handling complaints.

In a Memorandum dated September 9, 1996, RHS provided more detailed guidance. Copies of the 1930-C Handbook, Administrative Notices (AN's) and the September 9, 1996 Memorandum may be obtained by calling any State or Regional (District) Servicing Office of RHS (at the state and local level, RHS is referred to as Rural Development).

114 Special Requirements for Public Housing

Guidance addressing admission and occupancy requirements for Public Housing are contained in HUD's Public Occupancy Handbook 7465.1. This handbook provides public housing agencies (PHAs) with HUD policy and advice on occupancy matters related to the Lower Income Public Housing Program. In addition to the Fair Housing Act, PHAs are required to abide by the non-discrimination provisions of:

- Title VI of the Civil Rights Act of 1964

- Title VIII of the Civil Rights Act of 1968

- Section 504 of the Rehabilitation Act of 1973

- The Age Discrimination Act of 1975

- The Architectural Barriers Act

- Executive Order 11063.

- Title II of the ADA

115 What Are the Consequences of Non-Compliance with Fair Housing on a Housing Credit Property?

Fair Housing laws, of course, apply to Housing Credit properties in the same way as all other multifamily rental properties. In addition, however, violations of Fair Housing Laws on a Housing Credit property can lead to the recapture of all credits. This means, in effect, that Fair Housing violations on Housing Credit properties may have more severe consequences than on other properties, and owners and managers of these properties should take compliance very seriously.

Some specific Fair Housing issues raised in the operation of a Housing Credit project include:

- *Students* - Housing Credit regulations do not permit a household comprised entirely of students (with some exceptions) to occupy a unit. This is not a violation of fair housing laws, unless student status (matriculation) is a protected class in your state or local area.

- *Income Level* - Housing Credit apartments are designed to assist low- and moderate-income families. While households cannot earn over a certain amount in order to qualify for a Housing Credit apartment, there is no minimum income. It is not a violation of Fair Housing laws to require a minimum income, and prudent managers establish a minimum that ensures the household can afford the Housing Credit rent while also ensuring a sufficient number of eligible applicants.

- *Section 8* - While source of income is not a federally protected class according to the Fair Housing laws, Housing Credit regulations prohibit you from refusing to rent based solely on a household's receipt of Section 8 assistance (Section 8 applicants must, however, meet all other program eligibility criteria). In addition, source of income is a protected class in some states and localities.

- *Placement of Housing Credit Units* - In properties that have both market rate and income-restricted units, Fair Housing considerations affect the placement of units throughout the property:

  - Housing Credit apartments must have substantially the same features and amenities as market-rate apartments. In some states, they must be equivalent in size.

  See question 9.

  - It is generally thought to be easier to comply with the Housing Credit regulations if Housing Credit and market-rate units are segregated into different buildings. However, this may be viewed as discriminatory, particularly if there are any discernible differences in the quality of service, features, or location of the buildings. In other words, if your Housing Credit residents represent members of one or more protected classes, then any unequal treatment of Housing Credit residents will therefore result in unequal treatment of a protected class. Be aware that your state housing finance agency's approval of placement of Housing Credit units throughout the property will not provide you with any protection from Fair Housing complaints or enforcement action.

  - Properties at which all units are Housing Credit apartments but that have multiple set-asides (i.e. some units reserved for households earning less than 50 percent of median area income and some less than 80 percent) must also be careful how these units are distributed throughout the property.

Chapter Fifteen: Disability-Related Requirements in Federally-Assisted Housing

116   Who Is Protected by Section 504 of the Rehabilitation Act?

Section 504 of the Rehabilitation Act of 1973 protects against discrimination of "qualified individuals with handicaps" who participate in programs and activities conducted by HUD or that receive financial assistance from HUD. A qualified individual is one who is "eligible to participate in a program or activity" (in other words, who meets the housing program's eligibility requirements). This would include individuals who, if they were to receive a "reasonable accommodation" from the housing provider, could meet the housing program requirements.

117   What Is the Section 504 Definition of "Individual With Handicaps"?

In both the Fair Housing Act and Section 504, an "individual with handicap" is defined as:

"Any person who has a physical or mental impairment that substantially limits one or more major life activities; has a record of such an impairment; or is regarded as having such an impairment."

Refer to questions 60 and 62 for the definitions of disability according to the Fair Housing Act and Americans With Disabilities Act.

The similarity of the definitions in both laws is not accidental: the Preamble to the Fair Housing Regulations explains that:

"Congress intended that the definition of 'handicap' in the Fair Housing Amendments Act be interpreted in a manner that is consistent with regulations interpreting the meaning of the similar provision found in Section 504 of the Rehabilitation Act of 1973." [i]

---

i.   54 FR 3232 – Implementation of the Fair Housing Amendments Act of 1988

118 What Is the HUD Handbook Definition of Disability?

See also questions 60, 117, 120 and 121.

Some federally assisted properties are subject to HUD Occupancy Handbook 4350.3. This handbook defines disability for the purposes of admission to certain federal housing programs (Exhibit 2-1 of the Handbook), as well as for eligibility for protection under the Fair Housing Act and Section 504 of the Rehabilitation Act (Exhibit 2-2). Refer to these documents to ensure that you are applying the correct definitions for a given situation.

119 Does Section 504 Require Me To Modify My Procedures or My Property?

See questions 23, 24 and 130 for further information on the requirements of a self-evaluation and accessibility review.

Section 504 requires that "the [housing] program, when viewed in its entirety, is readily accessible to and useable by individuals with handicaps." Section 504 requires properties to perform a "self evaluation" (to ascertain the existence of barriers to accessibility) and prepare a "transition plan" (setting out a timetable and methodology for removing such barriers). A self-evaluation generally reviews policies, practices and procedures that the property may have in place and identifies any barriers to accessibility that are found to result from these policies, practices and procedures. In order to prepare the transition plan it may be necessary to perform an accessibility review to evaluate the nature and extent of any physical barriers to accessibility.

See question 64 on reasonable accommodation, and question 74 on reasonable modification.

Section 504 also requires housing providers to modify their procedures, practices and policies to ensure that they do not discriminate against a qualified individual with handicaps and to undertake reasonable modifications to dwelling units and common areas, when requested by applicants and residents with disabilities, as needed to provide accessibility. Section 504 requires that the housing provider pay for these changes.

See questions 123 and 127 for further information on what constitutes a fundamental alteration and undue financial and administrative burdens.

These changes do not have to be made, however, if making them would result in a fundamental alteration in the nature of the program under which the housing is provided or in undue financial and administrative burdens; however, changes have to be made up to the point that undue burdens are created.

120 What Are the Housing Assistance Program Definitions of Handicap and Disability?

See Chapter 5 for guidance on resident selection criteria.

In order to be admitted to federally-assisted housing, an applicant household must meet housing program eligibility requirements and also satisfy the housing provider's uniform, nondiscriminatory resident selection criteria. The remainder of this question will be devoted to questions of program eligibility (i.e. eligibility requirements that arise from the federal legislation, regulations, contracts and handbooks governing the particular housing programs under which a given property operates).

See also question 121.

Once admitted, households meeting program definitions of "disability" or "handicap" may be entitled to certain deductions that may reduce the amount of rent the household will pay.

Eligibility Requirements Common to All Programs

The following are the program eligibility requirements that are common to all regulated housing properties:

See also question 121.

- Household income must not exceed the income limit for the program (with rare exceptions).

- Household size must be appropriate for at least one of the unit types available at the property. Recent legislative and handbook changes provide that single persons are eligible for all HUD-regulated housing programs.

Additional Requirements for Family Properties

In general, for properties designed and operated for families, HUD housing programs impose no additional eligibility requirements. As discussed above, however, applicant households must also satisfy the housing provider's resident selection criteria.

Properties Exclusively for the Elderly

For the few HUD-assisted properties designed and operated solely for the elderly (i.e., with no provision for also serving non-elderly persons with disabilities), there is one additional program eligibility requirement: the head of household or spouse must be age 62 or over.

Properties for the Elderly and Non-elderly Persons with Disabilities

Historically, the majority of HUD-regulated housing properties serving the elderly also included a number of units (typically 10 percent of the total number of units) designed for persons with disabilities regardless of age (usually these apartments were designed to be accessible to wheelchair users). For these properties, households are required to meet one of the following additional program eligibility requirements:

- The head of household or spouse must be age 62 or over; or

- The household must meet the applicable program definition of "disabled" or "handicapped."

Housing Program Definition of "Disability"

The program definition of "disability" or "handicap" varies by housing program, with some programs offering a number of criteria under which a household might be eligible. Usually, it may be sufficient if any member of the household meets the criteria, but in some programs, either the head of household or spouse is required to have the disability or handicap condition.

Following is a summary of the most common regulated housing programs that have their own definition of "handicap" and/or "disability" for purposes of program eligibility. If a housing program in which you participate is not listed, you should check the applicable regulations to determine whether it, too, has its own definitions.

Some general principles should be kept in mind during the discussion of program definitions of "disability" and "handicap:"

- Typically, households with a member who has mobility impairments will be eligible under most of the programs. This is because the typical "handicap" accessible apartment was designed specifically to be accessible to wheelchair users.

- Whether households with other types of disabilities are eligible depends on HUD's determination of the purpose for which the housing program was enacted by Congress.

- Where, for instance, a given program requires non-elderly households to have a mobility impairment in order to be eligible, the existence of other disabilities in addition to the mobility impairment does not affect the eligibility. For example, a household with both a mobility impairment and a chronic mental illness would still be eligible.

- A household that meets the Section 504 definition of "individual with handicap" but which does not satisfy the other applicable housing program definition(s) would not be eligible for housing set aside for the disabled. This is because Section 504 protects "*otherwise* eligible individuals with handicap;" if the household does not meet the program eligibility requirements, then the protection provided by Section 504 does not apply.

The Section 8 Programs

The Housing and Community Development Act of 1992 ("the 1992 Act") changed the terms used in these programs. Prior to the 1992 Act, the terms "handicapped person" and "disabled person" were used. With the enactment of the 1992 Act, only one term is used: "person with disabilities," defined as a person who:

1 *"Has a disability as defined in Section 223 of the Social Security Act, which reads: "an inability to engage in any substantial gainful activity because of any physical or mental impairment that is expected to result in death or has lasted or can be expected to last continuously for at least 12 months; or, for a blind person at least 55 years old, inability because of blindness to engage in any substantial gainful activities comparable to those in which the person was previously engaged with some regularity and over a substantial period of time;" or*

2 *"Is determined, pursuant to regulations issued by the Secretary of HUD, to have a physical, mental, or emotional impairment which is expected to be of a long-continued and indefinite duration; substantially impedes the person's ability to live independently; and is such that this ability to live independently could be improved by more suitable housing conditions; or*

3 *Has a developmental disability as defined in Section 102 of the Developmental Disabilities Assistance and Bill of Rights Act, which reads: "a severe, chronic disability of a person 5 years of age or older which*

(A) is attributable to a mental or physical impairment or a combination of mental and physical impairments;

(B) is manifested before the person attains age 22;

(C) is likely to continue indefinitely;

(D) results in substantial functional limitations in three or more areas of the following areas of major life activity:

　(i)　self-care,

　(ii)　receptive and expressive language,

　(iii)　learning,

　(iv)　mobility,

　(v)　self-direction,

　(vi)　capacity for independent living; and

　(vii)　economic self-sufficiency.

(E) reflects the person's need for a combination and sequence of special, interdisciplinary, or generic care, treatment, or other services which are of lifelong or extended duration and are individually planned and coordinated; except that such term, when applied to infants and young children, means individuals from birth to age 5, inclusive, who have substantial developmental delay or specific congenital or acquired conditions with a high probability of resulting in developmental disabilities if services are not provided."

This definition, which merely combines the definitions of the previously used terms with little or no substantive changes, is applicable to all housing assisted under the Section 8 program. Prior to the 1992 Act, the terms in effect were defined as follows: "Handicapped person" (see definition (2) above) and the only change by the 1992 Act is the inclusion of "emotional impairment," and "disabled person." (See definitions (1) and (3) above). There were no changes to these definitions as a result of the 1992 Act.

See also Chapter 20 regarding Mixed Populations.

It should be noted that until the enactment of the 1992 Act, the Section 8 program had defined "elderly family" to include households whose members all were under age 62 but whose head, spouse or sole member was handicapped or disabled. The 1992

See Chapter 19 for
further information
on assisted properties
that are entitled to
provide a preference
for the elderly.Act provided a new definition of "elderly families" for properties that give a preference in admission to elderly families. This definition excludes from preferential admission non-elderly handicapped or disabled households and includes only those households where the head spouse or sole member is 62. (Eligible households, i.e. those with an elderly head or spouse can also include other members who are handicapped or disabled, however.) Properties that do not grant a preference to elderly families will continue to use the pre-1992 Act definition of elderly household.

Section 202 Of The Housing Act Of 1959 And Section 811 Of The National Affordable Housing Act

The Cranston-Gonzalez National Affordable Housing Act of 1990 ("the 1990 Act") made significant changes in the Section 202 program with respect to the manner in which housing under the program will be offered in the future. The 1990 Act provided that, in the future, separate housing would be provided for the elderly and for persons with disabilities: supportive housing for the elderly would be provided under Section 202 and supportive housing for persons with disabilities would be provided under Section 811. Under the Section 811 program disabilities are separated into three major categories: physical disability, developmental disability and chronic mental illness. An owner may, with HUD approval, limit occupancy of Section 811 housing to persons with similar disabilities.

As a result of the 1990 Act, the following definitions apply to properties approved as Section 202 or Section 811 properties on or after October 1, 1991, or such properties for which a loan had been approved but had not yet closed and were converted to the new category (referred to as "post 1990 Act property").

Post-1990 Act Section 202 program

For the post-1990 Act Section 202 program, the following definitions apply:

- "Elderly person" means a household composed of one or more persons, at least one of whom is age 62 or older.

See 24 CFR, Chapter VIII, Section 889.105 and Handbook 5471.3, Rev. 1, pp. 113.

- "Frail elderly" means an elderly person who is unable to perform at least three of five activities of daily living adopted by the Secretary for purposes of this program. The five activities of daily living are: (1) eating; (2) bathing; (3) grooming; (4)

dressing; (5) home management activities (for example housework, grocery shopping, laundry).

Section 811 Program

For the Section 811 program the following definitions apply:

- "Person with disabilities" means a household composed of one or more persons, at least one of whom has a disability.

- "Disability" means a physical, mental, or emotional impairment, which (a) is expected to be of a long-continued and indefinite duration; (b) substantially impedes the person's ability to live independently; and (c) is such that this ability to live independently could be improved by more suitable housing conditions.

- A person shall also be considered disabled if such person has a "developmental disability" (see definition 3 for the Section 8 program above).

Post-1990 Act properties are identified by the letters HD or EE in the HUD project number. The letters HH or EH identify a pre-1990 Act property.

Pre-1990 Act, Section 202

For pre-1990 Act Section 202 properties the following definitions apply:

- "Handicapped person" means any adult having a physical, mental, or emotional impairment which (1) is expected to be of a long-continued and indefinite duration; (2) substantially impedes the person's ability to live independently; and (3) is such that this ability to live independently could be improved by more suitable housing conditions.

- A person is also considered handicapped if he or she (1) has a 'developmental disability' (see definition 3 for the Section 8 program above), or (2) has a chronic mental illness (defined as a severe and persistent mental or emotional impairment that seriously limits his or her ability to live independently (e.g., by limiting functional capacities relative to primary aspects of daily living such as personal relations, living arrangements, work, recreation, etc.), and whose impairment could be improved by more suitable housing conditions.

Section 221   For purposes of Section 221 properties, persons are considered handicapped if they are handicapped within the definition which applies to pre 1990 Act Section 202 properties (see above).

Section 236   Under the Section 236 program, the definitions of "handicap" and "disability" are the same as those for the Section 8 program prior to the 1992 Act:

- "Handicapped person" means any adult having a physical or mental impairment which is expected to be of a long-continued and indefinite duration; substantially impedes the person's ability to live independently; and is such that this ability to live independently could be improved by more suitable housing conditions.

- "Disabled person" means a person who has a disability as defined in Section 223 of the Social Security Act (see Section 8, definition 1 above), or who has a developmental disability (see Section 8, definition 3 above).

121 Fair Housing Act vs. Program Definition

To the extent that being disabled/handicapped is a requirement of eligibility for admission to certain types of housing, the specific program definition of disability or handicap, which may be more restrictive than the Fair Housing Act or Section 504 definition, will prevail.

See question 87 for a discussion of inquiries.

The housing program definitions may come into play in two situations: firstly, when satisfying one of the applicable definitions is a prerequisite to establishing the household's eligibility; and secondly to establish eligibility for certain allowances against income. In both situations, it is acceptable to request verification of the existence of a disability. In the second situation, it is acceptable to request information regarding expected medical or assistance expenses.

To illustrate the first situation: a person applying for admission to a pre-October 1991 Section 202 property for the physically disabled must meet the housing program definition for having a "physical impairment" (in addition to all other applicable requirements for admission). In this instance, if the person has an impairment which meets the fair housing definition of "handicap" but which does not meet the applicable housing program definition, the housing provider must decline this person's application, because the person does not meet basic admission requirements for the particular housing program.

See question 87 for a discussion of inquiry technique, and question 88 for a general discussion of applicant screening and eligibility procedures.

To illustrate the second situation: if a four-person family, that includes a child with a disability, applies for an apartment in a Section 8 property for families, program eligibility is satisfied by virtue of the family status, and it is neither necessary nor appropriate to inquire about the disability for purposes of determining housing program eligibility. However, the household may be entitled to an allowance against income for certain expenses related to the child's disability condition. Therefore, at the point where the housing provider is determining final eligibility income, a limited inquiry into the disability condition is permissible in order to establish qualification for the allowance.

To decline the four-person household's application because of the child's disability condition would violate both Section 504 and the Fair Housing Act.

122 Are Drug or Alcohol Related Illnesses Considered Handicaps Under Section 504?

See questions 90 through 95.

Yes, both drug addiction and alcoholism are included in the definition of "individual with handicap" contained in the Fair Housing Act and Section 504. However, an individual who is engaged in the "current, illegal use of a controlled substance" (i.e. illegal drugs) is not protected and may be denied housing. The most detailed discussion of the meaning of "current illegal use" is found in DOJ's ADA regulations (see below). Individuals whose tenancy would pose a direct threat to the health or safety of others may also be denied housing.

This is not an artificial distinction. Congress intended to protect addicts who are drug free and in recovery, but not persons who are engaged in the current, illegal use of a controlled substance (whether addicted or not).

The Department of Justice, in its regulations implementing Titles II and III of the ADA, made the following points regarding "current, illegal use":

- Current illegal use is defined for ADA purposes as "illegal use of drugs that occurred recently enough to justify a reasonable belief that a person's drug use is current or that continuing use is a real and ongoing problem."[ii]

- "The key question is whether the individual's use of the substance is illegal, not whether the substance has recognized legal uses."

- Alcohol is not a controlled substance, so use of alcohol is not lawful grounds for denial of services or benefits under the "current illegal use" exception. Alcoholics are protected under the Fair Housing Act, the ADA and Section 504.

- "A distinction is also made between the use of a substance and the status of being addicted to that substance. Addiction is a disability, and addicts are individuals with disabilities protected by the [ADA]. The protection, however, does not extend to actions based on the illegal use of the substance. In other words, an addict cannot use the fact of his or her addiction as a defense to an action based on illegal use of drugs."

Some Housing providers may wish to require evidence of recovery. In its final report, the HUD Occupancy Task Force stated: "When an individual claims recovery, the regulations for all programs should authorize the housing provider to require the person to present evidence of recovery from a qualified, neutral third party in order to be admitted (in the case of an applicant) or allowed to continue to reside in the unit (in the case of a resident). See also 24 CFR 966.4(a)(5)(i): 'A PHA may require a family member who has engaged in the illegal use of drugs to present evidence of successful completion of a treatment program as a condition to being allowed to reside in the unit" (Occupancy Task Force Report, Chapter 3, page 3-10)

---

ii. Section 36.104

Examples of Drug Addiction as a Disability

*U.S. V Southern
Management
Corporation, 955 F.2d
914; US Court of
Appeals for the 4th
Circuit.

The claiming of a handicap on the basis of drug addiction was seen in one case where the managers of an apartment complex denied an application for housing. The application was made by the Board of a drug rehabilitation program which intended to house drug program participants at the property. The intended occupants were all in the second or "reentry" phase of the rehabilitation program, meaning that they had been drug-free for a year but would continue to be supervised and monitored by employees of the rehabilitation program. This supervision included twice-monthly drug tests with any participant testing positive for drugs being discharged from the program and evicted from the apartment. In reviewing the attitude of the housing managers to this application the court stated that "...we can see that there is no question that [the housing managers] denied housing to the Board on the basis of the substance abuser status of the prospective tenants; ...The clients are clearly impaired and their ability to obtain housing... was limited by the attitudes of [the leasing managers]. Thus we conclude that the clients qualify as having a handicap under the general definition at 42 USC "3602(h)(1)-(3)."*

The court went on to consider whether the exclusion of "current, illegal use of or addiction to a controlled substance" from the definition of handicap applied to the applicants. The housing managers contended that the term "addiction" included persons addicted to but no longer using controlled substances, that "once an addict always an addict" and addicts may not seek the Act's protection. In the view of the Court the question was whether "...a person who was previously using and is addicted to illegal drugs may, after a period of abstinence and rehabilitative efforts be said to no longer have an "addiction", as that term is used in the statutory exclusion." The court concluded that "...we believe that Congress intended to recognize that addiction is a disease from which, through rehabilitation efforts, a person may recover, and that an individual who makes the effort to recover should not be subject to housing discrimination based on society's "accumulated fears and prejudices" associated with drug addiction." The court therefore concluded that the refusal to rent was unlawful and awarded the Board substantial damages.

123 What Is a "Fundamental Alteration"?

A fundamental alteration is an action which would cause a basic change in the nature of the housing program offered at the property; for example an action requiring:

- The elimination or substantial modification of essential lease or housing program requirements;

- The property to provide supportive services; or

- The property to offer housing of a fundamentally different nature than the type of housing currently offered.

See question 64.

Actions that may be requested as "reasonable accommodations" may actually constitute fundamental alterations and thus would not have to be done. For example, a request to allow persons with disabilities to rent a dwelling by the day or by the week would be a fundamental alteration in an assisted housing program, where monthly or annual leases are the norm. On the other hand, making arrangements for residents to pay their rent by mail rather than in person might not result in a fundamental alteration.

A housing provider is not required to offer housing of a fundamentally different nature from the type of housing currently provided. Moreover, there must be a direct connection between the requested accommodation and the individual's disability.

See questions 64 and 69.

An example of a request for accommodation that is really a request for supportive services might involve a request for housekeeping or personal care services to enable an applicant with a disability to meet basic admissions requirements. Unless the property is designed as an assisted living facility where such services are provided routinely to all residents, agreeing to such an accommodation would likely constitute a fundamental alteration to the nature of the housing program.

124 Can Housing Providers Be Required to Provide Non-Housing Services as a Reasonable Accommodation?

See question 68.

As a general principle, housing providers are not required to provide supportive services for residents (e.g. counseling, medical or social services) that fall outside the scope of the property's housing program. The test of eligibility for admission is whether, with appropriate modifications or accommodations, the applicant or resident can comply with the requirements of the program offered, not whether he or she could benefit or obtain better results from some other program that the property does not offer.

Applicants who need supportive services may still qualify for regulated housing if they can obtain and arrange for these services on their own.

125 Does the Provision of "Auxiliary Aids" Constitute a Fundamental Alteration?

Auxiliary aids are services or devices that enable persons with impaired sensory, manual or speaking skills to have an equal opportunity to participate in, and enjoy the benefits of, programs or activities receiving federal financial assistance, by, for example facilitating effective communication. These do not include individually prescribed items or personal items.

Examples of auxiliary aids for persons with vision impairments include readers, Brailled materials, taped texts, large print materials and audio recordings.

For persons with hearing impairments, auxiliary aids include telecommunication devices for the deaf (TDDs), interpreters, note-takers, transcription services, closed caption decoders, open and closed captioning, videotext displays and written materials. Managers are generally not required to provide TDDs for a resident's personal use. You are required to either have a TDD on the property or an equivalent service. If, however, you have a gated community with a telephone available to call residents to have the gate opened, you might have to provide a TDD for both the resident and at the gate.[iii]

Auxiliary aids do not include individually prescribed items such as hearing aids, service animals or eyeglasses; or personal items such as telecommunications equipment in the resident's unit, personal readers, or personal interpreters.

Section 504 Regulations require housing providers to provide "appropriate auxiliary aids" where necessary to allow individuals with handicaps to have an equal opportunity to participate in and enjoy the benefits of the particular housing program. This includes providing TDDs or an equally effective alternative system for communicating with hearing-impaired persons. It does not, however, include taking any action that would result in a fundamental alteration in the nature of the program or in undue financial and administrative burdens.

RHS properties are also required to provide auxiliary aids (electronic, mechanical or personal assistance), excluding individually prescribed devices, to handicapped or disabled residents.

126 What About "Undue Administrative and Financial Burden"?

"Undue administrative and financial burdens" are justifications for failing to provide accessibility under Section 504 of the Rehabilitation Act and Title II of the ADA. They do not excuse a failure to provide reasonable accommodations as required by the Fair Housing Act. However, only accommodations that are "reasonable" have to be provided. Whether an accommodation is "reasonable" "is a question of fact, determined by a close examination of the particular circumstances." [iv] It has also been said, "The reasonable accommodation inquiry is highly fact-specific, requiring case-by-case determination." [v]

---

iii. Even though this is an 'individually prescribed item' the existence of a gate would make provision of a TDD necessary to afford the resident equal opportunity to use the property.

iv. Jankowski Lee & Associates et al V Cisneros & Rusinvo US Court of Appeal 7th Circuit, No. 95-3051

v. U.S. v. California Mobile Home Park Management Co. 29 F.3d 1413 (9th Circuit 1994)

A reasonable accommodation would not be required if it would impose an undue administrative and financial burden or would result in a fundamental alteration in the nature of the program or service offered (e.g., an owner who has previously not accepted Section 8 certificates may not be required to reasonably accommodate a disabled person by accepting Section 8 certificates).

Note that the standard is 'undue administrative *and* financial burden.' Owners should document both when rejecting a request for reasonable accommodation. Courts will consider the aggregate cost of both when hearing cases.

127 What Are "Undue Financial and Administrative Burdens" in Providing Accessibility?

See questions 134, 135 and 136.

The following discussion refers to the situation of an existing property that is not undergoing "substantial alteration" or undertaking "other alterations." For new construction and substantial alterations to existing buildings, accessibility must be provided. For existing properties undergoing "other alterations," accessibility must be provided "to the maximum extent feasible;" that is, other alterations to a dwelling unit or common area to provide accessibility need not be made if doing so would impose undue financial and administrative burdens.

Definition of Undue Financial and Administrative Burdens

Undue financial and administrative burdens are "modifications" or "accommodations" (i.e. procedural changes for accessibility); that would cause a property to incur an expense or undertake an activity that would put an unreasonable strain on the capacity of the property to operate in a manner consistent with the legal and contractual obligations of the owners. There must be both financial and administrative impact in order to create "undue financial and administrative burdens."

See also the following question for a discussion of how a housing provider might make a determination of undue burdens.

Housing providers are, however, required to make modifications and accommodations up to the point before undue burdens are created.

Undue Burdens and Physical Modifications

The Section 504 regulations contain a specific exception for accessibility modifications that "have little likelihood of being accomplished without removing or altering a load bearing structural member;" such modifications do not have to be performed.

A modification which entails a lesser redesign of a building or dwelling unit however, may not create undue burdens, depending upon the financial circumstances of the property and the needs of the resident or applicant.

If as a result of a proposed modification, basic maintenance to the property must be postponed, a defensible argument could be made that undue burdens would be created if the modification were undertaken. A determination of undue burdens will be based upon the specific circumstances of every property, taking into account such things as the constraints of the site and existing structure, plans for major renovations to the property, the needs of the resident, and the financial condition of the property. If major structural modifications (for instance, to create or enlarge bathrooms or bedrooms for wheelchair accessibility) would be required separate from a planned "substantial alteration" of the property, they could be considered undue burdens, depending significantly on the financial resources of the property and the specific needs of the resident or applicant.

Substitution of Alternative Methods

There is no requirement to make structural modifications if other methods of achieving accessibility are effective. For instance, the availability of suitable modified units in the buildings, or in other buildings in the area under control of the owner, or other properties in the area with which the owner has a referral agreement, may constitute an acceptable alternative to undertaking structural modifications. Similarly, there is no requirement to make a structural modification if accessibility can be accomplished via a less onerous procedural accommodation. Modifications (except in connection with a substantial alteration) may create undue burdens if they would cause the property to:

- Operate at a deficit or contribute to worsening of an existing deficit condition;

- Take funds away from necessary maintenance and repairs; or

- Result in a curtailment of basic services to the property.

**Adminis-
trative
Burdens**

Similarly, "undue administrative burdens" might result from an accommodation that requires a housing provider to provide support services to a person with disabilities, if the provision of such services would impair the ability of the provider to deliver basic administrative services to other residents. For example, if a provider were asked to provide trash collection services for a person with disabilities, and the provision of such services would result in a cutback in existing management services, it would pose an undue administrative burden.

*Management may
also have other
grounds for denying
requests; see
question 64.*

Undue administrative burdens might also result from accommodations that required a replacement of property staff with new staff having different qualifications and capabilities.

**Partial
Compliance**

If a housing provider determines that full compliance with a request would create undue burdens, it may be possible to comply partially without creating undue burdens. In this instance, the housing provider would be required to comply up to the point that undue burdens were created. For instance, a wheelchair user may request that the bathroom be enlarged and provided with grab bars; if the enlargement would constitute undue burdens and providing the grab bars would not, the housing provider would follow the steps outlined in the following question to determine if the disability could be accommodated in some other manner which would not create undue burdens. If alternatives are not feasible, the housing owner would provide the grab bars but not the enlargement.

The final report of the Public & Assisted Housing Occupancy Task Force contained a useful discussion on reaching agreement on reasonable accommodation methods.

128 Procedures for Making Undue Burden Determinations

The following discussion refers to the situation of an existing property that is not undergoing a "substantial alteration" or "other alteration." For new construction, and for existing properties undergoing "alterations," accessibility must be provided (and there is no "undue burdens" exception).

Experienced housing providers suggest that a determination that providing an accommodation or modification would result in undue burdens be made by a senior person, perhaps the supervisor or the off-site property manager responsible for the property, and that the determination be made in writing.

The goal is to place the applicant household in a unit that meets the household's needs. Thus, it is appropriate to consider all methods for accomplishing the goal, beyond the specific method that initially is being considered. Experienced housing providers advise that, in many instances, a creative solution can be found that does not create undue burdens, for example:

- Can the disability be accommodated within a reasonable period of time, say 30 days, at a nearby, similar property under the owner's control or with which the owner has a referral agreement?

- Can the disability be accommodated within a reasonable period of time at an existing accessible unit within the property?

- Are there any practicable non-structural methods for accommodating the disability? For instance, if a wheelchair user cannot access the laundry facility, the normal accommodation would be to make the laundry facility accessible. The owner might, however, incur less cost by offering to subsidize a laundry service that would pick up, clean and deliver the resident's laundry.

- Are there less burdensome structural methods for accommodating the disability? For instance, a wheelchair user may not be able to access the bathroom in its current configuration. Rather than tearing out, enlarging and reconstructing the existing bathroom, it may be possible for the resident to operate the wheelchair in the existing bathroom if (a) the vanity and lavatory are replaced with a wall-mounted lavatory and (b) the bathroom entry door is widened and made to swing out into the hall instead of into the bathroom itself.

- Has the housing provider discussed alternative methods for accommodating the disability with the person requesting the modification, and with local disability-oriented organizations?

Assuming that the housing provider has followed the above procedures, and has determined that undertaking the least burdensome method for accommodating the disability is not within the property's present financial and administrative resources:

See question 26.

• Document that you have acted in good faith, in an overall context of disability-awareness. If the determination of undue burdens results in an official complaint, this will be a key factor in the investigator's decision.

• Document your good faith efforts to consider seriously the household's request, and to accommodate the disability in a less burdensome manner.

• Demonstrate that the least burdensome method for accommodating the disability involves both financial and administrative burdens. The Section 504 regulations require that both types of burdens be present before a determination of undue burdens can be made.

• The Transition Plan includes timetables and funds sources for making structural modifications to the property over time, as needed to provide accessible routes plus a reasonable number of accessible units. If, in comparison to the timetables and funds sources contained in the Transition Plan, the requested modification occurs dramatically sooner, or at dramatically higher cost, or the anticipated financial or administrative resources do not exist, this would support a conclusion of undue burdens.

• Document the property's present financial condition. The HUD surplus cash calculation is a useful indicator; a property with zero surplus cash has exactly enough cash resources to cover its short-term financial obligations. If the property has negative surplus cash, or has insufficient positive surplus cash to cover the cost of the modification, this would support a conclusion of undue burdens.

• Is there any reason to expect that the property's financial condition will soon improve sufficiently to support the cost of the proposed modification? If so, it may be possible to accommodate the disability when the financial condition improves.

- Document your attempts to locate funding from third party sources. State and local governments and local disability-oriented organizations may have information about alternative funding sources.

129 What Are the Differences Between the ADA's "Readily Achievable" Standard, and 504's "Undue Burden" Standard?

The ADA and Section 504 use different standards for determining when a property should undertake modifications. For properties subject to Section 504, properties must make changes unless doing so poses an "undue financial and administrative burden". Properties or portions of properties that are subject to Title III of the ADA must make changes that are "readily achievable without too much difficulty or expense". These are tangibly different cost standards which could result in different decisions depending on which standard is used. If a property is affected by both standards, a safe approach is to follow the more restrictive approach (higher standard).

Chapter Sixteen: Accessibility and Federally-Assisted Properties

130 What Is a Section 504 Accessibility Review?

In general, the steps discussed in questions 23, 24 and 25 will meet Section 504's requirements for a "self evaluation" and "transition plan." However, the following additional points should be considered:

- For existing properties, the Section 504 regulations required nonstructural changes to be made not later than September 11, 1988.

See question 110 for the definition of "federal financial assistance."

- For existing properties, the transition plan was required to be completed by January 1, 1989. If your property has not completed a transition plan, this should be done as soon as possible. For properties not now subject to Section 504 but which receive Federal Financial Assistance in the future, a transition plan is required to be completed within six months following receipt of assistance.

- The 504 regulations require that you "consult with interested parties (local disability organizations and groups, disabled persons living in the property, etc.)" regarding the Accessibility Review, Self Evaluation and Transition Plan. Experienced housing providers advise that this participative process is valuable in developing a high quality approach to accessibility. In most areas, local disability-oriented organizations (such as Independent Living Centers) are available to participate in this process.

See question 125 for more on "Auxiliary Aides."

- The issue of communicating with residents or applicants with visual or hearing impairments should be addressed. Properties that are subject to the provisions of Section 504 of the Rehabilitation Act are required to provide auxiliary aids such as telecommunication devices for hearing impaired persons (TDD's) to ensure effective communication with these residents and applicants. Other properties should also consider the use of such devices.

131 What Are the Accessibility Requirements Under Section 504?

See question 108 for a description of subject properties.

Regulations under Section 504 of the Rehabilitation Act[i] define "accessible" to mean that a facility can be approached, entered and used by individuals with physical handicaps.

See question 133 for the accessibility requirements for new properties. See questions 119, 134, 135, 136 and 137 for further information on the accessibility requirements for properties undertaking various types of alterations.

Section 504 requires that all new multifamily housing projects (i.e. projects constructed after July 1988) that are subject to the Act must be designed and constructed to be readily accessible to and usable by individuals with handicaps. In the case of existing multifamily housing the regulations require that the housing program must be readily accessible to and usable by individuals with handicaps and that if certain types of alterations to such properties are undertaken that accessibility up to a specified level must be given.

132 Does RHS Impose Special Accessibility Review Requirements?

In general, the United States Department of Agriculture's Rural Housing Service (RHS) requirements for the self-evaluation and transition plan are identical to HUD requirements. USDA regulations implementing Section 504 were issued on June 11, 1982. These regulations address the self- evaluation and transition plan.

- Handbook 1930-C[ii] addresses Handicap signage (accessible parking spaces must have a sign showing the international symbol of accessibility), the use of Handicap logos and the need for an unobstructed accessible route through common areas and to the primary building entrance.

- Some state RHS offices required submission of transition plans for review by RHS.

---

i. 24 CFR Part 8 Section 8.22
ii. Exhibit B VI C 2b(2)

- RHS has taken the position that, to the extent possible, barriers to common use areas that prevent any mobility-impaired person from having full access will be removed.

133 Accessibility Requirements for New Construction of Federally Assisted Housing

See questions 110 and 138.

New apartment properties that receive federal financial assistance, and are thus subject to Section 504, must also meet the Section 504 accessibility standards. Section 504 requires that new developments have a minimum of 5 percent of the total dwelling units or at least one unit, whichever is greater, accessible for persons with mobility impairments. An additional 2 percent of the units must be accessible for persons who have hearing or vision impairments. For properties without an elevator, all ground floor units must meet the Fair Housing Act accessibility requirements; in properties with an elevator, all units must meet the Fair Housing Act accessibility requirements. HUD may prescribe a higher percentage of units to be accessible based upon the need for such units in the area.

Once the above test is met, no additional units need be made accessible unless:

- An eligible applicant with disabilities requiring an accessible unit reaches the top of the property's waiting list;

- There is no accessible unit in the subject property; and

- There is no accessible unit in a nearby (suitable) property with which the owner has a referral agreement.

For new construction, there is no exception for "undue financial and administrative burdens:" the property must be accessible to persons with disabilities.

Also see question 69 regarding accessibility requirements for new construction under the Fair Housing Act.

Section 504 accessibility standards are based on the Uniform Federal Accessibility Standards ("UFAS"), and Fair Housing Act accessibility standards are based on the ANSI standard. Providers who are considering new construction should consult with knowledgeable professionals regarding these standards and requirements.

134 What Is an "Alteration"?

In certain instances where alterations to an existing property are undertaken Section 504 requires that these alterations provide accessibility to persons with disabilities.

Maintenance, repair or replacement activities may fall under the Section 504 definition of alteration, which is defined as, "Any change in a facility or its permanent fixtures or equipment. It includes, but is not limited to, remodeling, renovation, rehabilitation, reconstruction, changes, or rearrangements in structural parts and extraordinary repairs. It does not include normal maintenance or repairs, re-roofing, interior decoration, or changes to mechanical systems."

See question 127.

Alterations may be categorized as either "substantial alterations" or "other alterations," and there are different accessibility requirements for each. If an alteration falls into the "other alteration" category, accessibility must be provided to the maximum extent feasible that would not impose undue burdens.

135 What Is a "Substantial Alteration"?

See question 133.

The accessibility requirements for new construction (including the requirement that 5 percent of the units must be accessible for the mobility impaired and 2 percent of the units must be accessible for persons with hearing or vision impairments), apply to an existing facility undergoing substantial alterations.

Section 504 defines "substantial alterations" as:

• *Alterations to properties with 15 or more units, and*

• *Where the cost of alteration is 75 percent or more of the replacement cost of the completed property.*

"Replacement cost" is defined as:

"...*the current cost of construction and equipment for a newly constructed housing facility of the size and type being altered. Construction and equipment costs do not include the cost of*

*land, demolition, site improvements, non-dwelling facilities
and administrative costs for project development activities."*

136 What Are "Other Alterations"?

Under Section 504, "other alterations" are modifications that go beyond normal maintenance into the "alterations" category, but that are of lesser cost than "substantial alterations."

"Other alterations" must, to the maximum extent feasible, make a property or dwelling, including common areas, readily accessible to and usable by a person with disabilities. Accessibility must be provided only up to the point of infeasibility or undue burdens.

If alterations to single elements or spaces of a dwelling unit amount to an alteration of the dwelling unit the entire dwelling must be made accessible. Once five percent of all the dwelling units at the property have been made accessible no additional elements within dwelling units or entire dwelling units are required to be made accessible.

Housing providers are cautioned that the "other alterations" definition may be construed to impose especially burdensome requirements. For instance, if a property's bathrooms are being renovated and if such renovations constitute "other alterations," each bathroom would have to be made accessible until at least 5 percent of the units are fully accessible. In this instance, the housing provider might incur lower costs by immediately making 5 percent of the units accessible, in order to avoid the additional costs in making 100 percent of the bathrooms accessible. As with new construction and substantial alteration, once the 5 percent threshold is met, the above requirements no longer apply.

The distinction between normal maintenance and "other alteration" is not as clear as housing providers might like. For instance, it is unclear whether restoration of a fire-damaged unit would constitute an "other alteration." In this case, it might be prudent to restore fire-damaged units to accessible or adaptable condition where unit design (and reconstruction cost) permits, and where the unit is on an accessible route, if the 5 percent requirement had not been met.

The purpose of the "other alteration" provision is to encourage providers to make 5 percent of dwelling units accessible immediately, in order to avoid the perhaps troublesome "other alteration" requirements. Providers who proceed quickly with accessibility modifications to dwelling units thus gain the benefit of exemption from a potentially problematic requirement.

Housing providers considering "alterations" should consult with professionals knowledgeable about accessibility requirements.

137 Requirements for Existing Housing

Section 504 also imposes accessibility requirements for existing properties that are not undergoing either "substantial alteration" or "other alterations."

Also see the discussion of Accessibility Review in questions 23, 24 and 25 for an introduction to accessibility in this global sense.

The requirement is that "the program, when viewed in its entirety, is readily accessible to and usable by individuals with handicaps." This requirement pertains to *program* accessibility rather than *physical* accessibility. The following discussion outlines the general areas of accessibility requirements, and refers to other portions of this guidebook for more detailed discussion of each area.

The program accessibility requirement does not necessarily mean that a housing provider must make each facility accessible to and usable by individuals with handicaps. A housing provider may meet its obligations through such means as referral to other properties, provision of services in an accessible building, or reassignment of services to an accessible building.

See questions 64 and 74 for discussions of reasonable accommodations [in procedures] and reasonable modifications [to structures]; see question 123 for a discussion on "fundamental alterations" and questions 127 and 128 on "undue burdens."

If requested by an applicant or resident with disabilities at the top of the waiting list, the provider must make a dwelling unit accessible, at the property's expense, unless to do so would result in a fundamental alteration in the nature of the program or in undue financial and administrative burdens.

Section 504 does not require a structural modification when a less troublesome procedural modification or method would be effective. For instance, the availability of suitable modified units in the buildings, or in other buildings in the area under control of the owner, or other properties in the area with which the owner has a referral agreement, would be such an alternative method.

If an accessibility modification is unreasonable, would result in a fundamental alteration, or would result in undue burdens, the modification does not have to be made. However, the Fair Housing Act provisions continue to be applicable.

See question 73 for the accessibility requirements under the Fair Housing Act.

The Section 504 regulations require that, in choosing among the methods for compliance, priority must be given to methods that offer housing to qualified persons in the most integrated setting appropriate (i.e. methods that do not have the effect of segregating residents with disabilities from residents without disabilities).

138 The 5-Percent/2-Percent Thresholds

Suppose an existing property has satisfied the five-percent/two-percent accessibility thresholds. Must an additional unit be made accessible if requested by an applicant with disabilities?

If at least 5 percent of a property's units are fully accessible (in the case of new construction, this would include having an additional 2 percent of the units accessible to persons with hearing and vision impairments), there is no obligation to make additional elements, or entire units, accessible unless an individual with disability requires an accessible unit (or some accessibility feature in a unit).

Thus, this new request for modifications must be granted (subject to the restrictions on undue burdens and fundamental alterations).

Housing providers are advised to treat accessible units as precious resources. If one of these units is rented to a household that does not need the accessibility features, it is advisable to require the household to execute a lease addendum agreeing to transfer to a non-accessible unit, when the accessible unit is required to accommodate a household that does need the accessibility features.

139 What Is RHS' Position On The 5-Percent/2-Percent Thresholds?

The USDA Section 504 regulations require that 5 percent of units built after June 11, 1982 be constructed as accessible units. The regulations also require that all new facilities be constructed in accordance with the Uniform Federal Accessibility Standards (UFAS).

Unlike the HUD Section 504 regulations, the USDA regulations are silent concerning units for the visually or hearing impaired. The RHS merely encourages developers to construct units that are designed for the hearing or visually impaired.

140 Applicability of the UFAS Standards for Physical Modifications

Section 504 Regulations provide that design, construction or alteration of buildings that conform to UFAS (or a substantially equivalent standard) will comply with accessibility requirements.

HUD's Occupancy Handbook 4350.3 Section 2-46(f) provides that after 5 percent of the property's units are accessible to persons with mobility impairments the owner must adapt additional units only if:

- The specific accessibility feature requested is reasonable;

- An accessible unit cannot be provided within a reasonable period of time; and

- Fulfilling the request will not result in undue financial and administrative burdens or in a fundamental alteration in the nature of the project or program.

See question 135.
If a "substantial alteration" is planned, all components of the modifications generally should conform with UFAS, or to another substantially equivalent standard acceptable under the Section 504 regulations. Providers who are considering substantial alterations should consult with qualified professionals concerning these standards.

For other properties (and for properties undertaking substantial alterations once the major renovation is completed), case-by-case modifications must be appropriate to the needs of specific applicants or residents. It will usually be appropriate for each component of such modifications to comply with UFAS or acceptable, equivalent specifications. For example, if a resident's disability can be accommodated by installation of grab bars in a bathroom, the housing provider is under no obligation to make other modifications in the bathroom; however, the grab bars should be installed to UFAS or an acceptable equivalent standard, unless the standard approach would not be effective in removing the resident's barriers to occupancy.

In general, there is a presumption in favor of the applicant's or resident's own assessment of the best methods for meeting his or her needs. Housing providers who feel that the modifications requested by a resident or applicant are beyond what is needed therefore bear the burden of proving this.

141 Sources of Funds for Reasonable Modifications

In Chapter 2 of HUD's Occupancy Handbook 4350.3, HUD indicated that it will allow the following funding approaches to cover modification costs:

- Residual Receipts funds may be used.

- Use of Replacement Reserve funds is discouraged; any Reserve funds withdrawn must be replaced, generally within one year. Often, this will require a rent increase; see further discussion below.

See also questions
127 and 128.
- Where a rent increase is necessary in order to fund a modification, this creates a presumption of undue burdens. Thus, the Handbook seems to indicate that modifications will often

constitute undue burdens unless the property currently has excess cash sufficient to pay for them.

- For properties using the Annual Adjustment Factor rent increase method, rents may not be increased to cover the cost of modifications.

Experienced housing providers recommend that, whenever a significant capital improvement plan is contemplated, needed accessibility modifications be taken into consideration and be made a part of the plan.

Housing providers should note that other resources may be available to pay for accessibility modifications. Examples might include Community Development Block Grant funds. Housing providers should network with local disability-related organizations, and with their state and local governments in order to obtain information on available sources of funding for undertaking alterations and modifications to provide accessibility.

Experienced housing providers also recommend that determinations of undue burdens be made carefully, because this is a volatile area of Fair Housing practice where significant differences of opinion can be expected between housing providers, advocates, regulatory agencies and the courts.

Chapter Seventeen: Occupancy, Persons With Disabilities, and Federally-Assisted Housing

142 How Can I Implement Federally Regulated Housing Programs in a Disability-Aware Manner?

For federal housing programs, disability status may sometimes determine program eligibility; hence it may be necessary to ascertain whether either the applicant or a member of the household has a disability. Generally, the rule of thumb is that the housing provider should verify the applicant's eligibility not disability. However, in order to determine eligibility, housing providers may sometimes have to ask questions related to the applicant's disability that would not be permissible in non-regulated properties (except when necessary to respond to a request for reasonable accommodation). In addition, inquiries about applicants' disabilities may be necessary because the amount of residents' medical expenses typically is a consideration in determining the amount of rent residents will pay.

See question 26.

These factors mean that providers of federally regulated housing must venture into areas that have high risk for fair housing complaints to arise. In addition to considerations applicable to all apartments, providers of federally regulated housing should also consider the following:

• If practical, develop your application procedures so that you will not be aware of disability conditions until the last possible moment. For most applicants at federally regulated properties, disability status and medical expenses can be determined and verified relatively late in the application process. If feasible, you will want to delay obtaining information on these matters until after you have decided to (tentatively) accept or decline the application.

See question 146.

• If your property normally has a waiting list (for example, because its rents are well below market), develop written procedures for filling vacancies in your accessible units. Some federal assistance programs have special waiting list priorities for applicants with disabilities.

• When you can't avoid a medical question, ask only what you absolutely need to know. Typically, when you inquire about medical expenses, you need to know only how much the applicant is likely to spend in the next 12 months; you do not need to know the diagnosis, details of the treatment plan, or the likely future course of the disease.

- When you can't avoid a disability question, ask only what you absolutely need to know. When you are verifying disability, you need only to find a qualified third party who will state in writing that the applicant meets one of the official or program definitions of a person with disabilities. Again, you do not need to know the medical details.

- When accepting applications, offer your accessible units. If your property has accessible or adaptable units, ask the applicant if anyone in the household needs the accessibility features only after you have made the tentative decision to accept the application. This can be done (in writing, requiring a written response) as a part of your normal process of deciding to which unit type the household will be assigned.

- When accepting applications, ask about modifications that may be required. For households who select standard (non-accessible) units, ask (in writing, requiring a written response) whether anyone in the household will need reasonable modifications to the unit in order to accommodate a disability condition.

- When responding to applicant requests for reasonable accommodations, remember that housing providers cannot be required to waive basic requirements for admission. For federally regulated programs, these basic requirements may include:

  - Compliance with housing program eligibility requirements.

See question 172.
  - Age (for properties which have appropriately elected to proceed under the 1992 Act and have established a preference for admission of the elderly).

143 Inquiries Concerning Disabilities, for Federally Regulated Properties

In general, an applicant, resident, guest or associate of an applicant/resident may not be asked whether he or she has a disability, or about the severity of a disability. For federally regulated housing, however, there are two scenarios where the owner can ask about the existence of a disability:

- The existence of a disability may often be a prime determinant of eligibility for admission; in these situations, an inquiry as to disability status is permissible. Additionally, an owner can ask for verification of a disability if a resident asks for a reasonable accommodation.

- Applicants and residents may not be asked to waive their right to confidentiality or be asked to reveal medical details about a disability. For instance, for an applicant to be eligible for an allowance for medical expenses, (available only to households whose head or spouse is "handicapped" or "disabled" as defined in the housing program), the provider must establish:

See questions 120 and 121.

- That the head or spouse meets at least one of the applicable housing program definitions, and that there is a qualified, neutral third party who can provide written verification that this is true.

- The amount of the household's expected qualified medical expenses over the next twelve month period, and that there are qualified, neutral third parties who can provide written verification of the expected medical expenses.

In this example, the provider does not need to know the medical diagnosis, the details of the treatment plan, or the likely future course of the disability. The inquiry and verification processes should be designed to prevent the inadvertent receipt of such unnecessary and unwanted information.

One good approach is to revise all application materials so that applicants are advised of situations where it may be to their advantage to disclose their disability status, for example:

- If disability will be a prime determinant of eligibility for admission (for instance, an applicant for a unit at a Section 811 property for the chronically mentally ill will need to establish that this particular disability exists); and

- If disability will entitle the household to an allowance (such as the allowance for medical expenses and the allowance for handicapped assistance and care costs).

Appendix 6 of HUD's Occupancy Handbook 4350.3 requires that owners tell applicants for certain assisted housing programs that they are permitted to verify the existence of a disability only if eligibility for admission is dependent on the existence of handicaps or disabilities or if the applicant is claiming allowances that are given to persons with handicaps or disabilities. Note that the applicant may elect to forego the benefit of any allowances available on the basis of disability, in which case a housing provider should not pursue any inquiry on the matter.

Rural Housing Service (RHS) provisions are similar to HUD's. In its September 1996 Memorandum entitled "Federally Assisted Programs and Accessibility Issues" RHS addressed disability-related requirements:

> *"Once a tenant/applicant requests their handicap status be considered, inquiries can be made but only to the extent necessary to verify disability. Management should not attempt to make any determination concerning a tenant/applicant's handicapping condition. The tenant/applicant may provide acceptable verification from a number of sources. For example, documentation that the tenant/applicant is eligible for Social Security Income Disability is preferable to requiring verification from their physician. The verification method that is least intrusive should be accepted."*

The Memo also advised against including the question, "Are you handicapped?" on application forms. Instead the Memo suggested that questions be designed to read from the perspective of eligibility. So, for example, the aforementioned question should read: "If you are applying for residence at an elderly project and you are under 62 are you aware that you must be handicapped or disabled to be eligible?" and "Are you requesting the elderly household deduction and medical expenses?" It is up to the household to answer these questions and provide documentation proving eligibility.

The application materials should include explanatory information that discusses how these allowances affect the amount of rent paid, so that the household can judge whether the potential benefit of lower rent outweighs any privacy concerns about disclosing disability status. Providers who use this approach will be able to avoid inquiry into disability status, until the applicant brings up the subject.

In addition, a federally regulated housing provider may ask all applicants for assisted housing:

*   Whether the applicant qualifies for a dwelling unit designed for persons with physical disabilities.

*   Whether the applicant qualifies for a medical expense deduction or another allowance which is a part of the housing program(s) offered at the property.

*   Whether any member of the applicant's household is engaged in the current illegal use of a controlled substance.

*   Whether any member of the applicant's household has been convicted of illegal manufacture or distribution of a controlled substance.

*   If the property has a priority for admission that is available to persons with disabilities, whether any member of the applicant's household qualifies for such a priority.

A number of housing providers have established a phased screening process to ensure that information is obtained only to the extent needed to determine eligibility. In these instances, in the application process providers obtain only the information that would affect a decision to accept or reject an applicant. Unless the condition of a disability is a factor in determining program eligibility, a provider has no need at the initial stage of the application process to make inquiries about the existence of a disability. If, however, the fact of a disability is a prime determinant of eligibility, a provider must from the start verify the existence of a disability condition as defined in the applicable housing program.

When the tentative decision is made to accept the applicant to the property's waiting list, the provider then inquires as to the applicant's need for a unit with accessibility modifications.

See questions 95 and 150 for discussions of procedures regarding applicants who are denied housing.

Later, when a unit becomes available and the applicant approaches the top of the waiting list, the provider will seek to obtain the more detailed information relevant to the determination of eligibility for an accessible unit and rent payment, including provision for any allowances.

144 For Federally Regulated Properties, What Additional Considerations Affect My Decisions When Applicants and Residents Request Changes to My Property and Procedures?

Would Granting These Requests Create Undue Financial and Administrative Burdens?

With respect to persons with disabilities, reasonable modifications to dwelling units, or reasonable accommodations in rules and regulations, need not be made if they pose undue financial and administrative burdens to the property. Modifications must be made, however, up to the point at which further modifications would result in undue burdens. To sustain an argument that an undue burden would be created if a request is granted, providers must show real and credible evidence, such as the impairment of the ability of the property to provide essential services or to meet basic financial obligations.

Would Granting These Requests Result in a Fundamental Alteration of the Housing Program Under Which the Property Operates?

A fundamental change in the nature of the housing program, for example in the type or extent of services provided, is not required to accommodate the needs of a person with disabilities. An example of a request that would result in a fundamental alteration of a program if it were to be granted is a request from an applicant who suffers from a neurological disorder for 24 hour nursing care. The owner does not provide this type of medical service in the housing that he offers. Although he must allow the applicant to obtain the nursing care on his own, it would constitute a fundamental alteration in the nature of the program if the owner were required to provide this medical service at the owner's expense. Again, however, requests for accommodations to provide accessibility must be granted up to the point that further accommodations would result in a fundamental alteration in the nature of the housing program under which the property operates. See also questions 67 and 123.

Limit Inquiries to What You Need To Know

Follow an objective process for reviewing eligibility for residency. Where the applicant has protected status and this status is related to eligibility under a federally regulated housing program (e.g., a mentally disabled person applying for a Section 811 property for the chronically mentally ill), use the least intrusive means available to verify the existence of a disability. Ask only those questions which tell you whether a person is eligible for admission. In this example, ask simply, does a disability, as defined in the program regulation, exist? Ask disability-related questions in a sensitive manner. Ask only at the point you need to know, not before.

145 "Independent Living" and Federally Regulated Properties

See question 89.

Housing providers may *not* make the ability to live independently a requirement for admission or continuing occupancy. Both HUD and RHS explicitly prohibit use of an "independent living" requirement.

146 Are There Any Occupancy Requirements for Accessible Units in Federally Assisted Housing?

See question 152.

Yes, the Section 504 regulations are specific on this issue. There are two requirements, one dealing with marketing and the other with priority for housing.

First, housing providers who have accessible units must adopt marketing approaches that ensure that eligible persons with disabilities are aware of this availability. The marketing efforts should be focused on the populations that would benefit from the particular accessibility features offered at the property. Housing providers should note that this marketing requirement is applicable regardless of the length of the waiting list.

See question 180.

Second, accessible units are allocated using a special priority approach. When accessible units become available, the housing provider must offer the units in the following order (for properties that have appropriately elected to proceed under the 1992 Act):

- First, to current residents (of the property or of nearby properties under common ownership or control) having disabilities which would benefit from the available unit's accessibility features, but whose current units do not have such features. These households with disabilities should be ranked in the order indicated by the priorities and preferences included in the housing provider's resident selection plan.

- Second, to eligible households on the waiting list having disabilities which would benefit from the available unit's accessibility features. These households with disabilities should be ranked in the order indicated by the priorities and preferences included in the housing provider's resident selection plan.

- Third, to other eligible and qualified households on the waiting list (i.e. those without disabilities), in which case the provider is permitted (and advised) to require the household to agree, in writing, to transfer to an available non-accessible unit at the provider's request.

When an accessible unit becomes available, households that need the unit's accessibility features move to the top of the waiting list, ahead of households with earlier application dates.

This requirement implies that housing providers must determine, at or soon after the time of application, whether applicant households would benefit from accessibility features. Because this determination involves inquiry into the existence of disabilities, it is a sensitive process that providers will want to handle with care and tact, using standard written forms as opposed to less formal methods of communication.

147 Is Eligibility for Section 202 Properties Affected By the Type of "Handicap"?

Yes. In the case of Section 202 properties constructed prior to October 1991, HUD required owners to specify the target population which each property would serve, from among four distinct sub populations—elderly, physically handicapped, developmentally disabled, and chronically mentally ill. Note, however, that it is permissible to serve more than one of those categories, for example many properties serve the elderly and physically handicapped. HUD approval must be obtained if the property intends to serve another or different target population.

Consider a Section 202 assisted elderly housing property that was originally designed only for the elderly and the mobility impaired. In this example, the property would admit only those applicants who were "elderly" and/or "mobility impaired" as defined in the program regulations. Note that non-elderly persons with mobility impairments are eligible only for accessible units. Of course, applicants who meet the appropriate program definition would remain eligible regardless of any additional disabilities: an elderly person who is also vision impaired would be eligible, as would a mobility impaired person who is also chronically mentally ill.

148 Can Physician's Statements Be Required as a Condition of Eligibility, in Federally Regulated Housing?

See question 149 for a discussion of acceptable means of verification.

No. If the existence of a disability must be verified, a physician's statement is only one of a number of acceptable verification methods. HUD's Public Housing Occupancy Handbook 7465.1 in fact prohibits a Public Housing Authority from requiring verification from a physician when adequate verification is available from other sources.

HUD Handbook 4350.3 does not permit housing providers to require either a physical examination or any form of medical test as a condition of eligibility.

149 What Are Acceptable Methods For Verifying Disability Status, in Federally Regulated Housing?

Experienced owners and managers recommend the use of verification methods that take into account the following guidelines:

- Providers should not inquire into the nature or extent of the disability. For instance, in determining eligibility, the provider need only establish that the applicant meets one of the applicable housing program definitions. It is not necessary or lawful to inquire into the precise nature or medical details of the disability.

- Given a choice of verification methods, choose the method that is least likely to reveal unwanted medical details. Receipt of SSI disability benefits is, by itself, proof of disability status. Note, however, that HUD's Occupancy Handbook 4350.3 provides guidelines for methods of verifying the existence of a disability and its suggested third-party verification form includes a question (requiring a "Yes" or "No" answer) whether the person has a disability as defined in Section 223 of the Social Security Act.

The RHS Occupancy Handbook states, *"Receipt of veteran's or Social Security Disability payments benefits for disability...does not automatically establish disability."*[i] However, in practice, the RHS apparently recognizes that these disability payments do constitute proof of disability.

Limit the verification to what is needed. For example, to determine the allowance for medical expenses, the housing provider needs only to establish the amount expected to be spent over the next twelve months, and to identify a neutral, qualified third party with whom the amount can be verified. There is no need to establish the medical details of the treatment plan.

A requirement that third party verifications come only from a physician is not reasonable if other available sources (for example, a therapist or a counselor) are qualified to give the verification.

An approach used by one provider is to send a letter to a qualified healthcare professional listing the applicable housing program definitions of a person with disabilities, and asking the professional to indicate whether the applicant meets at least one of those definitions.

---

i.   RHS 1930-C, Exhibit B(II)

Similarly, HUD's suggested disability verification form (referred to above) recommends that the form contain the definition of "disability" or "handicap" applicable to the particular program under which the property operates and should ask the third party to identify any of the relevant definitions that apply to the individual by indicating "Yes" or "No."

150 In Federally Regulated Housing, May Managers Deny Applicants Who Display Threatening Behavior?

See question 90 for a discussion of this issue. Experienced providers advise that it may be more effective to concentrate on the issue of lease compliance, rather than the "direct threat" provision.

The Fair Housing Act and Section 504 include specific provisions that providers may properly decline applicants whose tenancy would pose a "direct threat to the health and safety of others" or would result in substantial physical damage to the property of others. RHS regulations also provide that applications for housing may be refused if the proposed tenancy would threaten the health and safety of other individuals or would result in substantial physical damage to the property of others, *unless the threat can be removed by applying a reasonable accommodation*. (Our emphasis).

Federally regulated housing leases impose a specific obligation on residents to observe standards of conduct that do not interfere with the right of others to the full and safe enjoyment of their dwelling and common facilities. The screening process to determine an applicant's qualification for residency must be based on the applicant's demonstrated ability and willingness to meet this and all other terms of the lease (for example: timely payment of rent, proper care of the dwelling, and adherence to reasonable rules and regulations).

If the application and screening materials, taken as a whole, do not support a conclusion that the terms of the lease will be complied with, the applicant may be rejected.

Experienced housing providers suggest that, prior to rejecting an applicant with a known disability, the housing provider offer an informal meeting, to explore whether there is a reasonable accommodation that would make the applicant acceptable. In fact HUD's Occupancy Handbook 4350.3 provides that upon receiving written notice of the rejection of an application for housing all applicant may, within fourteen days, request a meeting to discuss the rejection. Be aware that neither the Fair Housing Act nor Section 504 require this formal rejection notification and appeals process, and so this requirement applies only to properties governed by the 4350.3.

Applicants who are rejected because they have histories of noncompliance with lease provisions may have disability conditions of which the housing provider is unaware. The rejection letter should offer rejected applicants with disabilities the opportunity to request a reasonable accommodation that would enable the applicant to meet the terms of the lease. For example, if it is disclosed that an applicant's disruptive or threatening behavior is related to his or her failure to medicate, it may be a reasonable accommodation to accept the applicant if he or she can arrange for a live-in or visiting aide who would administer medication as needed. In order to meet this requirement, a housing provider might include language such as this in each rejection letter: "If you are a person with disabilities, and the reason your application is being denied is related to your disability, you may contact us not later than (date, time) to discuss whether a reasonable accommodation by us would allow your application to be acceptable."

If this discussion identifies a possible accommodation, the housing provider may require verification of the information and must then determine whether the accommodation is sufficient to overcome the reason for rejection of the application.

See question 64.

HUD's Occupancy Handbook 4350.3 Section 2-25(h) provides that owners may include the consideration of "extenuating circumstances" in their screening criteria. If a property's screening practices allow for the consideration of extenuating circumstances, then the extent to which an applicant's disability has affected his or her application should be considered. In addition, regardless of any such provision in a property's screening criteria, the Fair Housing Act requires all properties to make reasonable accommodations for persons with disabilities.

151 Do Federally Regulated Housing Providers Have Any Special Requirements for Communicating With Individuals With Hearing or Vision Impairments?

Yes. Section 504 requires housing providers to communicate effectively with applicants, residents and members of the public. Housing providers must provide communications in alternative formats (for example, taped readings of the lease and related documents for vision-impaired persons; and printed copies of materials normally delivered orally, for hearing-impaired persons).

The choice of communication method should give primary consideration to the requests of individuals with handicaps. Local Independent Living Centers, or similar organizations, can provide information to assist in making these choices.

See question 125.

If the housing provider communicates with applicants or residents by telephone, then the provider must use a TDD [Telecommunications Device for the Deaf] for communicating with persons with hearing impairments, or an "equally effective" communication system or provide auxiliary aids, if necessary for communicating with persons with hearing impairments

RHS regulations also require housing providers to take appropriate steps to ensure effective communication with applicants and tenants with handicaps and disabilities including providing auxiliary aids (electronic, mechanical or personal assistance) where necessary.

152 Do HUD and RHS Allow Accessible Apartments to Be Rented to Households Who Do Not Need the Accessibility Features?

In certain cases, yes.

HUD-Regulated Properties

In HUD-regulated housing, Handbook 4350.3 provides that accessible units must be assigned in accordance with the order set out in question 146. However, if there are no current tenants or qualified applicants on the property's waiting list who have disabilities requiring the accessibility features of the particular unit the owner may offer the unit to another household and may incorporate into the lease an agreement that the tenant will move to a non-accessible unit of the proper size within the same property when one becomes available. The lease provision should state who would pay for the cost of the move.

RHS-Regulated Properties

Handbook 1930-C[ii] provides that units may be rented to households not needing the accessibility features, when:

- No applicants needing the features have applied for housing, and management has made a diligent effort to identify such individuals;[iii] and,

- The non-disabled resident agrees to transfer to another apartment when one becomes available and someone has applied who needs the accessibility features. The leasing section of the RHS Handbook includes a lease clause for this situation.[iv] If a non-disabled applicant refuses to sign this lease clause , the housing provider would not be required to rent to that household. If an applicant who signs the lease clause later refuses to move, this would constitute grounds to terminate the tenancy or not renew a lease.

153 What Is a "Live-In Care Attendant"?

Both RHS and HUD[v] use the same definition. A Live-in Care Attendant is a person who resides with an individual with disabilities or who is elderly, and who:

- Is determined to be essential to the care and well-being of the person;

- Is not obligated for the support of the person; and

- Would not be living in the unit except to provide the necessary supportive services.

A family member may serve as a Live-in Care Attendant, so long as the above criteria are met.

---

ii.   Exhibit B, VI, D, 2, g
iii. These instructions are attached to the AFHMP (Affirmative Fair Housing Market Plan) form.
iv.   Exhibit B VIII C
v.   HUD 4350.3 CHG-26 Exhibit 2-1(i).

154 Does RHS Require That Residents Be Able to Sign Their Own Legal Documents?

The Rural Housing Service allows guardian signatures in all RHS programs as a reasonable accommodation for applicants with disabilities.[vi]

155 Does RHS Impose Special "Reasonable Accommodation" Requirements?

The RHS Handbook 1930-C addresses the issue of reasonable accommodation:

- The Project Management Plan must discuss reasonable accommodations in communication, and how the borrower will make reasonable accommodation decisions.[vii]

- The borrower must establish and enforce rules to ensure there are reasonable accommodations to persons who are handicapped or disabled.[viii]

- The management section of the Handbook[ix] restates fair housing law in regard to reasonable accommodations, stressing parking and service/companion animal issues—two of the most common that managers must face.

156 Does RHS Impose Special "Reasonable Modification" Requirements?

On September 9, 1996, RHS issued a memo addressing accessibility issues. The Memo restates Section 504 policies and adds Agency guidance in dealing with modifications. In part, the Memo reads:

"The borrower is responsible for bearing the expense of providing these modifications or other special accommodations,

---

vi. See USDA Memo dated September 9, 1996
vii. Exhibit B-1 of Handbook 1930 C
viii. Exhibit B VIII G 11
ix. Exhibit B VI D 3a

needed by individuals with handicaps unless the borrower can show that it would cause an 'undue financial burden.' If this position is taken, the borrower must prove such a burden exists in order to receive a waiver from the Secretary. Reserve funds and subsequent loans, operating funds, and alternative funding sources such as State and local Agencies, must be considered. Most modifications are not expected to create undue financial/administrative burdens. All waiver reports will be reviewed for approval by the Secretary of Agriculture."

Section 504 requires that at least 5 percent of units in buildings constructed after June 1982 meet the Uniform Federal Accessibility Standards. The September 9, 1999 RHS Memorandum clarifies that on RHS-regulated properties these accessible units must be comparable in variety (of unit types) to other units at the property.

In addition, the Project Management Plan[x] must discuss any planned accessibility modifications.

---

x.   Exhibit B-1 of Handbook 1930 C

Chapter Eighteen: Fair Housing Marketing and Admissions Issues for Federally-Assisted Properties

157 *Affirmative Fair Housing Marketing Requirements*

Affirmative Fair Housing Marketing Plans (AFHMPs) are required for many rental properties and programs that receive FHA mortgage insurance, HUD subsidies, RHS loans, and/or RHS subsidies. The purpose of the plan is to attract renters of all groups regardless of sex, disability and familial status. Some examples of multifamily programs that require the submission of a written AFHMP are:

- Multifamily mortgage insurance under sections 207, 220, 221(d)(3) and 221(d)(4) of the National Housing Act.

- Project-based Section 8 Rental Assistance.

- Housing for the Elderly or Handicapped under Section 202 of the Housing Act.

- Projects financed under Section 515 of the Housing Act of 1949 by the Farmers Home Administration Section 8 Set-Aside.

- Supportive housing for persons with disabilities under Section 811 of the National Housing Act.

Many other affordable housing programs do not require a formal plan, but are required to conceive, implement and maintain records of their affirmative marketing efforts with special emphasis on attracting the "least likely to apply" segment of the population.

The AFHMP process is particularly concerned with attracting those segments of the population that are considered "least likely to apply" for housing at the particular property unless special outreach efforts are implemented. For example, if the property is built in an area with a low percentage of African-Americans, they would be judged "least likely to apply," and the AFHMP rules would require additional "outreach" to African-American applicants. This outreach might include advertising in media that reach that audience predominately, and/or provision of marketing materials to organizations that serve that community. Some populations may require marketing materials in a language other than English.

AFHMPs will frequently need to include a description of outreach efforts geared towards persons with disabilities in the community because they are considered among those 'least likely to apply' without special outreach activities.

An AFHMP must include a description of the methods to be used to market the property generally and the special outreach steps that will be taken to attract the group(s) identified as being least likely to apply. Details about the commercial media to be used in advertising must also be included in the plan. AFHMP's must also include a description of the indicators that will be used to measure the success of the marketing program and an indication of the capacity to provide staff with training on fair housing laws.

The AFHMP must be submitted to HUD for approval on HUD Form 935.2. The same form is used for HUD and for RHS, although RHS uses slightly different instructions.

HUD Require-
ments

HUD's approval of the Plan is based on whether HUD determines that the Plan has the potential to effectively attract renters from all groups within the property's market area, whether it has the potential to attract persons with disabilities and their families to the property, whether the provider has identified the appropriate group(s) for special outreach and whether the fair housing training proposed for the management staff is adequate.

On HUD-regulated properties the Plan must be available for public inspection in the property office. The Plan remains in force throughout the life of a multifamily project mortgage and/or the period for which a HUD subsidy is provided.

Rural
Housing
Service
Requirements

In the case of RHS properties the approved AFHMP must be posted at the property's project site, rental office or any other location where tenant applications are received.[i]

Unlike HUD, RHS requires that Affirmative Marketing be done at least once a year even if there are an adequate number of applicants on the property's waiting list.

Unlike HUD, RHS does NOT allow waiting lists to be closed. Applications must always be made available.[ii]

---

i. See RHS Handbook 1930-C, Exhibit B1(3)
ii. Handbook 1930-C Exhibit VI C 2 a(1)(2)

158 Additional RHS Requirements for Fair Housing Posters

RHS requires two additional items to be displayed in the property's rental office:

- The "And Justice for All" poster (a USDA Equal Opportunity Non-Discrimination poster);[iii] and,

- A copy of the Applicant/Tenant 1944-L Grievance and Appeal Procedure.

If the rental office is not on site these items must be displayed in a prominent place on the site.

See question 41.

All properties, regardless of federal financial assistance are required to display the Fair Housing poster.

159 What Household Types Are Eligible for RHS "Family" Properties?

Occupancy[iv] requirements for the four different types of RHS properties are as follows:

- Family housing may be occupied by any combination of elderly, disabled or handicapped and/or nonelderly, nondisabled or nonhandicapped tenants including tenants with minor children,

- Elderly housing must be occupied by tenants who are elderly, disabled and/or handicapped but children cannot be excluded if they are members of the elderly household,

- Mixed housing (i.e. housing that consists of specific units in a project designated as family housing and other units designated as elderly housing units) occupancy is governed by the family and elderly housing provisions, and

- Congregate housing and group homes must be occupied by elderly, handicapped or disabled persons or families requiring the supportive services provided by the property.

---

iii. Available at http://www.usda.gov/da/cr/just.htm
iv. Handbook 1930-C Exhibit B, VI DI(h)

The RHS definition of familial status, as found in Exhibit B of the RHS Handbook, defines who has protection from familial status discrimination under the Fair Housing Act. It is not an eligibility definition.

160 Does RHS Allow Single Person Households to Be Admitted to RHS "Family" Housing?

Yes, in fact "Household" is defined as "One or more persons who maintain or will maintain residency in one rental or cooperative unit."[v] However, RHS typically does not allow single person households to be admitted to units larger than one bedroom.

Although RHS has always permitted reasonable accommodations for single applicants with disabilities, or pregnant women, who may request two bedrooms, an Administrative Notice (AN #3285) was issued on August 30, 1996 reminding housing providers not to permanently fill large units with single people. Managers are permitted some flexibility if warranted by market conditions such as high vacancy or physical conditions such as projects with all two bedroom units.

161 Criminal Background Checks on Federally Regulated Properties

See also questions 9 and 47.

Increasingly, managers are using criminal background checks as an additional screening measure. In fact, HUD guidelines contained in PIH Notice 96-16 require Public Housing Authorities to review the police and court records of public housing applicants as well as members of their household aged 16 and older. It is proposed to extend this requirement to all Section 8 assisted housing programs as well as other HUD assisted housing programs such as Section 221(d)(3) BMIR programs, Section 202 and 811 programs and Section 236 programs. In the case of properties that can exercise their own discretion on whether or not to use such screening, the use of criminal background checks will be considered discriminatory *only* if the basis of checking or not checking is related to membership in a protected class. For

---

v.   See RHS Handbook 1930-C, Exhibit BII, page 11

example, such checks are only performed on applicants who are members of a particular race.

Managers must get written consent from an applicant before undertaking a criminal background check. Even where such checks are required (for example in public housing) the tenant or applicant must give his or her signed consent for this information to be released. In the case of public housing the PHA may obtain criminal conviction records directly from the National Crime Information Center, police departments and other law enforcement agencies under the Housing Opportunity Program Extension Act. Owners of project-based section 8 properties may request the PHA in whose jurisdiction the property is located to obtain criminal records and perform determinations for the owner regarding screening applicants. The owner is not entitled to receive the record or be informed of its contents. Instead, the PHA uses the record to screen or evaluate the applicant based on the owner's standards of admission and occupancy.

When refusing admission to an applicant because of information uncovered by a criminal background check, the applicant should be told—in writing—the reason for the refusal.

Chapter Nineteen: Familial Status Issues in Federally-
Assisted Housing

162 Verifications and Familial Status

In assisted housing, the size and composition of an applicant's household may often determine:

- Eligibility for residence at the particular property;

- The amount of rent that should be charged; and/or

- The size of the rental unit that will be offered to the applicant.

As a general rule housing providers must verify any factor that is a prime determinant of eligibility for federal housing assistance at the property. This may include verifying the familial status of applicants for such housing by ascertaining, for example whether the applicant:

- Has children;

- Is pregnant; or,

- Is in the process of obtaining custody of a minor child.

See question 121 for further information on the eligibility of single persons for the Section 8 program.

Single people are eligible for admission to assisted housing, so that the fact that an applicant is childless, unmarried or intends to live alone would not be a disqualifying factor. However, it may limit the applicant's choice of the size unit to be assigned.

The methods for verifying familial status must be reasonable. Acceptable verification methods are minimally intrusive, and are geared towards obtaining the basic information necessary for ensuring compliance with the program requirements under which the particular property operates.

Housing providers are advised to interpret the above guidelines as prohibiting the requirement of any type of medical examination or medical test (including sonogram testing) in order to verify any familial status assertions. The RHS Handbook 1930-C does, however, provide that a housing provider can request written verification of an unborn child by a doctor or other qualified third party.

See question 163 for a discussion of "minimum occupancy standards."

As stated at the outset, the size and composition of an applicant's family will often determine the size of the unit that will be offered to the applicant, because assisted properties typically apply minimum occupancy standards for each type of unit at the property.

See question 56.
HUD's Occupancy Handbook 4350.3 advises housing providers against making recommendations or decisions about whether or not to rent based on the housing provider's opinion of what is in a family's best interest.

HUD's Occupancy Handbooks (Public Housing 7465.1 and Assisted Housing 4350.3) also require that in establishing occupancy standards owners comply with State and local laws as well as the Handbooks. Owners therefore need to familiarize themselves with these codes.

163 What Is a "Minimum Occupancy Standard"

A minimum occupancy standard is a requirement that each unit type be occupied by a minimum number of persons. The purpose of a minimum occupancy standard is to make the best use of scarce affordable housing resources by avoiding under-utilization of affordable rental units.

Owners of HUD-assisted housing are required to adopt minimum occupancy standards. These standards must be both acceptable to HUD and defensible under the Fair Housing Act (i.e. should not have the effect of discriminating against any members of a protected class). HUD's guidelines for occupancy standards are contained in Handbook 4350.3 for Subsidized Multifamily Housing Programs and in Handbook 7465.1 REV 2 for Lower Income Public Housing Programs. RHS properties must also adopt occupancy standards that will prevent overcrowding (maximum occupancy standards) and under-utilization (minimum occupancy standards). Guidelines for these properties are contained in Handbook Number 1930-C.

Minimum occupancy standard violations ("under-utilized" apartments) typically occur when members of a family leave the household, resulting in too few household members for the apartment size. HUD's Occupancy Guidelines for Subsidized Multifamily Housing Programs (Handbook 4350.3) provides that if a unit becomes under-utilized because of changes in household composition, the owner should require the family to move to an appropriate size unit within the property when one becomes available.

RHS guidance also provides that when a unit becomes over-crowded or under-utilized and there is a waiting list for a unit of that size the tenant must move to another unit of adequate size when one becomes available. If the tenant refuses to move or there is no such available unit, the tenant must vacate the property within a reasonable time period. All RHS lease agreements must contain these provisions.

164 May Housing Providers Base Minimum Occupancy Standards on the Age, Gender or Relationship of Household Members?

No. Minimum occupancy standards should refer to the number of persons required to occupy a unit of a particular size and not the gender of the occupants or their age or relationship to each other. HUD permits housing providers to consider age, gender and family relationship in certain circumstances. However, the *initial* designation of the number of persons required for each unit size should be based strictly on the number of persons in the household.

Following this initial designation, the housing provider might offer a larger unit, based on legitimate need including accommodation of a disability, and/or considerations of gender, age or relationship of household members. For example it may be reasonable for young siblings of the opposite sex to share a bedroom. To require adolescent siblings of the opposite sex to do so may not be. Therefore, despite a minimum occupancy standard that provides for a minimum of five persons in a three bedroom unit, in the case of a household that consists of two parents and two adolescent children of the opposite sex, offering them a three bedroom unit on request may be appropriate. It is most unlikely that a policy of this type would be found to unfairly exclude or discriminate against families with children.

HUD's Handbooks require that occupancy standards:

• Must consider the number of persons residing (or anticipated to reside) in the unit.

- May consider, when it is reasonable to do so, both the number of persons in the household and the relationship and sex of those persons.

- Should consider the size of the unit as well as the size and number of bedrooms.

Regarding relationship and gender, HUD allows owners to use the following guidelines in developing occupancy standards:

- Children of the same sex may share a bedroom.

- No more than two persons would be required to occupy a bedroom.

- Unrelated adults would not be required to share a bedroom.

- Persons of the opposite sex (other than spouses) would not be required to share a bedroom.

- A child may share a bedroom with a parent if the parent so wishes. However, children, with the possible exception of infants, would not be required to share a bedroom with persons of different generations, including their parents.

Persons of different generations (for example, grandparent and grandchild) would not be required to share a bedroom.

These approaches suggested above (initial assignment based strictly on number of persons, then giving the household an opportunity to request a larger or smaller unit size) will allow families to choose smaller or larger units, depending on the family's needs. For example a family may request a smaller unit on the basis that they wish their two children of the opposite sex to share a bedroom, even though the property's occupancy policy does not require this.

RHS Guidelines are virtually identical to HUD's and can be found at Handbook 1930-C Exhibit B VI D 1 Section 2.

165 Typical Minimum and Maximum Occupancy Standards for Federally-Assisted Housing

In assisted housing, most households can be appropriately accommodated at two persons per bedroom. However, some households will need larger units as a result of disability, privacy considerations, or other legitimate needs. Generally, providers can choose to adopt a flexible standard, where applicant households choose from, at most, two unit types; or a more structured standard, where applicant households are assigned to one unit type but allowed to request one additional bedroom if there are acceptable reasons for this request.

An Example of a Flexible Occupancy Standard

Number of Bedrooms	Number of Persons	
	Minimum	Maximum
One	1	2
Two	2	4
Three	3	5
Four	5	8

The applicant may select any unit size for which the household size qualifies.

An Example of a Structured Occupancy Standard

Number of Bedrooms	Number of Persons	
	Minimum	Maximum
Zero	1	1
One	1	2
Two	3	4
Three	5	6
Four	7	8

The applicant household may request a unit that is one bedroom larger than shown above, on the basis of disability, or other acceptable reasons.

Some housing providers choose to disregard infants for purposes of their occupancy standards. For example, two adults and an infant would qualify as two persons and may therefore, on request, be accommodated in a one-bedroom unit.

166 How Should Assisted Housing Providers Determine Overcrowding and Under-utilization, for Purposes of Making Needed Unit Transfers?

Written occupancy standards for assisted housing should address the issues of overcrowding (i.e., too many occupants in a unit) and under-utilization (i.e., too few occupants to justify the governmental subsidy for the unit size).

Over-crowding

Typical occupancy standards provide that households with more than the maximum number of occupants are considered overcrowded and are subject to unit transfer. HUD requires that occupancy standards must comply with all reasonable State or local restrictions regarding the maximum number of occupants permitted to occupy a dwelling. Failure to abide by these standards will constitute a breach of both HUD's directives and local and State laws. RHS goes even further than HUD in providing not only that occupancy standards must comply with State or local restrictions but that in the absence of such restrictions a dwelling will be considered overcrowded if its occupancy level exceeds 2 people per habitable sleeping room; however, an additional person may be accommodated if a habitable room provides at least 50 square feet per person. For example, a one-bedroom unit has a large bedroom of 175 square feet (excluding closets); the RHS would consider occupancy of three persons to be reasonable (175 square feet divided by three persons equals more than 50 square feet per person). In practice, the RHS does not take a position on overcrowding of units, and allows owners to set maximum occupancy above two persons per bedroom, regardless of bedroom size.

Under-utilization

Typical occupancy standards provide that households with less than the required minimum number of occupants are considered to be under-utilizing the governmental subsidy and are subject to unit transfer. This will usually occur where, during the course of the tenancy, there is a reduction in the number of family members occupying the unit. However, transfer is generally not required if at the inception of the tenancy the unit size, though inappropriate, was approved by management. This typically happens when, to reduce vacancies at the property, a family is allowed to rent a unit that is larger than appropriate for the family size. In those circumstances it is advisable that the lease provide that the family will move to a smaller unit when another family needs the larger one and a suitable smaller unit is available.

It is generally recommended that the property's standard lease provide that, in the event of overcrowding or under-utilization, the household will agree to be transferred to a unit of the appropriate size if and when one becomes available. In the case of under-utilization, HUD's Occupancy Handbook 4350.3 provides that if a family refuses to move, after a request to do so has been made, they may be permitted to remain in the unit but must pay the HUD-approved market rent for it. If they fail to pay this rent they may be evicted. HUD's model lease for multifamily subsidized housing also provides that families in under-utilized units will be required to move within thirty days of the availability of an appropriate size unit or pay the market rent for the occupied unit.

167 May Federally Assisted Elderly Properties Exclude Children?

Also see question 59 for exceptions which allow certain properties to exclude children.

Generally the answer is no, even though under the Fair Housing Act certain elderly properties are exempted from the provisions prohibiting discrimination on the ground of familial status. HUD has determined that the various mortgage insurance programs under the National Housing Act (including Sections 220, 221, 223, 231, and 236) contain a statutory requirement that households with children may not be excluded. Thus, properties developed under these mortgage insurance programs may not exclude otherwise eligible households with children (for example, a grandchild living with grandparent), even if the property was designed and operated for the elderly. Excluding households with children from residing at those elderly properties will therefore constitute illegal discrimination on the basis of familial status.

For federally assisted properties for the elderly not developed under these mortgage insurance programs (for instance, Section 202 properties, or Section 8 with a non-FHA-insured mortgage loan), the Fair Housing Act also prohibits discrimination against families with children.

168 What Is the RHS Definition of "Elderly"?

"Elderly" is defined[i] as a person who is at least 62 years old. The term elderly also means individuals with handicaps or disabilities regardless of age as separately defined in the Handbook. RHS therefore uses the term "elderly" to denote a person of age 62 or older, a person with a handicap, or a person with a disability. "Elderly family" means a household where the tenant, cotenant, member *or* co-member is at least 62 years old, disabled or handicapped.

Like HUD, in RHS practice the term "elderly" does not refer to a nonelderly household that includes an "elderly" relative or a handicapped child. The tenant, cotenant, member or co-member (in the case of cooperative housing) must be either elderly or disabled or handicapped.

The RHS definition of tenant/cotenant is a person who has signed a lease and is, or will be, an occupant of a unit.

169 Are Any RHS Elderly Programs Exempted from the Familial Status Requirements of the Fair Housing Act?

The practical answer is no. On July 9, 1991, the Department of Housing and Urban Development determined that certain RHS housing qualified for an exemption from the prohibitions against discrimination because of familial status. The exemption applies to housing RHS designated as housing for the elderly or handicapped under the Section 515 program. The determination stated that the exemption would exist as long as the units are rented to elderly persons in accordance with the terms of the program.

---

i.   Handbook 1930-C Exhibit B II

However, if an owner were to prevent an elderly household from occupying a unit because the household included children, the owner would not be complying with the terms of the program. Therefore, although the exemption is technically available, in actual practice owners may not exclude elderly households with children from RHS properties.

170 Are Families With Children Eligible for Admission to RHS Elderly Housing?

Yes, provided that the household otherwise qualifies. The RHS provisions governing elderly housing[ii] state that "Elderly Housing must be occupied by tenants who are elderly, disabled and/or handicapped but not at the exclusion of children if they are members of the 'elderly' household, nor shall it be restricted exclusively for use by tenants who are disabled and/or handicapped." In addition, leases on RHS properties are forbidden from including any provisions that prohibit occupancy by families with children under 18, and this applies also to housing designated as elderly.

ii. Handbook 1930-C Exhibit B(VI)(D)(1XhX2)

Chapter Twenty: "Mixed Population" Issues in Federally-Assisted Elderly Properties

171 Which Properties May Provide a Preference for the Elderly?

See 184 for further information on these programs.

There are various types of properties that are entitled to limit admission to the elderly, for example:

- Section 202 Supportive Housing for the Elderly properties; and,

- Section 221 and 236 properties, if they were originally designed for occupancy by elderly families.

See question 112 for a definition of "mixed populations."

In addition, the Housing and Community Development Act allows certain properties to provide a preference for the elderly while still admitting other categories of residents in certain circumstances.

Properties that are entitled to provide this preference for the elderly are properties that were originally designed primarily for occupancy by the elderly and were assisted in their construction or substantial rehabilitation under one of the following Section 8 programs:

- The Section 8 New Construction Program;

- The Section 8 Substantial Rehabilitation Program;

- The State Housing Agencies Program (if it involves new construction and substantial rehabilitation);

- The New Construction Set-Aside for Section 515 Rural Rental Housing Program; and

- The Section 8 Housing Assistance Program for the Disposition of HUD-Owned Projects (if it involves substantial rehabilitation).

It does not matter if a property is FHA-insured or not. If a property falls within one of the above programs and it was originally designed primarily for occupancy by households whose head, spouse or sole member is elderly, the manner in which the property was financed is irrelevant: the property is entitled to provide a preference for the elderly.

172 Providing a Preference for the Elderly

Before an owner elects to provide a preference to the elderly, it must first determine whether the property was originally designed primarily for occupancy by the elderly. The 1992 Act is silent on how an owner should make this determination. Regulations made under the Act,[i] on the other hand, do provide detailed guidance on this issue.

Documentation Requirement

The regulations include a "documentation requirement." This requirement states that elections be supported by at least one "primary source" or at least two "secondary sources."

Primary Sources

Primary sources include, but are not necessarily limited to, identification of the project (or portion of the project) as serving elderly families in one of the following documents:

- The application in response to the notice of funding availability;

- The terms of the notice of funding availability under which the application was solicited;

- The regulatory agreement;

- The loan commitment;

- The bid invitation;

- The owner's management plan; or

- Any other underwriting or financial document collected at or before the loan closing.

Secondary Sources

Secondary sources include, but are not necessarily limited to:

- Lease records from the earliest two years of occupancy, for which records are available, showing that occupancy had been restricted primarily to households whose head, spouse or sole member was 62 or older;

- Evidence that services for the elderly have been provided, such as services funded by the Older Americans Act, transportation to senior citizen centers, or programs coordinated with the Area Agency on Aging;

---

i.   *These Regulations may be found at 24 CFR Ch. VIII 880.612a.*

- Property unit mix with a higher percentage of efficiencies and one bedroom units (HUD's Occupancy Handbook 4350.3 for Subsidized Multifamily Housing provides that virtually no project with a large percentage of two, three or four bedroom units would have been approved as elderly housing); or

- Any other relevant type of historical data.

When to Consider Secondary Sources

If there is a conflict between primary sources as to the original design of the property, the owner may not make an election by relying on primary sources alone. In these cases, the owner would need to rely on secondary sources to support the election. In other words, two or more secondary sources may be used in the event that primary sources conflict or do not provide clear evidence of the property's original design.

If there are no primary or secondary sources to support a claim that the property was originally designed to house the elderly, then a preference for the elderly cannot be given and all eligible applicants must be housed in the appropriate order.

Making the Election

Once an owner has determined that the property was originally designed primarily for occupancy by the elderly, the owner does not have to take any formal action. The owner need only revise the property's admissions policies to reflect the election and to conform to the statutory and regulatory provisions. In certain circumstances the owner will also need to inform non-elderly applicants who are currently on the property's waiting list that an election in favor of the elderly has been made and that it may affect their application for housing. This notification is required if all the units set-aside for non-elderly disabled families are already occupied or if there are no units required to be set-aside for non-elderly disabled families. In either of those events there may be a reduced likelihood that the property will be able to accommodate non-elderly applicants. Nevertheless, such applicants should not be removed from the waiting list.

See question 174 for set-aside requirements.

173 Is HUD Approval of the Preference for the Elderly Necessary?

See question 172.

No. However, an owner, if challenged on its election; must be able to produce evidence that supports the property's eligibility to give a preference in admission to the elderly. In addition, HUD may, at any time, review and determine whether the property was eligible to elect such a preference.

It would be wise for an owner to keep all documentation which was relied upon in making the election. That way, if challenged, it will be a simple matter to produce the requisite proof.

174 Calculating The Set-Aside

The law requires that even if a property has elected to exercise a preference for elderly families the owner must nevertheless reserve a specific number of units in the property for occupancy by disabled applicants who are neither elderly nor near-elderly (i.e., aged 50 and over but less than 62).

See the next page for an example.

To calculate the number of units which must be set aside for this purpose, the owner must first determine the percentage of units occupied by households whose head, spouse or sole member was a person with disabilities under the age of 50, as of January 1, 1992, and as of October 28, 1992. The owner should take the number of units corresponding to the higher percentage and compare it to 10 percent of the property's units. Whichever of those two numbers is less is the number of units that must be reserved or set aside for non-elderly disabled occupants. In no case will the maximum number of units that must be set aside exceed ten percent of the total number of units at the property.[ii]

---

ii.   24 CFR 880.612a (c) (1)

Example: Calculating the Set-Aside

> *You have a 100-unit property. On January 1, 1992, 5 percent of the units were occupied by residents with disabilities under the age of 50; on October 28, 1992, 12% of the units were occupied by such residents. Since the October 28 percentage is greater, you take that number, which amounts to 12 units and compare it to 10 percent of the property's units (10 units). The lesser of those two numbers is the number of units required to be set aside; in this case, 10 units or 10%.*
>
> *In contrast, if on January 1, 1992, 6% of the units were occupied by residents with disabilities under the age of 50, and 8% of the units so occupied on October 28, 1992. Taking the larger of the two numbers, 8% which amounts to 8 units, and comparing it to 10 percent of the units, (10 units), the number of units required to be set aside would be 8% or 8 units. Of course, if no units were occupied by non-elderly disabled persons at January 1, 1992 or October 28, 1992 then no set-aside will have to be made.*

Keep a copy of the resident profile information, and a written record of the set-aside calculation in the property's permanent files.

175 Can I Exceed the Set-Aside?

The number of units required to be reserved at any time is the number calculated based on the formula outlined in question 174.

Yes. The regulations state that the calculated set-aside is only a minimum. Accordingly, an owner may, at any time, reserve a higher number of units for the non-elderly disabled. Moreover, the regulations state that an owner who chooses to exceed its set-aside is not obligated to continue to provide that greater number of units.

However, an owner who chooses to exceed its set-aside and then return to the set-aside should not do so in a manner that could be interpreted as discriminatory. For example: choosing to exceed the set-aside for physically disabled non-elderly applicants but returning to the set-aside when a mentally disabled person applies or reaches the top of the property's waiting list.

176 How Do I Comply With the Set-Aside Requirements When Filling Vacant Units?

In selecting applicants to fill vacant units, the owner must first determine the property's current position in relation to set-aside compliance. If the required number of non-elderly disabled units has been set aside the owner would fill vacancies with elderly families. If the required number of non-elderly disabled units has not been set-aside the owner must fill vacant units, up to the number of units required to be set aside, with households whose head, spouse, or sole member of the household is under age 50 and is a person with disabilities.

It is advisable to perform the set-aside compliance calculation each time an admission decision is made, and to retain a written record of the calculation in the property's permanent files.

177 What Is the Secondary Preference for Near-Elderly?

In certain circumstances, properties that provide a preference to the elderly may elect to provide a secondary preference to "near elderly" persons with disabilities (i.e., 50 and over but less than 62) rather than "younger" or non-elderly persons with disabilities. This preference can be exercised in two situations:

- If all the units required to be set-aside for non-elderly disabled families have been so reserved, and there are no elderly applicants on the waiting list then near-elderly disabled applicants can be housed in units reserved for the elderly; or

- If the number of units set-aside for non-elderly disabled residents exceeds the number of applicants eligible for those units then near-elderly disabled applicants can be housed in those units.

178 What If There Are an Insufficient Number of Applicants?

What if the owner elects to exercise the secondary preference, but there are an insufficient number of near-elderly disabled applicants to fill existing vacancies?

See question 172.

If there are an insufficient number of applicants in any of the three preferential categories (i.e., elderly, non-elderly disabled and near-elderly disabled) to fill vacant units, the units are to be made generally available to any otherwise eligible applicant on the waiting list, without regard to the preferences or reservation of units provided by Title VI of the Housing and Community Development Act of 1992 and its regulations. Likewise, if the secondary preference is not exercised and there are no elderly or non-elderly disabled applicants on the waiting list, vacant units can be made available to any eligible applicant on the waiting list. This is why applicants who do not fall within any of the preferential categories should be kept on the waiting list. They may still become eligible for housing if there are vacancies at the property and no preferential category applicants on the waiting list.

See question 157.

However, the regulations provide that before an owner determines that there are an insufficient number of applicants who qualify for housing on the basis of any of the preferences, the owner must first conduct marketing and other outreach activities in accordance with applicable HUD regulations to attract such applicants. These regulations require an owner to undertake marketing of the property in accordance with the property's HUD-approved Affirmative Fair Housing Marketing Plan and all Fair Housing and Equal Opportunity requirements.

179 What If Non-Elderly Residents With Disabilities Exceed the Set-Aside?

If the number of units occupied by non-elderly disabled residents exceeds the number of units required to be set-aside for them, the owner may *not* evict those residents in order to reduce the number of units occupied by the non-elderly disabled to the level of the required set-aside. However, as non-elderly persons with disabilities move out of the property, the owner may fill the resulting vacancies with elderly families until the number of units occupied by the non-elderly disabled is equivalent to the property's set-aside.

It is also forbidden for owners to evict residents solely because the units occupied by them are required in order to satisfy any preference or set-aside.

180 Resident Selection for Accessible Units

There is nothing explicit in either the regulations or the statute governing how owners should fill accessible units. However, the preamble to the regulations makes it clear that an accessible unit need not be given to the next applicant on the waiting list in need of such a unit if that applicant would not otherwise be eligible pursuant to the new preference provisions.

An Example of Unit-Assignment

> *A property has reached its set-aside. The only applicant in need of an available accessible unit is under age 50. The property may, nevertheless, make the unit available to an elderly person (or a near-elderly disabled person if there are no elderly on the waiting list) not in need of the unit's accessibility features.*

See also questions 146 and 138.

With respect to projects or parts of projects for the elderly, to be eligible for a unit made accessible under Section 504 of the Rehabilitation Act of 1973 the applicant must meet the definition of elderly family and a member of the household must have a disability requiring the accessibility features of the unit.[iii] On the other hand, the preamble also states that when the next eligible applicant for a unit (elderly or non-elderly) is in need of an accessible unit and the only available unit is not accessible, then the owner is to accommodate the applicant either by:

- Making that unit accessible; or

- By transferring a resident who is living in an accessible unit and who does not need the unit's features.

181 What If I Make No Election?

If an owner does not elect to give a preference to the elderly, the property must continue to admit residents pursuant to the rules in effect prior to the 1992 Act. In other words, applicants with disabilities who are under age 62 must be admitted as if they were elderly, without any numerical limitation.

---

iii. HUD's Occupancy Handbook #4350.3 Section 2-6

182 Do I Have To Decide Now?

No. Although it is not specifically stated, the regulations seem to sanction the making of the election to give a preference to the elderly at any time the owner chooses. Consequently, an election could be made in the future.

Regardless of when the owner makes the election, in determining the number of units to be set aside for the non-elderly disabled occupancy levels by that group as at January 1, and October 28, 1992 must be calculated as set out above.

183 Other Mixed Populations Provisions

Two changes are noteworthy: the definition of "elderly families," and the status of older properties designed for elderly occupancy.

This definition applies to all Section 8 programs, not just to those listed in question 171.

Prior to the 1992 Act, the term "elderly families" was defined under the United States Housing Act of 1937 to include persons with disabilities under the age of 62. It was this inclusion that required the admission of non-elderly persons with disabilities into Section 8 elderly properties prior to the 1992 Act. The 1992 Act changed the definition of "elderly families" to mean specifically those whose head, spouse or sole member is age 62 or older.

Title VI of the 1992 Act also made it clear that properties designed exclusively for elderly occupancy under the 236 program, the 221(d)(3) BMIR program and the 202 program may continue to restrict occupancy to elderly families in accordance with the rules, standards, and agreements governing occupancy in such housing in effect at the time of the development of the housing. Owners should carefully study these rules, standards and agreements, to determine whether their property was designed exclusively for elderly occupancy.

184 Are Federally Assisted Apartment Properties for the Elderly Allowed to Exclude or Restrict the Number of Non-Elderly Persons With Disabilities?

Yes, certain programs permit the number of non-elderly disabled admissions to be restricted, and other programs permit the total exclusion of the non-elderly disabled. Following is a summary of the most common programs and what they permit:

Section 202 and Section 811

Section 202 Supportive Housing Program for the Elderly provides capital advances to finance the construction and rehabilitation of structures that will serve as supportive housing for very low-income elderly persons (i.e. aged 62 years and older) and provides rent subsidies for the properties to help make them affordable. Prior to the 1990 National Affordable Housing Act applicants for admission to Section 202 housing had to be either elderly or disabled and low-income. This Act established a separate program for the disabled—"Supportive Housing Program for Persons with Disabilities" - under Section 811.

See question 120 for additional information on the eligibility requirements for these programs.

Occupancy in Section 202 housing is open to any household comprised of one or more persons (one of whom is 62 years of age or more at the time of initial occupancy), if other occupancy requirements are met (for example, income eligibility). On the question of adult children of Section 202 residents coming to live with an elderly parent, HUD has ruled that this is permissible only where the adult children are essential for the care or well being of the elderly tenant(s).[iv] In other words adult children qualify for occupancy only as long as the tenant requires their supportive services.

Under Section 811, owners are expressly authorized, with HUD approval, to limit occupancy of housing for persons with disabilities to persons with similar disabilities.

Sections 221 and 236

Admission to Section 221 and 236 properties may be restricted to the group of persons for whom the property was originally designed, for example all Section 236 programs were originally designed to serve either families or the elderly and/or disabled. Section 221 properties were originally intended to serve the elderly or disabled.

Under Section 658 of the Housing and Community Development Act an owner of any federally assisted project that was designed for occupancy by elderly families may continue to restrict occupancy in such projects to elderly families. Section 221 and 236

---

iv. HUD Directive Number 97-74 "Occupancy In Section 202/8 Projects properties fall within that provision and can limit admission exclusively to elderly families (i.e., families whose heads or their spouses or whose sole members are at least 62 years of age) if that was the group for whom the project was specifically designed. The non-elderly disabled would have no rights of admission to such elderly properties. If, however, the properties have accessible units then non-elderly disabled persons requiring accessibility features must be accepted for accessible units. In order to identify the particular group that the project was intended to serve, HUD's Occupancy Handbook 4350.3 provides that documents such as regulatory agreements, loan commitment papers and financial documents should be examined. If the property documentation is unclear as to the category of persons intended to be served and the owner claims that it was originally designed for the elderly, then approval must be obtained from the Director of Housing Management. It is recommended that owners obtain the advice of counsel before designating their property as one designed for exclusive occupancy by a particular class.

185 Does RHS Allow Persons With Disabilities, Under the Age of 62, to Live in Elderly Housing?

Yes. Under RHS Handbook 1930-C the term "Elderly" includes individuals with handicaps or disabilities regardless of age and "Elderly family" includes a household where the tenant, cotenant, member or co-member is disabled or handicapped. It is also expressly provided that elderly housing must be occupied by tenants who are either elderly, disabled and/or handicapped.

186 Does RHS Allow Non-Elderly or Non-Disabled Persons to Live in Elderly Housing?

Yes, non-elderly and non-disabled persons may live in elderly housing but they do so as part of the elderly or disabled tenant's household and they may not themselves be the qualifying tenant. RHS Handbook 1930-C expressly provides that elderly housing must be occupied by tenants who are elderly, disabled and/or handicapped but not at the exclusion of children if they are members of the "elderly" household. In addition, surviving members of an elderly, disabled and/or handicapped tenant's household may continue occupancy of the elderly unit even if they are not elderly, disabled or handicapped.

SUBCHAPTER A—FAIR HOUSING

PART 100—DISCRIMINATORY CONDUCT UNDER THE FAIR HOUSING ACT

Subpart A—General

Subpart B—Discriminatory Housing Practices

Subpart C—Discrimination in Residential Real Estate-Related Transactions

Subpart D—Prohibition Against Discrimination Because of Handicap

Subpart E—Housing for Older Persons

Subpart F—Interference, Coercion or Intimidation

AUTHORITY : 42 U.S.C. 3535(d), 3600±3620.

SOURCE : 54 FR 3283, Jan. 23, 1989, unless otherwise noted.

Subpart A—General

§100.1   Authority.

This regulation is issued under the authority of the Secretary of Housing and Urban Development to administer and enforce title VIII of the Civil Rights Act of 1968, as amended by the Fair Housing Amendments Act of 1988 (the Fair Housing Act).

§100.5   Scope.

(a) It is the policy of the United States to provide, within constitutional limitations, for fair housing throughout the United States. No person shall be subjected to discrimination because of race, color, religion, sex, handicap, familial status, or national origin in the sale, rental, or advertising of dwellings, in the provision of brokerage services, or in the availability of residential real estate-related transactions.

(b) This part provides the Department's interpretation of the coverage

541

§ 100.10

of the Fair Housing Act regarding discrimination related to the sale or rental of dwellings, the provision of services in connection therewith, and the availability of residential real estate-related transactions.

(c) Nothing in this part relieves persons participating in a Federal or Federally-assisted program or activity from other requirements applicable to buildings and dwellings.

§ 100.10 Exemptions.

(a) This part does not:

(1) Prohibit a religious organization, association, or society, or any non-profit institution or organization operated, supervised or controlled by or in conjunction with a religious organization, association, or society, from limiting the sale, rental or occupancy of dwellings which it owns or operates for other than a commercial purpose to persons of the same religion, or from giving preference to such persons, unless membership in such religion is restricted because of race, color, or national origin;

(2) Prohibit a private club, not in fact open to the public, which, incident to its primary purpose or purposes, provides lodgings which it owns or operates for other than a commercial purpose, from limiting the rental or occupancy of such lodgings to its members or from giving preference to its members;

(3) Limit the applicability of any reasonable local, State or Federal restrictions regarding the maximum number of occupants permitted to occupy a dwelling; or

(4) Prohibit conduct against a person because such person has been convicted by any court of competent jurisdiction of the illegal manufacture or distribution of a controlled substance as defined in section 102 of the Controlled Substances Act (21 U.S.C. 802).

(b) Nothing in this part regarding discrimination based on familial status applies with respect to housing for older persons as defined in subpart E of this part.

(c) Nothing in this part, other than the prohibitions against discriminatory advertising, applies to:

(1) The sale or rental of any single family house by an owner, provided the following conditions are met:

(i) The owner does not own or have any interest in more than three single family houses at any one time.

(ii) The house is sold or rented without the use of a real estate broker, agent or salesperson or the facilities of any person in the business of selling or renting dwellings. If the owner selling the house does not reside in it at the time of the sale or was not the most recent resident of the house prior to such sale, the exemption in this paragraph (c)(1) of this section applies to only one such sale in any 24-month period.

(2) Rooms or units in dwellings containing living quarters occupied or intended to be occupied by no more than four families living independently of each other, if the owner actually maintains and occupies one of such living quarters as his or her residence.

§ 100.20 Definitions.

The terms Department, Fair Housing Act, and Secretary are defined in 24 CFR part 5.

Aggrieved person includes any person whoÐ

(a) Claims to have been injured by a discriminatory housing practice; or

(b) Believes that such person will be injured by a discriminatory housing practice that is about to occur.

Broker or Agent includes any person authorized to perform an action on behalf of another person regarding any matter related to the sale or rental of dwellings, including offers, solicitations or contracts and the administration of matters regarding such offers, solicitations or contracts or any residential real estate-related transactions.

Discriminatory housing practice means an act that is unlawful under section 804, 805, 806, or 818 of the Fair Housing Act.

Dwelling means any building, structure or portion thereof which is occupied as, or designed or intended for occupancy as, a residence by one or more families, and any vacant land which is offered for sale or lease for the construction or location thereon of any such building, structure or portion thereof.

Office of Asst. Secy., Equal Opportunity, HUD §100.50

Familial status means one or more individuals (who have not attained the age of 18 years) being domiciled withÐ

(a) A parent or another person having legal custody of such individual or individuals; or

(b) The designee of such parent or other person having such custody, with the written permission of such parent or other person.

The protections afforded against discrimination on the basis of familial status shall apply to any person who is pregnant or is in the process of securing legal custody of any individual who has not attained the age of 18 years.

Handicap is defined in §100.201.

Person includes one or more individuals, corporations, partnerships, associations, labor organizations, legal representatives, mutual companies, joint-stock companies, trusts, unincorporated organizations, trustees, trustees in cases under title 11 U.S.C., receivers, and fiduciaries.

Person in the business of selling or renting dwellings means any person who:

(a) Within the preceding twelve months, has participated as principal in three or more transactions involving the sale or rental of any dwelling or any interest therein;

(b) Within the preceding twelve months, has participated as agent, other than in the sale of his or her own personal residence, in providing sales or rental facilities or sales or rental services in two or more transactions involving the sale or rental of any dwelling or any interest therein; or

(c) Is the owner of any dwelling designed or intended for occupancy by, or occupied by, five or more families.

State means any of the several states, the District of Columbia, the Commonwealth of Puerto Rico, or any of the territories and possessions of the United States.

[54 FR 3283, Jan. 23, 1989, as amended at 61 FR 5205, Feb. 9, 1996]

Subpart B—Discriminatory Housing Practices

§100.50 Real estate practices prohibited.

(a) This subpart provides the Department's interpretation of conduct that is unlawful housing discrimination under section 804 and section 806 of the Fair Housing Act. In general the prohibited actions are set forth under sections of this subpart which are most applicable to the discriminatory conduct described. However, an action illustrated in one section can constitute a violation under sections in the subpart. For example, the conduct described in § 100.60(b)(3) and (4) would constitute a violation of § 100.65(a) as well as § 100.60(a).

(b) It shall be unlawful to:

(1) Refuse to sell or rent a dwelling after a bona fide offer has been made, or to refuse to negotiate for the sale or rental of a dwelling because of race, color, religion, sex, familial status, or national origin, or to discriminate in the sale or rental of a dwelling because of handicap.

(2) Discriminate in the terms, conditions or privileges of sale or rental of a dwelling, or in the provision of services or facilities in connection with sales or rentals, because of race, color, religion, sex, handicap, familial status, or national origin.

(3) Engage in any conduct relating to the provision of housing which otherwise makes unavailable or denies dwellings to persons because of race, color, religion, sex, handicap, familial status, or national origin.

(4) Make, print or publish, or cause to be made, printed or published, any notice, statement or advertisement with respect to the sale or rental of a dwelling that indicates any preference, limitation or discrimination because of race, color, religion, sex, handicap, familial status, or national origin, or an intention to make any such preference, limitation or discrimination.

(5) Represent to any person because of race, color, religion, sex, handicap, familial status, or national origin that a dwelling is not available for sale or rental when such dwelling is in fact available.

(6) Engage in blockbusting practices in connection with the sale or rental of dwellings because of race, color, religion, sex, handicap, familial status, or national origin.

(7) Deny access to or membership or participation in, or to discriminate against any person in his or her access

§ 100.60

to or membership or participation in, any multiple-listing service, real estate brokers' assocation, or other service organization or facility relating to the business of selling or renting a dwelling or in the terms or conditions or membership or participation, because of race, color, religion, sex, handicap, familial status, or national origin.

(c) The application of the Fair Housing Act with respect to persons with handicaps is discussed in subpart D of this part.

§ 100.60 Unlawful refusal to sell or rent or to negotiate for the sale or rental.

(a) It shall be unlawful for a person to refuse to sell or rent a dwelling to a person who has made a   bona fide offer, because of race, color, religion, sex, familial status, or national origin or to refuse to negotiate with a person for the sale or rental of a dwelling because of race, color, religion, sex, familial status, or national origin, or to discriminate against any person in the sale or rental of a dwelling because of handicap.

(b) Prohibited actions under this section include, but are not limited to:

(1) Failing to accept or consider a bona fide offer because of race, color, religion, sex, handicap, familial status, or national origin.

(2) Refusing to sell or rent a dwelling to, or to negotiate for the sale or rental of a dwelling with, any person because of race, color, religion, sex, handicap, familial status, or national origin.

(3) Imposing different sales prices or rental charges for the sale or rental of a dwelling upon any person because of race, color, religion, sex, handicap, familial status, or national origin.

(4) Using different qualification criteria or applications, or sale or rental standards or procedures, such as income standards, application requirements, application fees, credit analysis or sale or rental approval procedures or other requirements, because of race, color, religion, sex, handicap, familial status, or national origin.

(5) Evicting tenants because of their race, color, religion, sex, handicap, familial status, or national origin or be-

cause of the race, color, religion, sex, handicap, familial status, or national origin of a tenant's guest.

§ 100.65 Discrimination in terms, conditions and privileges and in services and facilities.

(a) It shall be unlawful, because of race, color, religion, sex, handicap, familial status, or national origin, to impose different terms, conditions or privileges relating to the sale or rental of a dwelling or to deny or limit services or facilities in connection with the sale or rental of a dwelling.

(b) Prohibited actions under this section include, but are not limited to:

(1) Using different provisions in leases or contracts of sale, such as those relating to rental charges, security deposits and the terms of a lease and those relating to down payment and closing requirements, because of race, color, religion, sex, handicap, familial status, or national origin.

(2) Failing or delaying maintenance or repairs of sale or rental dwellings because of race, color, religion, sex, handicap, familial status, or national origin.

(3) Failing to process an offer for the sale or rental of a dwelling or to communicate an offer accurately because of race, color, religion, sex, handicap, familial status, or national origin.

(4) Limiting the use of privileges, services or facilities associated with a dwelling because of race, color, religion, sex, handicap, familial status, or national origin of an an owner, tenant or a person associated with him or her.

(5) Denying or limiting services or facilities in connection with the sale or rental of a dwelling, because a person failed or refused to provide sexual favors.

§ 100.70 Other prohibited sale and rental conduct.

(a) It shall be unlawful, because of race, color, religion, sex, handicap, familial status, or national origin, to restrict or attempt to restrict the choices of a person by word or conduct in connection with seeking, negotiating for, buying or renting a dwelling so as to perpetuate, or tend to perpetuate, segregated housing patterns, or to discourage or obstruct choices in a

544

Office of Asst. Secy., Equal Opportunity, HUD §100.75

community, neighborhood or development.

(b) It shall be unlawful, because of race, color, religion, sex, handicap, familial status, or national origin, to engage in any conduct relating to the provision of housing or of services and facilities in connection therewith that otherwise makes unavailable or denies dwellings to persons.

(c) Prohibited actions under paragraph (a) of this section, which are generally referred to as unlawful steering practices, include, but are not limited to:

(1) Discouraging any person from inspecting, purchasing or renting a dwelling because of race, color, religion, sex, handicap, familial status, or national origin, or because of the race, color, religion, sex, handicap, familial status, or national origin of persons in a community, neighborhood or development.

(2) Discouraging the purchase or rental of a dwelling because of race, color, religion, sex, handicap, familial status, or national origin, by exaggerating drawbacks or failing to inform any person of desirable features of a dwelling or of a community, neighborhood, or development.

(3) Communicating to any prospective purchaser that he or she would not be comfortable or compatible with existing residents of a community, neighborhood or development because of race, color, religion, sex, handicap, familial status, or national origin.

(4) Assigning any person to a particular section of a community, neighborhood or development, or to a particular floor of a building, because of race, color, religion, sex, handicap, familial status, or national origin.

(d) Prohibited activities relating to dwellings under paragraph (b) of this section include, but are not limited to:

(1) Discharging or taking other adverse action against an employee, broker or agent because he or she refused to participate in a discriminatory housing practice.

(2) Employing codes or other devices to segregate or reject applicants, purchasers or renters, refusing to take or to show listings of dwellings in certain areas because of race, color, religion, sex, handicap, familial status, or na-

tional origin, or refusing to deal with certain brokers or agents because they or one or more of their clients are of a particular race, color, religion, sex, handicap, familial status, or national origin.

(3) Denying or delaying the processing of an application made by a purchaser or renter or refusing to approve such a person for occupancy in a cooperative or condominium dwelling because of race, color, religion, sex, handicap, familial status, or national origin.

(4) Refusing to provide municipal services or property or hazard insurance for dwellings or providing such services or insurance differently because of race, color, religion, sex, handicap, familial status, or national origin.

§100.75 Discriminatory advertisements, statements and notices.

(a) It shall be unlawful to make, print or publish, or cause to be made, printed or published, any notice, statement or advertisement with respect to the sale or rental of a dwelling which indicates any preference, limitation or discrimination because of race, color, religion, sex, handicap, familial status, or national origin, or an intention to make any such preference, limitation or discrimination.

(b) The prohibitions in this section shall apply to all written or oral notices or statements by a person engaged in the sale or rental of a dwelling. Written notices and statements include any applications, flyers, brochures, deeds, signs, banners, posters, billboards or any documents used with respect to the sale or rental of a dwelling.

(c) Discriminatory notices, statements and advertisements include, but are not limited to:

(1) Using words, phrases, photographs, illustrations, symbols or forms which convey that dwellings are available or not available to a particular group of persons because of race, color, religion, sex, handicap, familial status, or national origin.

(2) Expressing to agents, brokers, employees, prospective sellers or renters or any other persons a preference for or limitation on any purchaser or renter

545

§ 100.80

because of race, color, religion, sex, handicap, familial status, or national origin of such persons.

(3) Selecting media or locations for advertising the sale or rental of dwellings which deny particular segments of the housing market information about housing opportunities because of race, color, religion, sex, handicap, familial status, or national origin.

(4) Refusing to publish advertising for the sale or rental of dwellings or requiring different charges or terms for such advertising because of race, color, religion, sex, handicap, familial status, or national origin.

(d) 24 CFR part 109 provides information to assist persons to advertise dwellings in a nondiscriminatory manner and describes the matters the Department will review in evaluating compliance with the Fair Housing Act and in investigating complaints alleging discriminatory housing practices involving advertising.

§ 100.80 Discriminatory representations on the availability of dwellings.

(a) It shall be unlawful, because of race, color, religion, sex, handicap, familial status, or national origin, to provide inaccurate or untrue information about the availability of dwellings for sale or rental.

(b) Prohibited actions under this section include, but are not limited to:

(1) Indicating through words or conduct that a dwelling which is available for inspection, sale, or rental has been sold or rented, because of race, color, religion, sex, handicap, familial status, or national origin.

(2) Representing that covenants or other deed, trust or lease provisions which purport to restrict the sale or rental of dwellings because of race, color, religion, sex, handicap, familial status, or national origin preclude the sale of rental of a dwelling to a person.

(3) Enforcing covenants or other deed, trust, or lease provisions which preclude the sale or rental of a dwelling to any person because of race, color, religion, sex, handicap, familial status, or national origin.

(4) Limiting information, by word or conduct, regarding suitably priced dwellings available for inspection, sale

or rental, because of race, color, religion, sex, handicap, familial status, or national origin.

(5) Providing false or inaccurate information regarding the availability of a dwelling for sale or rental to any person, including testers, regardless of whether such person is actually seeking housing, because of race, color, religion, sex, handicap, familial status, or national origin.

§ 100.85 Blockbusting.

(a) It shall be unlawful, for profit, to induce or attempt to induce a person to sell or rent a dwelling by representations regarding the entry or prospective entry into the neighborhood of a person or persons of a particular race, color, religion, sex, familial status, or national origin or with a handicap.

(b) In establishing a discriminatory housing practice under this section it is not necessary that there was in fact profit as long as profit was a factor for engaging in the blockbusting activity.

(c) Prohibited actions under this section include, but are not limited to:

(1) Engaging, for profit, in conduct (including uninvited solicitations for listings) which conveys to a person that a neighborhood is undergoing or is about to undergo a change in the race, color, religion, sex, handicap, familial status, or national origin of persons residing in it, in order to encourage the person to offer a dwelling for sale or rental.

(2) Encouraging, for profit, any person to sell or rent a dwelling through assertions that the entry or prospective entry of persons of a particular race, color, religion, sex, familial status, or national origin, or with handicaps, can or will result in undesirable consequences for the project, neighborhood or community, such as a lowering of property values, an increase in criminal or antisocial behavior, or a decline in the quality of schools or other services or facilities.

§ 100.90 Discrimination in the provision of brokerage services.

(a) It shall be unlawful to deny any person access to or membership or participation in any multiple listing service, real estate brokers' organization or other service, organization, or facility

546

Office of Asst. Secy., Equal Opportunity, HUD §100.125

relating to the business of selling or renting dwellings, or to discriminate against any person in the terms or conditions of such access, membership or participation, because of race, color, religion, sex, handicap, familial status, or national origin.

(b) Prohibited actions under this section include, but are not limited to:

(1) Setting different fees for access to or membership in a multiple listing service because of race, color, religion, sex, handicap, familial status, or national origin.

(2) Denying or limiting benefits accruing to members in a real estate brokers' organization because of race, color, religion, sex, handicap, familial status, or national origin.

(3) Imposing different standards or criteria for membership in a real estate sales or rental organization because of race, color, religion, sex, handicap, familial status, or national origin.

(4) Establishing geographic boundaries or office location or residence requirements for access to or membership or participation in any multiple listing service, real estate brokers' organization or other service, organization or facility relating to the business of selling or renting dwellings, because of race, color, religion, sex, handicap, familial status, or national origin.

Subpart C—Discrimination in Residential Real Estate-Related Transactions

§100.110 Discriminatory practices in residential real estate-related transactions.

(a) This subpart provides the Department's interpretation of the conduct that is unlawful housing discrimination under section 805 of the Fair Housing Act.

(b) It shall be unlawful for any person or other entity whose business includes engaging in residential real estate-related transactions to discriminate against any person in making available such a transaction, or in the terms or conditions of such a transaction, because of race, color, religion, sex, handicap, familial status, or national origin.

§100.115 Residential real estate-related transactions.

The term residential real estate-related transactions means:

(a) The making or purchasing of loans or providing other financial assistanceÐ

(1) For purchasing, constructing, improving, repairing or maintaining a dwelling; or

(2) Secured by residential real estate; or

(b) The selling, brokering or appraising of residential real property.

§100.120 Discrimination in the making of loans and in the provision of other financial assistance.

(a) It shall be unlawful for any person or entity whose business includes engaging in residential real estate-related transactions to discriminate against any person in making available loans or other financial assistance for a dwelling, or which is or is to be secured by a dwelling, because of race, color, religion, sex, handicap, familial status, or national origin.

(b) Prohibited practices under this section include, but are not limited to, failing or refusing to provide to any person, in connection with a residential real estate-related transaction, information regarding the availability of loans or other financial assistance, application requirements, procedures or standards for the review and approval of loans or financial assistance, or providing information which is inaccurate or different from that provided others, because of race, color, religion, sex, handicap, familial status, or national origin.

§100.125 Discrimination in the purchasing of loans.

(a) It shall be unlawful for any person or entity engaged in the purchasing of loans or other debts or securities which support the purchase, construction, improvement, repair or maintenance of a dwelling, or which are secured by residential real estate, to refuse to purchase such loans, debts, or securities, or to impose different terms or conditions for such purchases, because of race, color, religion, sex, handicap, familial status, or national origin.

547

§ 100.130

(b) Unlawful conduct under this section includes, but is not limited to:

(1) Purchasing loans or other debts or securities which relate to, or which are secured by dwellings in certain communities or neighborhoods but not in others because of the race, color, religion, sex, handicap, familial status, or national origin of persons in such neighborhoods or communities.

(2) Pooling or packaging loans or other debts or securities which relate to, or which are secured by, dwellings differently because of race, color, religion, sex, handicap, familial status, or national origin.

(3) Imposing or using different terms or conditions on the marketing or sale of securities issued on the basis of loans or other debts or securities which relate to, or which are secured by, dwellings because of race, color, religion, sex, handicap, familial status, or national origin.

(c) This section does not prevent consideration, in the purchasing of loans, of factors justified by business necessity, including requirements of Federal law, relating to a transaction's financial security or to protection against default or reduction of the value of the security. Thus, this provision would not preclude considerations employed in normal and prudent transactions, provided that no such factor may in any way relate to race, color, religion, sex, handicap, familial status or national origin.

§ 100.130 Discrimination in the terms and conditions for making available loans or other financial assistance.

(a) It shall be unlawful for any person or entity engaged in the making of loans or in the provision of other financial assistance relating to the purchase, construction, improvement, repair or maintenance of dwellings or which are secured by residential real estate to impose different terms or conditions for the availability of such loans or other financial assistance because of race, color, religion, sex, handicap, familial status, or national origin.

(b) Unlawful conduct under this section includes, but is not limited to:

(1) Using different policies, practices or procedures in evaluating or in deter-

mining creditworthiness of any person in connection with the provision of any loan or other financial assistance for a dwelling or for any loan or other financial assistance which is secured by residential real estate because of race, color, religion, sex, handicap, familial status, or national origin.

(2) Determining the type of loan or other financial assistance to be provided with respect to a dwelling, or fixing the amount, interest rate, duration or other terms for a loan or other financial assistance for a dwelling or which is secured by residential real estate, because of race, color, religion, sex, handicap, familial status, or national origin.

§ 100.135 Unlawful practices in the selling, brokering, or appraising of residential real property.

(a) It shall be unlawful for any person or other entity whose business includes engaging in the selling, brokering or appraising of residential real property to discriminate against any person in making available such services, or in the performance of such services, because of race, color, religion, sex, handicap, familial status, or national origin.

(b) For the purposes of this section, the term appraisal means an estimate or opinion of the value of a specified residential real property made in a business context in connection with the sale, rental, financing or refinancing of a dwelling or in connection with any activity that otherwise affects the availability of a residential real estate-related transaction, whether the appraisal is oral or written, or transmitted formally or informally. The appraisal includes all written comments and other documents submitted as support for the estimate or opinion of value.

(c) Nothing in this section prohibits a person engaged in the business of making or furnishing appraisals of residential real property from taking into consideration factors other than race, color, religion, sex, handicap, familial status, or national origin.

(d) Practices which are unlawful under this section include, but are not limited to, using an appraisal of residential real property in connection

Office of Asst. Secy., Equal Opportunity, HUD §100.143

with the sale, rental, or financing of any dwelling where the person knows or reasonably should know that the appraisal improperly takes into consideration race, color, religion, sex, handicap, familial status or national origin.

§100.140   General rules.

(a) Voluntary self-testing and correction. The report or results of a self-test a lender voluntarily conducts or authorizes are privileged as provided in this subpart if the lender has taken or is taking appropriate corrective action to address likely violations identified by the self-test. Data collection required by law or any governmental authority (federal, state, or local) is not voluntary.

(b) Other privileges.   This subpart does not abrogate any evidentiary privilege otherwise provided by law.

[62 FR 66432, Dec. 18, 1997]

§100.141   Definitions.

As used in this subpart:

Lender means a person who engages in a residential real estate-related lending transaction.

Residential real estate-related lending transaction means the making of a loan:

(1) For purchasing, constructing, improving, repairing, or maintaining a dwelling; or

(2) Secured by residential real estate.

Self-test means any program, practice or study a lender voluntarily conducts or authorizes which is designed and used specifically to determine the extent or effectiveness of compliance with the Fair Housing Act. The self-test must create data or factual information that is not available and cannot be derived from loan files, application files, or other residential real estate-related   lending   transaction records. Self-testing includes, but is not limited to, using fictitious credit applicants (testers) or conducting surveys of applicants or customers, nor is it limited to the pre-application stage of loan processing.

[62 FR 66432, Dec. 18, 1997]

§100.142   Types of information.

(a) The privilege under this subpart covers:

(1) The report or results of the self-test;

(2) Data or factual information created by the self-test;

(3) Workpapers, draft documents and final documents;

(4) Analyses, opinions, and conclusions if they directly result from the self-test report or results.

(b) The privilege does not cover:

(1) Information about whether a lender conducted a self-test, the methodology used or scope of the self-test, the time period covered by the self-test or the dates it was conducted;

(2) Loan files and application files, or other residential real estate-related lending transaction records (e.g., property appraisal reports, loan committee meeting minutes or other documents reflecting the basis for a decision to approve or deny a loan application, loan policies or procedures, underwriting   standards,   compensation records) and information or data derived from such files and records, even if such data has been aggregated, summarized or reorganized to facilitate analysis.

[62 FR 66432, Dec. 18, 1997]

§100.143   Appropriate   corrective   action.

(a) The report or results of a self-test are privileged as provided in this subpart if the lender has taken or is taking appropriate corrective action to address likely violations identified by the self-test. Appropriate corrective action is required when a self-test shows it is more likely than not that a violation occurred even though no violation was adjudicated formally.

(b) A lender must take action reasonably likely to remedy the cause and effect of the likely violation and must:

(1) Identify the policies or practices that are the likely cause of the violation, such as inadequate or improper lending policies, failure to implement established policies, employee conduct, or other causes; and

(2) Assess the extent and scope of any likely violation, by determining which areas of operation are likely to be affected by those policies and practices, such as stages of the loan application

549

process, types of loans, or the particular branch where the likely violation has occurred. Generally, the scope of the self-test governs the scope of the appropriate corrective action.

(c) Appropriate corrective action may include both prospective and remedial relief, except that to establish a privilege under this subpart:

(1) A lender is not required to provide remedial relief to a tester in a self-test;

(2) A lender is only required to provide remedial relief to an applicant identified by the self-test as one whose rights were more likely than not violated;

(3) A lender is not required to provide remedial relief to a particular applicant if the statute of limitations applicable to the violation expired before the lender obtained the results of the self-test or the applicant is otherwise ineligible for such relief.

(d) Depending on the facts involved, appropriate corrective action may include, but is not limited to, one or more of the following:

(1) If the self-test identifies individuals whose applications were inappropriately processed, offering to extend credit if the applications were improperly denied; compensating such persons for any damages, both out-of-pocket and compensatory;

(2) Correcting any institutional policies or procedures that may have contributed to the likely violation, and adopting new policies as appropriate;

(3) Identifying, and then training and/or disciplining the employees involved;

(4) Developing outreach programs, marketing strategies, or loan products to serve more effectively the segments of the lender's market that may have been affected by the likely violation; and

(5) Improving audit and oversight systems to avoid a recurrence of the likely violations.

(e) Determination of appropriate corrective action is fact-based. Not every corrective measure listed in paragraph (d) of this section need be taken for each likely violation.

(f) Taking appropriate corrective action is not an admission by a lender that a violation occurred.

[62 FR 66432, Dec. 18, 1997]

§ 100.144   Scope of privilege.

The report or results of a self-test may not be obtained or used by an aggrieved person, complainant, department or agency in any:

(a) Proceeding or civil action in which a violation of the Fair Housing Act is alleged; or

(b) Examination or investigation relating to compliance with the Fair Housing Act.

[62 FR 66432, Dec. 18, 1997]

§ 100.145   Loss of privilege.

(a) The self-test report or results are not privileged under this subpart if the lender or person with lawful access to the report or results:

(1) Voluntarily discloses any part of the report or results or any other information privileged under this subpart to any aggrieved person, complainant, department, agency, or to the public; or

(2) Discloses the report or results or any other information privileged under this subpart as a defense to charges a lender violated the Fair Housing Act; or

(3) Fails or is unable to produce self-test records or information needed to determine whether the privilege applies.

(b) Disclosures or other actions undertaken to carry out appropriate corrective action do not cause the lender to lose the privilege.

[62 FR 66432, Dec. 18, 1997]

§ 100.146   Limited use of privileged information.

Notwithstanding § 100.145, the self-test report or results may be obtained and used by an aggrieved person, applicant, department or agency solely to determine a penalty or remedy after the violation of the Fair Housing Act has been adjudicated or admitted. Disclosures for this limited purpose may be used only for the particular proceeding in which the adjudication or admission is made. Information disclosed under this section remains otherwise privileged under this subpart.

[62 FR 66433, Dec. 18, 1997]

Office of Asst. Secy., Equal Opportunity, HUD § 100.201

§ 100.147 Adjudication.

An aggrieved person, complainant, department or agency that challenges a privilege asserted under § 100.144 may seek a determination of the existence and application of that privilege in:

(a) A court of competent jurisdiction; or

(b) An administrative law proceeding with appropriate jurisdiction.

[62 FR 66433, Dec. 18, 1997]

§ 100.148 Effective date.

The privilege under this subpart applies to self-tests conducted both before and after January 30, 1998, except that a self-test conducted before January 30, 1998 is not privileged:

(a) If there was a court action or administrative proceeding before January 30, 1998, including the filing of a complaint alleging a violation of the Fair Housing Act with the Department or a substantially equivalent state or local agency; or

(b) If any part of the report or results were disclosed before January 30, 1998 to any aggrieved person, complainant, department or agency, or to the general public.

[62 FR 66433, Dec. 18, 1997]

Subpart D—Prohibition Against Discrimination Because of Handicap

§ 100.200 Purpose.

The purpose of this subpart is to effectuate sections 6 (a) and (b) and 15 of the Fair Housing Amendments Act of 1988.

§ 100.201 Definitions.

As used in this subpart:

Accessible, when used with respect to the public and common use areas of a building containing covered multifamily dwellings, means that the public or common use areas of the building can be approached, entered, and used by individuals with physical handicaps. The phrase readily accessible to and usable by is synonymous with accessible. A public or common use area that complies with the appropriate requirements of ANSI A117.1±1986 or a comparable standard is accessible within the meaning of this paragraph.

Accessible route means a continuous unobstructed path connecting accessible elements and spaces in a building or within a site that can be negotiated by a person with a severe disability using a wheelchair and that is also safe for and usable by people with other disabilities. Interior accessible routes may include corridors, floors, ramps, elevators and lifts. Exterior accessible routes may include parking access aisles, curb ramps, walks, ramps and lifts. A route that complies with the appropriate requirements of ANSI A117.1±1986 or a comparable standard is an accessible route .

ANSI A117.1±1986 means the 1986 edition of the American National Standard for buildings and facilities providing accessibility and usability for physically handicapped people. This incorporation by reference was approved by the Director of the Federal Register in accordance with 5 U.S.C. 552(a) and 1 CFR part 51. Copies may be obtained from American National Standards Institute, Inc., 1430 Broadway, New York, NY 10018. Copies may be inspected at the Department of Housing and Urban Development, 451 Seventh Street, SW., room 10276, Washington, DC, or at the Office of the Federal Register, 800 North Capitol Street, NW., suite 700, Washington, DC.

Building means a structure, facility or portion thereof that contains or serves one or more dwelling units.

Building entrance on an accessible route means an accessible entrance to a building that is connected by an accessible route to public transportation stops, to accessible parking and passenger loading zones, or to public streets or sidewalks, if available. A building entrance that complies with ANSI A117.1±1986 or a comparable standard complies with the requirements of this paragraph.

Common use areas means rooms, spaces or elements inside or outside of a building that are made available for the use of residents of a building or the guests thereof. These areas include hallways, lounges, lobbies, laundry rooms, refuse rooms, mail rooms, recreational areas and passageways among and between buildings.

551

§ 100.201

Controlled substance means any drug or other substance, or immediate precursor included in the definition in section 102 of the Controlled Substances Act (21 U.S.C. 802).

Covered multifamily dwellings means buildings consisting of 4 or more dwelling units if such buildings have one or more elevators; and ground floor dwelling units in other buildings consisting of 4 or more dwelling units.

Dwelling unit means a single unit of residence for a family or one or more persons. Examples of dwelling units include: a single family home; an apartment unit within an apartment building; and in other types of dwellings in which sleeping accommodations are provided but toileting or cooking facilities are shared by occupants of more than one room or portion of the dwelling, rooms in which people sleep. Examples of the latter include dormitory rooms and sleeping accommodations in shelters intended for occupancy as a residence for homeless persons.

Entrance means any access point to a building or portion of a building used by residents for the purpose of entering.

Exterior means all areas of the premises outside of an individual dwelling unit.

First occupancy means a building that has never before been used for any purpose.

Ground floor means a floor of a building with a building entrance on an accessible route. A building may have more than one ground floor.

Handicap means, with respect to a person, a physical or mental impairment which substantially limits one or more major life activities; a record of such an impairment; or being regarded as having such an impairment. This term does not include current, illegal use of or addiction to a controlled substance. For purposes of this part, an individual shall not be considered to have a handicap solely because that individual is a transvestite. As used in this definition:

(a) Physical or mental impairment includes:

(1) Any physiological disorder or condition, cosmetic disfigurement, or anatomical loss affecting one or more of the following body systems: Neurological; musculoskeletal; special sense organs; respiratory, including speech organs; cardiovascular; reproductive; disgestive; genito-urinary; hemic and lymphatic; skin; and endocrine; or

(2) Any mental or psychological disorder, such as mental retardation, organic brain syndrome, emotional or mental illness, and specific learning disabilities. The term physical or mental impairment includes, but is not limited to, such diseases and conditions as orthopedic, visual, speech and hearing impairments, cerebral palsy, autism, epilepsy, muscular dystrophy, multiple sclerosis, cancer, heart disease, diabetes, Human Immunodeficiency Virus infection, mental retardation, emotional illness, drug addiction (other than addiction caused by current, illegal use of a controlled substance) and alcoholism.

(b) Major life activities means functions such as caring for one's self, performing manual tasks, walking, seeing, hearing, speaking, breathing, learning and working.

(c) Has a record of such an impairment means has a history of, or has been misclassified as having, a mental or physical impairment that substantially limits one or more major life activities.

(d) Is regarded as having an impairment means:

(1) Has a physical or mental impairment that does not substantially limit one or more major life activities but that is treated by another person as constituting such a limitation;

(2) Has a physical or mental impairment that substantially limits one or more major life activities only as a result of the attitudes of other toward such impairment; or

(3) Has none of the impairments defined in paragraph (a) of this definition but is treated by another person as having such an impairment.

Interior means the spaces, parts, components or elements of an individual dwelling unit.

Modification means any change to the public or common use areas of a building or any change to a dwelling unit.

552

Office of Asst. Secy., Equal Opportunity, HUD   **§ 100.203**

Premises means the interior or exterior spaces, parts, components or elements of a building, including individual dwelling units and the public and common use areas of a building.

Public use areas means interior or exterior rooms or spaces of a building that are made available to the general public. Public use may be provided at a building that is privately or publicly owned.

Site means a parcel of land bounded by a property line or a designated portion of a public right or way.

§ 100.202 General prohibitions against discrimination because of handicap.

(a) It shall be unlawful to discriminate in the sale or rental, or to otherwise make unavailable or deny, a dwelling to any buyer or renter because of a handicap ofÐ

(1) That buyer or renter;

(2) A person residing in or intending to reside in that dwelling after it is so sold, rented, or made available; or

(3) Any person associated with that person.

(b) It shall be unlawful to discriminate against any person in the terms, conditions, or privileges of the sale or rental of a dwelling, or in the provision of services or facilities in connection with such dwelling, because of a handicap ofÐ

(1) That buyer or renter;

(2) A person residing in or intending to reside in that dwelling after it is so sold, rented, or made available; or

(3) Any person associated with that person.

(c) It shall be unlawful to make an inquiry to determine whether an applicant for a dwelling, a person intending to reside in that dwelling after it is so sold, rented or made available, or any person associated with that person, has a handicap or to make inquiry as to the nature or severity of a handicap of such a person. However, this paragraph does not prohibit the following inquiries, provided these inquiries are made of all applicants, whether or not they have handicaps:

(1) Inquiry into an applicant's ability to meet the requirements of ownership or tenancy;

(2) Inquiry to determine whether an applicant is qualified for a dwelling available only to persons with handicaps or to persons with a particular type of handicap;

(3) Inquiry to determine whether an applicant for a dwelling is qualified for a priority available to persons with handicaps or to persons with a particular type of handicap;

(4) Inquiring whether an applicant for a dwelling is a current illegal abuser or addict of a controlled substance;

(5) Inquiring whether an applicant has been convicted of the illegal manufacture or distribution of a controlled substance.

(d) Nothing in this subpart requires that a dwelling be made available to an individual whose tenancy would constitute a direct threat to the health or safety of other individuals or whose tenancy would result in substantial physical damage to the property of others.

§ 100.203 Reasonable modifications of existing premises.

(a) It shall be unlawful for any person to refuse to permit, at the expense of a handicapped person, reasonable modifications of existing premises, occupied or to be occupied by a handicapped person, if the proposed modifications may be necessary to afford the handicapped person full enjoyment of the premises of a dwelling. In the case of a rental, the landlord may, where it is reasonable to do so, condition permission for a modification on the renter agreeing to restore the interior of the premises to the condition that existed before the modification, reasonable wear and tear excepted. The landlord may not increase for handicapped persons any customarily required security deposit. However, where it is necessary in order to ensure with reasonable certainty that funds will be available to pay for the restorations at the end of the tenancy, the landlord may negotiate as part of such a restoration agreement a provision requiring that the tenant pay into an interest bearing escrow account, over a reasonable period, a reasonable amount of money not to exceed the cost of the restorations. The interest in any such account shall accrue to the benefit of the tenant.

(b) A landlord may condition permission for a modification on the renter

553

§ 100.204

providing a reasonable description of the proposed modifications as well as reasonable assurances that the work will be done in a workmanlike manner and that any required building permits will be obtained.

(c) The application of paragraph (a) of this section may be illustrated by the following examples:

Example (1): A tenant with a handicap asks his or her landlord for permission to install grab bars in the bathroom at his or her own expense. It is necessary to reinforce the walls with blocking between studs in order to affix the grab bars. It is unlawful for the landlord to refuse to permit the tenant, at the tenant's own expense, from making the modifications necessary to add the grab bars. However, the landlord may condition permission for the modification on the tenant agreeing to restore the bathroom to the condition that existed before the modification, reasonable wear and tear excepted. It would be reasonable for the landlord to require the tenant to remove the grab bars at the end of the tenancy. The landlord may also reasonably require that the wall to which the grab bars are to be attached be repaired and restored to its original condition, reasonable wear and tear excepted. However, it would be unreasonable for the landlord to require the tenant to remove the blocking, since the reinforced walls will not interfere in any way with the landlord's or the next tenant's use and enjoyment of the premises and may be needed by some future tenant.

Example (2): An applicant for rental housing has a child who uses a wheelchair. The bathroom door in the dwelling unit is too narrow to permit the wheelchair to pass. The applicant asks the landlord for permission to widen the doorway at the applicant's own expense. It is unlawful for the landlord to refuse to permit the applicant to make the modification. Further, the landlord may not, in usual circumstances, condition permission for the modification on the applicant paying for the doorway to be narrowed at the end of the lease because a wider doorway will not interfere with the landlord's or the next tenant's use and enjoyment of the premises.

§ 100.204   Reasonable accommodations.

(a) It shall be unlawful for any person to refuse to make reasonable accommodations in rules, policies, practices, or services, when such accommodations may be necessary to afford a handicapped person equal opportunity to use and enjoy a dwelling unit, including public and common use areas.

(b) The application of this section may be illustrated by the following examples:

Example (1): A blind applicant for rental housing wants live in a dwelling unit with a seeing eye dog. The building has a no pets policy. It is a violation of § 100.204 for the owner or manager of the apartment complex to refuse to permit the applicant to live in the apartment with a seeing eye dog because, without the seeing eye dog, the blind person will not have an equal opportunity to use and enjoy a dwelling.

Example (2): Progress Gardens is a 300 unit apartment complex with 450 parking spaces which are available to tenants and guests of Progress Gardens on a first come first served basis. John applies for housing in Progress Gardens. John is mobility impaired and is unable to walk more than a short distance and therefore requests that a parking space near his unit be reserved for him so he will not have to walk very far to get to his apartment. It is a violation of § 100.204 for the owner or manager of Progress Gardens to refuse to make this accommodation. Without a reserved space, John might be unable to live in Progress Gardens at all or, when he has to park in a space far from his unit, might have great difficulty getting from his car to his apartment unit. The accommodation therefore is necessary to afford John an equal opportunity to use and enjoy a dwelling. The accommodation is reasonable because it is feasible and practical under the circumstances.

§ 100.205   Design and construction requirements.

(a) Covered multifamily dwellings for first occupancy after March 13, 1991 shall be designed and constructed to have at least one building entrance on an accessible route unless it is impractical to do so because of the terrain or unusual characteristics of the site. For purposes of this section, a covered multifamily dwelling shall be deemed to be designed and constructed for first occupancy on or before March 13, 1991, if the dwelling is occupied by that date, or if the last building permit or renewal thereof for the dwelling is issued by a State, County or local government on or before June 15, 1990. The burden of establishing impracticality because of terrain or unusual site characteristics is on the person or persons who designed or constructed the housing facility.

554

Office of Asst. Secy., Equal Opportunity, HUD §100.205

(b) The application of paragraph (a) of this section may be illustrated by the following examples:

Example (1): A real estate developer plans to construct six covered multifamily dwelling units on a site with a hilly terrain. Because of the terrain, it will be necessary to climb a long and steep stairway in order to enter the dwellings. Since there is no practical way to provide an accessible route to any of the dwellings, one need not be provided.

Example (2): A real estate developer plans to construct a building consisting of 10 units of multifamily housing on a waterfront site that floods frequently. Because of this unusual characteristic of the site, the builder plans to construct the building on stilts. It is customary for housing in the geographic area where the site is located to be built on stilts. The housing may lawfully be constructed on the proposed site on stilts even though this means that there will be no practical way to provide an accessible route to the building entrance.

Example (3): A real estate developer plans to construct a multifamily housing facility on a particular site. The developer would like the facility to be built on the site to contain as many units as possible. Because of the configuration and terrain of the site, it is possible to construct a building with 105 units on the site provided the site does not have an accessible route leading to the building entrance. It is also possible to construct a building on the site with an accessible route leading to the building entrance. However, such a building would have no more than 100 dwelling units. The building to be constructed on the site must have a building entrance on an accessible route because it is not impractical to provide such an entrance because of the terrain or unusual characteristics of the site.

(c) All covered multifamily dwellings for first occupancy after March 13, 1991 with a building entrance on an accessible route shall be designed and constructed in such a manner thatÐ

(1) The public and common use areas are readily accessible to and usable by handicapped persons;

(2) All the doors designed to allow passage into and within all premises are sufficiently wide to allow passage by handicapped persons in wheelchairs; and

(3) All premises within covered multifamily dwelling units contain the following features of adaptable design:

(i) An accessible route into and through the covered dwelling unit;

(ii) Light switches, electrical outlets, thermostats, and other environmental controls in accessible locations;

(iii) Reinforcements in bathroom walls to allow later installation of grab bars around the toilet, tub, shower, stall and shower seat, where such facilities are provided; and

(iv) Usable kitchens and bathrooms such that an individual in a wheelchair can maneuver about the space.

(d) The application of paragraph (c) of this section may be illustrated by the following examples:

Example (1): A developer plans to construct a 100 unit condominium apartment building with one elevator. In accordance with paragraph (a), the building has at least one accessible route leading to an accessible entrance. All 100 units are covered multifamily dwelling units and they all must be designed and constructed so that they comply with the accessibility requirements of paragraph (c) of this section.

Example (2): A developer plans to construct 30 garden apartments in a three story building. The building will not have an elevator. The building will have one accessible entrance which will be on the first floor. Since the building does not have an elevator, only the ground floor units are covered multifamily units. The ground floor is the first floor because that is the floor that has an accessible entrance. All of the dwelling units on the first floor must meet the accessibility requirements of paragraph (c) of this section and must have access to at least one of each type of public or common use area available for residents in the building.

(e) Compliance with the appropriate requirements of ANSI A117.1±1986 suffices to satisfy the requirements of paragraph (c)(3) of this section.

(f) Compliance with a duly enacted law of a State or unit of general local government that includes the requirements of paragraphs (a) and (c) of this section satisfies the requirements of paragraphs (a) and (c) of this section.

(g)(1) It is the policy of HUD to encourage States and units of general local government to include, in their existing procedures for the review and approval of newly constructed covered multifamily dwellings, determinations as to whether the design and construction of such dwellings are consistent with paragraphs (a) and (c) of this section.

(2) A State or unit of general local government may review and approve

555

§ 100.300

newly constructed multifamily dwellings for the purpose of making determinations as to whether the requirements of paragraphs (a) and (c) of this section are met.

(h) Determinations of compliance or noncompliance by a State or a unit of general local government under paragraph (f) or (g) of this section are not conclusive in enforcement proceedings under the Fair Housing Amendments Act.

(i) This subpart does not invalidate or limit any law of a State or political subdivision of a State that requires dwellings to be designed and constructed in a manner that affords handicapped persons greater access than is required by this subpart.

[54 FR 3283, Jan. 23, 1989, as amended at 56 FR 11665, Mar. 20, 1991]

Subpart E—Housing for Older Persons

§ 100.300   Purpose.

The purpose of this subpart is to effectuate the exemption in the Fair Housing Amendments Act of 1988 that relates to housing for older persons.

§ 100.301   Exemption.

(a) The provisions regarding familial status in this part do not apply to housing which satisfies the requirements of §§ 100.302, 100.303 or § 100.304.

(b) Nothing in this part limits the applicability of any reasonable local, State, or Federal restrictions regarding the maximum number of occupants permitted to occupy a dwelling.

§ 100.302   State   and   Federal   elderly housing programs.

The provisions regarding familial status in this part shall not apply to housing provided under any Federal or State program that the Secretary determines is specifically designed and operated to assist elderly persons, as defined in the State or Federal program.

§ 100.303   62 or over housing.

(a) The provisions regarding familial status in this part shall not apply to housing intended for, and solely occupied by, persons 62 years of age or

older. Housing satisfies the requirements of this section even though:

(1) There are persons residing in such housing on September 13, 1988 who are under 62 years of age, provided that all new occupants are persons 62 years of age or older;

(2) There are unoccupied units, provided that such units are reserved for occupancy by persons 62 years of age or over;

(3) There are units occupied by employees of the housing (and family members residing in the same unit) who are under 62 years of age provided they perform substantial duties directly related to the management or maintenance of the housing.

(b) The following examples illustrate the application of paragraph (a) of this section:

Example (1): John and Mary apply for housing at the Vista Heights apartment complex which is an elderly housing complex operated for persons 62 years of age or older. John is 62 years of age. Mary is 59 years of age. If Vista Heights wishes to retain its "62 or over" exemption it must refuse to rent to John and Mary because Mary is under 62 years of age. However, if Vista Heights does rent to John and Mary, it might qualify for the "55 or over" exemption in § 100.304.

Example (2): The Blueberry Hill retirement community has 100 dwelling units. On September 13, 1988, 15 units were vacant and 35 units were occupied with at least one person who is under 62 years of age. The remaining 50 units were occupied by persons who were all 62 years of age or older. Blueberry Hill can qualify for the "62 or over" exemption as long as all units that were occupied after September 13, 1988 are occupied by persons who were 62 years of age or older. The people under 62 in the 35 units previously described need not be required to leave for Blueberry Hill to qualify for the "62 or over" exemption.

§ 100.304   55 or over housing.

(a) The provisions regarding familial status shall not apply to housing intended and operated for occupancy by at least one person 55 years of age or older per unit pursuant to this section.

(b) In order to qualify as housing for older persons under this section, at least 80 percent of the units in the housing facility must be occupied by at least one person 55 years of age or older, except that a newly constructed housing facility for first occupancy

556

after March 12, 1989, need not comply with this section until 25 percent of the units in the facility are occupied.

(c) Housing satisfies the requirements of this section even though:

(1) On September 13, 1988, under 80 percent of the occupied units in the housing facility are occupied by at least one person 55 years of age or older per unit, provided that at least 80 percent of the units that are occupied after September 13, 1988, are occupied by at least one person 55 years of age or older.

(2) There are unoccupied units, provided that at least 80 percent of the occupied units are occupied by at least one person 55 years of age or older.

(3) There are units occupied by employees of the housing provider (and family members residing in the same unit) who are under 55 years of age, provided the employees perform substantial duties directly related to the management or maintenance of the housing.

[61 FR 18249, Apr. 25, 1996]

Subpart F—Interference, Coercion or Intimidation

§ 100.400 Prohibited interference, coercion or intimidation.

(a) This subpart provides the Department's interpretation of the conduct that is unlawful under section 818 of the Fair Housing Act.

(b) It shall be unlawful to coerce, intimidate, threaten, or interfere with any person in the exercise or enjoyment of, or on account of that person having exercised or enjoyed, or on account of that person having aided or encouraged any other person in the exercise or enjoyment of, any right granted or protected by this part.

(c) Conduct made unlawful under this section includes, but is not limited to, the following:

(1) Coercing a person, either orally, in writing, or by other means, to deny or limit the benefits provided that person in connection with the sale or rental of a dwelling or in connection with a residential real estate-related transaction because of race, color, religion, sex, handicap, familial status, or national origin.

(2) Threatening, intimidating or interfering with persons in their enjoyment of a dwelling because of the race, color, religion, sex, handicap, familial status, or national origin of such persons, or of visitors or associates of such persons.

(3) Threatening an employee or agent with dismissal or an adverse employment action, or taking such adverse employment action, for any effort to assist a person seeking access to the sale or rental of a dwelling or seeking access to any residential real estate-related transaction, because of the race, color, religion, sex, handicap, familial status, or national origin of that person or of any person associated with that person.

(4) Intimidating or threatening any person because that person is engaging in activities designed to make other persons aware of, or encouraging such other persons to exercise, rights granted or protected by this part.

(5) Retaliating against any person because that person has made a complaint, testified, assisted, or participated in any manner in a proceeding under the Fair Housing Act.

PART 103—FAIR HOUSING— COMPLAINT PROCESSING

Subpart A—Purpose and Definitions

Subpart B—Complaints

Subpart C—Referral of Complaints to State and Local Agencies

Tuesday
December 22, 1998

federal register

Part V

Department of Housing and Urban Development

Fair Housing Enforcement—Occupancy
Standards; Statement of Policy; Notice;
Republication

70982   Federal Register / Vol. 63, No. 245 / Tuesday, December 22, 1998 / Notices

DEPARTMENT OF HOUSING AND URBAN DEVELOPMENT

[Docket No. FR–4405–N–01]

Fair Housing Enforcement— Occupancy Standards; Notice of Statement of Policy

Note: This document, FR Doc. 98±33568, was originally published on December 18, 1998 at 63 FR 70256±70257. It is being republished to reproduce the camera copy of the appendix furnished by the agency.

AGENCY: Office of the Assistant Secretary for Fair Housing and Equal Opportunity, HUD.

ACTION: Notice of Statement of Policy.

SUMMARY: This statement of policy advises the public of the factors that HUD will consider when evaluating a housing provider's occupancy policies to determine whether actions under the provider's policies may constitute discriminatory conduct under the Fair Housing Act on the basis of familial status (the presence of children in a family). Publication of this notice meets the requirements of the Quality Housing and Work Responsibility Act of 1998.

DATES: Effective date: December 18, 1998.

FOR FURTHER INFORMATION CONTACT: Sara Pratt, Director, Office of Investigations, Office of Fair Housing and Equal Opportunity, Room 5204, 451 Seventh Street, SW, Washington, DC 20410, telephone (202) 708±2290 (not a toll-free number). For hearing- and speech-impaired persons, this telephone number may be accessed via TTY (text telephone) by calling the Federal Information Relay Service at 1±800± 877±8339 (toll-free).

SUPPLEMENTARY INFORMATION:

Statutory and Regulatory Background

Section 589 of the Quality Housing and Work Responsibility Act of 1998 (Pub. L. 105±276, 112 Stat. 2461, approved October 21, 1998, ``QHWRA'') requires HUD to publish a notice in the Federal Register that advises the public of the occupancy standards that HUD uses for enforcement purposes under the Fair Housing Act (42 U.S.C. 3601± 3619). Section 589 requires HUD to publish this notice within 60 days of enactment of the QHWRA, and states that the notice will be effective upon publication. Specifically, section 589 states, in relevant part, that:

[T]he specific and unmodified standards provided in the March 20, 1991, Memorandum from the General Counsel of [HUD] to all Regional Counsel shall be the policy of [HUD] with respect to complaints of discrimination under the Fair Housing Act * * * on the basis of familial status which involve an occupancy standard established by a housing provider.

The Fair Housing Act prohibits discrimination in any aspect of the sale, rental, financing or advertising of dwellings on the basis of race, color, religion, national origin, sex or familial status (the presence of children in the family). The Fair Housing Act also provides that nothing in the Act ``limits the applicability of any reasonable local, State or Federal restrictions regarding the maximum number of occupants permitted to occupy a dwelling.'' The Fair Housing Act gave HUD responsibility for implementation and enforcement of the Act's requirements. The Fair Housing Act authorizes HUD to receive complaints alleging discrimination in violation of the Act, to

investigate these complaints, and to engage in efforts to resolve informally matters raised in the complaint. In cases where the complaint is not resolved, the Fair Housing Act authorizes HUD to make a determination of whether or not there is reasonable cause to believe that discrimination has occurred. HUD's regulations, implementing the Fair Housing Act (42 U.S.C. 3614) are found in 24 CFR part 100.

In 1991, HUD's General Counsel, Frank Keating, determined that some confusion existed because of the absence of more detailed guidance regarding what occupancy restrictions are reasonable under the Act. To address this confusion, General Counsel Keating issued internal guidance to HUD Regional Counsel on factors that they should consider when examining complaints filed with HUD under the Fair Housing Act, to determine whether or not there is reasonable cause to believe discrimination has occurred.

This Notice

Through this notice HUD implements section 589 of the QHWRA by adopting as its policy on occupancy standards, for purposes of enforcement actions under the Fair Housing Act, the standards provided in the Memorandum of General Counsel Frank Keating to Regional Counsel dated March 20, 1991, attached as Appendix A.

Authority: 42 U.S.C. 3535(d), 112 Stat. 2461.

Dated: December 14, 1998.

Eva M. Plaza,

Assistant Secretary for Fair Housing and Equal Opportunity.

BILLING CODE 4210–28–P

Federal Register / Vol. 63, No. 245 / Tuesday, December 22, 1998 / Notices   70983

U. S. Department of Housing and Urban Development
Washington, D.C. 20410-0500

APPENDIX A

March 20, 1991

OFFICE OF GENERAL COUNSEL

MEMORANDUM FOR: All Regional Counsel

FROM: Frank Keating, G

SUBJECT: Fair Housing Enforcement Policy: Occupancy Cases

On February 21, 1991, I issued a memorandum designed to
facilitate your review of cases involving occupancy policies
under the Fair Housing Act. The memorandum was based on my
review of a significant number of such cases and was intended to
constitute internal guidance to be used by Regional Counsel in
reviewing cases involving occupancy restrictions. It was not
intended to create a definitive test for whether a landlord or
manager would be liable in a particular case, nor was it intended
to establish occupancy policies or requirements for any
particular type of housing.

However, in discussions within the Department, and with the
Department of Justice and the public, it is clear that the
February 21 memorandum has resulted in a significant
misunderstanding of the Department's position on the question
of occupancy policies which would be reasonable under the Fair
Housing Act. In this respect, many people mistakenly viewed the
February 21 memorandum as indicating that the Department was
establishing an occupancy policy which it would consider
reasonable in any fair housing case, rather than providing
guidance to Regional Counsel on the evaluation of evidence in
familial status cases which involve the use of an occupancy
policy adopted by a housing provider.

For example, there is a HUD Handbook provision regarding
the size of the unit needed for public housing tenants. See
Handbook 7465.1 REV-2, Public Housing Occupancy Handbook:
Admission, revised section 5-1 (issued February 12, 1991). While
that Handbook provision states that HUD does not specify the
number of persons who may live in public housing units of various
sizes, it provides guidance about the factors public housing
agencies may consider in establishing reasonable occupancy
policies. Neither this memorandum nor the memorandum of February
21, 1991 overrides the guidance that Handbook provides about
program requirements.

70984   Federal Register / Vol. 63, No. 245 / Tuesday, December 22, 1998 / Notices

As you know, assuring Fair Housing for all is one of Secretary Kemp's top priorities. Prompt and vigorous enforcement of all the provisions of the Fair Housing Act, including the protections in the Act for families with children, is a critical responsibility of mine and every person in the Office of General Counsel. I expect Headquarters and Regional Office staff to continue their vigilant efforts to proceed to formal enforcement in all cases in which there is reasonable cause to believe that a discriminatory housing practice under the Act has occurred or is about to occur. This is particularly important in cases where occupancy restrictions are used to exclude families with children or to unreasonably limit the ability of families with children to obtain housing.

In order to assure that the Department's position in the area of occupancy policies is fully understood, I believe that it is imperative to articulate more fully the Department's position on reasonable occupancy policies and to describe the approach that the Department takes in its review of occupancy cases.

Specifically, the Department believes that an occupancy policy of two persons in a bedroom, as a general rule, is reasonable under the Fair Housing Act. The Department of Justice has advised us that this is the general policy it has incorporated in consent decrees and proposed orders, and such a general policy also is consistent with the guidance provided to housing providers in the HUD handbook referenced above. However, the reasonableness of any occupancy policy is rebuttable, and neither the February 21 memorandum nor this memorandum implies that the Department will determine compliance with the Fair Housing Act based solely on the number of people permitted in each bedroom. Indeed, as we stated in the final rule implementing the Fair Housing Amendments Act of 1988, the Department's position is as follows:

> [T]here is nothing in the legislative history which indicates any intent on the part of Congress to provide for the development of a national occupancy code. . . .

> On the other hand, there is no basis to conclude that Congress intended that an owner or manager of dwellings would be unable to restrict the number of occupants who could reside in a dwelling. Thus, the Department believes that in appropriate circumstances, owners and managers may develop and implement reasonable occupancy requirements based on factors such as the number and size of sleeping areas or bedrooms and the overall size of the dwelling unit. In this regard, it must be noted that, in connection with a complaint alleging discrimination on the basis of familial status, the Department will carefully examine any such

Federal Register / Vol. 63, No. 245 / Tuesday, December 22, 1998/ Notices   70985

nongovernmental restriction to determine whether it operates unreasonably to limit or exclude families with children.

24 C.F.R. Chapter I, Subchapter A. Appendix I at 566-67 (1990).

Thus, in reviewing occupancy cases, HUD will consider the size and number of bedrooms and other special circumstances. The following principles and hypothetical examples should assist you in determining whether the size of the bedrooms or special circumstances would make an occupancy policy unreasonable.

Size of bedrooms and unit

Consider two theoretical situations in which a housing provider refused to permit a family of five to rent a two-bedroom dwelling based on a "two people per bedroom" policy. In the first, the complainants are a family of five who applied to rent an apartment with two large bedrooms and spacious living areas. In the second, the complainants are a family of five who applied to rent a mobile home space on which they planned to live in a small two-bedroom mobile home. Depending on the other facts, issuance of a charge might be warranted in the first situation, but not in the second.

The size of the bedrooms also can be a factor suggesting that a determination of no reasonable cause is appropriate. For example, if a mobile home is advertised as a "two-bedroom" home, but one bedroom is extremely small, depending on all the facts, it could be reasonable for the park manager to limit occupancy of the home to two people.

Age of children

The following hypotheticals involving two housing providers who refused to permit three people to share a bedroom illustrate this principle. In the first, the complainants are two adult parents who applied to rent a one-bedroom apartment with their infant child, and both the bedroom and the apartment were large. In the second, the complainants are a family of two adult parents and one teenager who applied to rent a one-bedroom apartment. Depending on the other facts, issuance of a charge might be warranted in the first hypothetical, but not in the second.

Configuration of unit

The following imaginary situations illustrate special circumstances involving unit configuration. Two condominium associations each reject a purchase by a family of two adults and three children based on a rule limiting sales to buyers who satisfy a "two people per bedroom" occupancy policy. The first association manages a building in which the family of the five sought to purchase a unit consisting of two bedrooms plus a den or

70986   Federal Register / Vol. 63, No. 245 / Tuesday, December 22, 1998 / Notices

study. The second manages a building in which the family of five sought to purchase a two-bedroom unit which did not have a study or den. Depending on the other facts, a charge might be warranted in the first situation, but not in the second.

Other physical limitations of housing

In addition to physical considerations such as the size of each bedroom and the overall size and configuration of the dwelling, the Department will consider limiting factors identified by housing providers, such as the capacity of the septic, sewer, or other building systems.

State and local law

If a dwelling is governed by State or local governmental occupancy requirements, and the housing provider's occupancy policies reflect those requirements, HUD would consider the governmental requirements as a special circumstance tending to indicate that the housing provider's occupancy policies are reasonable.

Other relevant factors

Other relevant factors supporting a reasonable cause recommendation based on the conclusion that the occupancy policies are pretextual would include evidence that the housing provider has: (1) made discriminatory statements; (2) adopted discriminatory rules governing the use of common facilities; (3) taken other steps to discourage families with children from living in its housing; or (4) enforced its occupancy policies only against families with children. For example, the fact that a development was previously marketed as an "adults only" development would militate in favor of issuing a charge. This is an especially strong factor if there is other evidence suggesting that the occupancy policies are a pretext for excluding families with children.

An occupancy policy which limits the number of <u>children</u> per unit is less likely to be reasonable than one which limits the number of <u>people</u> per unit.

Special circumstances also may be found where the housing provider limits the total number of dwellings he or she is willing to rent to families with children. For example, assume a landlord owns a building of two-bedroom units, in which a policy of four people per unit is reasonable. If the landlord adopts a four person per unit policy, but refuses to rent to a family of two adults and two children because twenty of the thirty units already are occupied by families with children, a reasonable cause recommendation would be warranted.

Federal Register / Vol. 63, No. 245 / Tuesday, December 22, 1998 / Notices   70987

If your review of the evidence indicates that these or other special circumstances are present, making application of a "two people per bedroom" policy unreasonably restrictive, you should prepare a reasonable cause determination. The Executive Summary should explain the special circumstances which support your recommendation.

[FR Doc. 98±33568 Filed 12±17±98; 8:45 am]
BILLING CODE BILLING CODE 4210-28-C

Office of the Secretary, HUD

Department's policy of equal employment opportunity.

§7.37 Rights of appeal.

The provisions of 29 CFR part 1614, subpart D, shall govern rights of appeal.

§7.38 Relationship to other HUD appellate procedures.

(a) An aggrieved individual covered by a collective bargaining agreement that permits allegations of discrimination to be raised in a negotiated grievance procedure can file a complaint under these procedures or a negotiated grievance, but not both. An election to proceed under this part is indicated only by filing of a written complaint. An election to proceed under a negotiated grievance procedure is indicated by the filing of a timely grievance.

(b) An aggrieved individual alleging discrimination on the basis of race, color, religion, sex, national origin, age or disability related to or stemming from an action that can be appealed to the Merit Systems Protection Board (MSPB) can file a complaint under these procedures, or an appeal with the MSPB, but not both. Whichever is filed first, the complaint or the appeal, is considered an election to proceed in that forum.

Subpart B [Reserved]

PART 8—NONDISCRIMINATION BASED ON HANDICAP IN FEDERALLY ASSISTED PROGRAMS AND ACTIVITIES OF THE DEPARTMENT OF HOUSING AND URBAN DEVELOPMENT

Subpart A—General Provisions

Sec.
8.1   Purpose.
8.2   Applicability.
8.3   Definitions.
8.4   Discrimination prohibited.
8.5   [Reserved]
8.6   Communications.

Subpart B—Employment

8.10 General prohibitions against employment discrimination.
8.11 Reasonable accommodation.
8.12 Employment criteria.

§ 8.1

8.13 Preemployment inquiries.

Subpart C—Program Accessibility

8.20 General requirement concerning program accessibility.
8.21 Non-housing facilities.
8.22 New constructionÐhousing facilities.
8.23 Alterations of existing housing facilities.
8.24 Existing housing programs.
8.25 Public housing and multi-family Indian housing.
8.26 Distribution of accessible dwelling units.
8.27 Occupancy of accessible dwelling units.
8.28 Housing certificate and housing voucher programs.
8.29 Homeownership programs (sections 235(i) and 235(j), Turnkey III and Indian Housing Mutual Self-Help Programs).
8.30 Rental rehabilitation program.
8.31 Historic properties.
8.32 Accessibility standards.
8.33 Housing adjustments.

Subpart D—Enforcement

8.50 Assurances required.
8.51 Self-evaluation.
8.52 Remedial and affirmative action.
8.53 Designation of responsible employee and adoption of grievance procedures.
8.54 Notice.
8.55 Compliance information.
8.56 Conduct of investigations.
8.57 Procedure for effecting compliance.
8.58 Hearings.

AUTHORITY : 29 U.S.C. 794; 42 U.S.C. 3535(d) and 5309.

SOURCE : 53 FR 20233, June 2, 1988, unless otherwise noted.

Subpart A—General Provisions

§8.1   Purpose.

(a) The purpose of this part is to effectuate section 504 of the Rehabilitation Act of 1973, as amended (29 U.S.C 794), to the end that no otherwise qualified individual with handicaps in the United States shall, solely by reason of his or her handicap, be excluded from the participation in, be denied the benefits of, or be subjected to discrimination under any program or activity receiving Federal financial assistance from the Department of Housing and Urban Development. This part also implements section 109 of the Housing and Community Development Act of 1974, as amended (42 U.S.C. 5309). This part does not effectuate section 504 as

81

§8.2   24 CFR Subtitle A (4-1-98 Edition)

it applies to any program or activity conducted by the Department. Compliance with this part does not assure compliance with requirements for accessibility by physically-handicapped persons imposed under the Architectural Barriers Act of 1968 (42 U.S.C. 4151±4157; 24 CFR part 40).

(b) The policies and standards for compliance established by this part are established in contemplation of, and with a view to enforcement through, the Department's administration of programs or activities receiving Federal financial assistance and the administrative procedures described in subparts D and E (including, without limitation, judicial enforcement under §8.57(a)).

§8.2 Applicability.

This part applies to all applicants for, and recipients of, HUD assistance in the operation of programs or activities receiving such assistance. Such assistance includes, but is not limited to, that which is listed in appendix A of this part.

§8.3 Definitions.

As used in this part:

Accessible, when used with respect to the design, construction, or alteration of a facility or a portion of a facility other than an individual dwelling unit, means that the facility or portion of the facility when designed, constructed or altered, can be approached, entered, and used by individuals with physical handicaps. The phrase accessible to and usable by is synonomous with accessible.

Accessible, when used with respect to the design, construction, or alteration of an individual dwelling unit, means that the unit is located on an accessible route and when designed, constructed, altered or adapted can be approached, entered, and used by individuals with physical handicaps. A unit that is on an accessible route and is adaptable and otherwise in compliance with the standards set forth in § 8.32 is accessible within the meaning of this paragraph. When a unit in an existing facility which is being made accessible as a result of alterations is intended for use by a specific qualified individual with handicaps (e.g., a current oc-

cupant of such unit or of another unit under the control of the same recipient, or an applicant on a waiting list), the unit will be deemed accessible if it meets the requirements of applicable standards that address the particular disability or impairment of such person.

Accessible route means a continuous unobstructed path connecting accessible elements and spaces in a building or facility that complies with the space and reach requirements of applicable standards prescribed by § 8.32. An accessible route that serves only accessible units occupied by persons with hearing or vision impairments need not comply with those requirements intended to effect accessibility for persons with mobility impairments.

Adaptability means the ability of certain elements of a dwelling unit, such as kitchen counters, sinks, and grab bars, to be added to, raised, lowered, or otherwise altered, to accommodate the needs of persons with or without handicaps, or to accommodate the needs of persons with different types or degrees of disability. For example, in a unit adaptable for a hearing-impaired person, the wiring for visible emergency alarms may be installed but the alarms need not be installed until such time as the unit is made ready for occupancy by a hearing-impaired person.

Alteration means any change in a facility or its permanent fixtures or equipment. It includes, but is not limited to, remodeling, renovation, rehabilitation, reconstruction, changes or rearrangements in structural parts and extraordinary repairs. It does not include normal maintenance or repairs, reroofing, interior decoration, or changes to mechanical systems.

Applicant for assistance means one who submits an application, request, plan, or statement required to be approved by a Department official or by a primary recipient as a condition of eligibility for Federal financial assistance. An application means such a request, plan or statement.

Auxiliary aids means services or devices that enable persons with impaired sensory, manual, or speaking skills to have an equal opportunity to participate in, and enjoy the benefits of, programs or activities receiving

82

Office of the Secretary, HUD

Federal financial assistance. For example, auxiliary aids for persons with impaired vision may include readers, Brailled materials, audio recordings, and other similar services and devices. Auxiliary aids for persons with impaired hearing may include telephone handset amplifiers, telephones compatible with hearing aids, telecommunication devices for deaf persons (TDD's), interpreters, notetakers, written materials, and other similar services and devices.

Department or HUD means the Department of Housing and Urban Development.

Facility means all or any portion of buildings, structures, equipment, roads, walks, parking lots, rolling stock or other real or personal property or interest in the property.

Federal financial assistance means any assistance provided or otherwise made available by the Department through any grant, loan, contract or any other arrangement, in the form of:

(a) Funds;

(b) Services of Federal personnel; or

(c) Real or personal property or any interest in or use of such property, including:

(1) Transfers or leases of the property for less than fair market value or for reduced consideration; and

(2) Proceeds from a subsequent transfer or lease of the property if the Federal share of its fair market value is not returned to the Federal Government.

Federal financial assistance includes community development funds in the form of proceeds from loans guaranteed under section 108 of the Housing and Community Development Act of 1974, as amended, but does not include assistance made available through direct Federal procurement contracts or payments made under these contracts or any other contract of insurance or guaranty.

Handicap means any condition or characteristic that renders a person an individual with handicaps.

Historic preservation programs or activities means programs or activities receiving Federal financial assistance that have preservation of historic properties as a primary purpose.

Historic properties means those properties that are listed or are eligible for listing in the National Register of Historic Places, or such properties designated as historic under a statute of the appropriate State or local government body.

Individual with handicaps means any person who has a physical or mental impairment that substantially limits one or more major life activities; has a record of such an impairment; or is regarded as having such an impairment. For purposes of employment, this term does not include: Any individual who is an alcoholic or drug abuser whose current use of alcohol or drugs prevents the individual from performing the duties of the job in question, or whose employment, by reason of current alcohol or drug abuse, would constitute a direct threat to property or the safety of others; or any individual who has a currently contagious disease or infection and who, by reason of such disease or infection, would constitute a direct threat to the health or safety of other individuals or who, by reason of the currently contagious disease or infection, is unable to perform the duties of the job. For purposes of other programs and activities, the term does not include any individual who is an alcoholic or drug abuser whose current use of alcohol or drugs prevents the individual from participating in the program or activity in question, or whose participation, by reason of such current alcohol or drug abuse, would constitute a direct threat to property or the safety of others. As used in this definition, the phrase:

(a) Physical or mental impairment includes:

(1) Any physiological disorder or condition, cosmetic disfigurement, or anatomical loss affecting one or more of the following body systems: Neurological; musculoskeletal; special sense organs; respiratory, including speech organs; cardiovascular; reproductive; digestive; genito-urinary; hemic and lymphatic; skin; and endocrine; or

(2) Any mental or psychological disorder, such as mental retardation, organic brain syndrome, emotional or mental illness, and specific learning disabilities. The term physical or mental impairment includes, but is not limited

83

to, such diseases and conditions as orthopedic, visual, speech and hearing impairments, cerebral palsy, autism, epilepsy, muscular dystrophy, multiple sclerosis, cancer, heart disease, diabetes, mental retardation, emotional illness, drug addiction and alcoholism.

(b) *Major life activities* means functions such as caring for one's self, performing manual tasks, walking, seeing, hearing, speaking, breathing, learning and working.

(c) *Has a record of such an impairment* means has a history of, or has been misclassified as having, a mental or physical impairment that substantially limits one or more major life activities.

(d) *Is regarded as having an impairment* means:

(1) Has a physical or mental impairment that does not substantially limit one or more major life activities but that is treated by a recipient as constituting such a limitation;

(2) Has a physical or mental impairment that substantially limits one or more major life activities only as a result of the attitudes of others toward such impairment; or

(3) Has none of the impairments defined in paragraph (a) of this section but is treated by a recipient as having such an impairment.

Multifamily housing project means a project containing five or more dwelling units.

Primary recipient means a person, group, organization, State or local unit of government that is authorized or required to extend Federal financial assistance to another recipient for the purpose of carrying out a program or activity.

Program or activity means all of the operations of:

(a)(1) A department, agency, special purpose district, or other instrumentality of a State or of a local government; or

(2) The entity of such State or local government that distributes such assistance and each such department or agency (and each other State or local government entity) to which the assistance is extended, in the case of assistance to a State or local government;

(b)(1) A college, university, or other post-secondary institution, or a public system of higher education; or

(2) A local educational agency (as defined in section 198(a)(10) of the Elementary and Secondary Education Act of 1965), system of vocational education, or other school system;

(c)(1) An entire corporation, partnership, or other private organization, or an entire sole proprietorshipÐ

(i) If assistance is extended to such corporation, partnership, private organization, or sole proprietorship as a whole; or

(ii) Which is principally engaged in the business of providing education, health care, housing, social services, or parks and recreation; or

(2) The entire plant or other comparable, geographically separate facility to which Federal financial assistance is extended, in the case of any other corporation, partnership, private organization, or sole proprietorship; or

(d) Any other entity which is established by two or more of the entities described in paragraphs (a), (b), or (c) of this section;

any part of which is extended Federal financial assistance.

Project means the whole of one or more residential structures and appurtenant structures, equipment, roads, walks, and parking lots which are covered by a single contract for Federal financial assistance or application for assistance, or are treated as a whole for processing purposes, whether or not located on a common site.

Qualified individual with handicaps means:

(a) With respect to employment, an individual with handicaps who, with reasonable accommodation, can perform the essential functions of the job in question; and

(b) With respect to any non-employment program or activity which requires a person to perform services or to achieve a level of accomplishment, an individual with handicaps who meets the essential eligibility requirements and who can achieve the purpose of the program or activity without modifications in the program or activity that the recipient can demonstrate would result in a fundamental alteration in its nature; or

84

Office of the Secretary, HUD   **§8.4**

(c) With respect to any other non-employment program or activity, an individual with handicaps who meets the essential eligibility requirements for participation in, or receipt of benefits from, that program or activity. Essential eligibility requirements include stated eligibility requirements such as income as well as other explicit or implicit requirements inherent in the nature of the program or activity, such as requirements that an occupant of multifamily housing be capable of meeting the recipient's selection criteria and be capable of complying with all obligations of occupancy with or without supportive services provided by persons other than the recipient. For example, a chronically metally ill person whose particular condition poses a significant risk of substantial interference with the safety or enjoyment of others or with his or her own health or safety in the absence of necessary supportive services may be qualified for occupancy in a project where such supportive services are provided by the recipient as part of the assisted program. The person may not be qualified for a project lacking such services.

Recipient means any State or its political subdivision, any instrumentality of a State or its political subdivision, any public or private agency, institution, organization, or other entity, or any person to which Federal financial assistance is extended for any program or activity directly or through another recipient, including any successor, assignee, or transferee of a recipient, but excluding the ultimate beneficiary of the assistance. An entity or person receiving housing assistance payments from a recipient on behalf of eligible families under a housing assistance payments program or a voucher program is not a recipient or subrecipient merely by virtue of receipt of such payments.

Replacement cost of the completed facility means the current cost of construction and equipment for a newly constructed housing facility of the size and type being altered. Construction and equipment costs do not include the cost of land, demolition, site improvements, non-dwelling facilities and administrative costs for project development activities.

Secretary means the Secretary of Housing and Urban Development.

Section 504 means section 504 of the Rehabilitation Act of 1973, as amended, 29 U.S.C. 794, as it applies to programs or activities receiving Federal financial assistance.

Substantial impairment means a significant loss of the integrity of finished materials, design quality, or special character resulting from a permanent alteration.

[53 FR 20233, June 2, 1988; 54 FR 8188, Feb. 27, 1989]

§8.4 Discrimination prohibited.

(a) No qualified individual with handicaps shall, solely on the basis of handicap, be excluded from participation in, be denied the benefits of, or otherwise be subjected to discrimination under any program or activity that receives Federal financial assistance from the Department.

(b)(1) A recipient, in providing any housing, aid, benefit, or service in a program or activity that receives Federal financial assistance from the Department may not, directly or through contractual, licensing, or other arrangements, solely on the basis of handicap:

(i) Deny a qualified individual with handicaps the opportunity to participate in, or benefit from, the housing, aid, benefit, or service;

(ii) Afford a qualified individual with handicaps an opportunity to participate in, or benefit from, the housing, aid, benefit, or service that is not equal to that afforded to others;

(iii) Provide a qualified individual with handicaps with any housing, aid, benefit, or service that is not as effective in affording the individual an equal opportunity to obtain the same result, to gain the same benefit, or to reach the same level of achievement as that provided to others;

(iv) Provide different or separate housing, aid, benefits, or services to individuals with handicaps or to any class of individuals with handicaps from that provided to others unless such action is necessary to provide qualified individuals with handicaps with housing, aid, benefits, or services that are as effective as those provided to others.

85

§ 8.4   **24 CFR Subtitle A (4-1-98 Edition)**

(v) Aid or perpetuate discrimination against a qualified individual with handicaps by providing significant assistance to an agency, organization, or person that discriminates on the basis of handicap in providing any housing, aid, benefit, or service to beneficiaries in the recipient's federally assisted program or activity;

(vi) Deny a qualified individual with handicaps the opportunity to participate as a member of planning or advisory boards;

(vii) Deny a dwelling to an otherwise qualified buyer or renter because of a handicap of that buyer or renter or a person residing in or intending and eligible to reside in that dwelling after it is sold, rented or made available; or

(viii) Otherwise limit a qualified individual with handicaps in the enjoyment of any right, privilege, advantage, or opportunity enjoyed by other qualified individuals receiving the housing, aid, benefit, or service.

(2) For purposes of this part, housing, aids, benefits, and services, to be equally effective, are not required to produce the identical result or level of achievement for individuals with handicaps and non-handicapped persons, but must afford individuals with handicaps equal opportunity to obtain the same result, to gain the same benefit, or to reach the same level of achievement.

(3) A recipient may not deny a qualified individual with handicaps the opportunity to participate in any federally assisted program or activity that is not separate or different despite the existence of permissibly separate or different programs or activities.

(4) In any program or activity receiving Federal financial assistance from the Department, a recipient may not, directly or through contractual or other arrangements, utilize criteria or methods of administration the purpose or effect of which would:

(i) Subject qualified individuals with handicaps to discrimination solely on the basis of handicap;

(ii) Defeat or substantially impair the accomplishment of the objectives of the recipient's federally assisted program or activity for qualified individuals with a particular handicap involved in the program or activity, un-

less the recipient can demonstrate that the criteria or methods of administration are manifestly related to the accomplishment of an objective of a program or activity; or

(iii) Perpetuate the discrimination of another recipient if both recipients are subject to common administrative control or are agencies of the same State.

(5) In determining the site or location of a federally assisted facility, an applicant for assistance or a recipient may not make selections the purpose or effect of which would:

(i) Exclude qualified individuals with handicaps from, deny them the benefits of, or otherwise subject them to discrimination under, any program or activity that receives Federal financial assistance from the Department, or

(ii) Defeat or substantially impair the accomplishment of the objectives of the program or activity with respect to qualified individuals with handicaps.

(6) As used in this section, the housing, aid, benefit, or service provided under a program or activity receiving Federal financial assistance includes any housing, aid, benefit, or service provided in or through a facility that has been constructed, altered, leased or rented, or otherwise acquired, in whole or in part, with Federal financial assistance.

(c)(1) Non-handicapped persons may be excluded from the benefits of a program if the program is limited by Federal statute or executive order to individuals with handicaps. A specific class of individuals with handicaps may be excluded from a program if the program is limited by Federal statute or Executive order to a different class of individuals.

(2) Certain Department programs operate under statutory definitions of handicapped person that are more restrictive than the definition of individual with handicaps contained in § 8.3 (see appendix B). Those definitions are not superseded or otherwise affected by this regulation.

(d) Recipients shall administer programs and activities receiving Federal financial assistance in the most integrated setting appropriate to the needs of qualified individuals with handicaps.

(e) The obligation to comply with this part is not obviated or alleviated

86

Office of the Secretary, HUD

§ 8.10

by any State or local law or other requirement that, based on handicap, imposes inconsistent or contradictory prohibitions or limits upon the eligibility of qualified individuals with handicaps to receive services or to practice any occupation or profession.

(f) The enumeration of specific forms of prohibited discrimination in paragraphs (b) through (e) of this section does not limit the general prohibition in paragraph (a) of this section.

[53 FR 20233, June 2, 1988; 53 FR 28115, July 26, 1988]

§ 8.5 [Reserved]

§ 8.6 Communications.

(a) The recipient shall take appropriate steps to ensure effective communication with applicants, beneficiaries, and members of the public.

(1) The recipient shall furnish appropriate auxiliary aids where necessary to afford an individual with handicaps an equal opportunity to participate in, and enjoy the benefits of, a program or activity receiving Federal financial assistance.

(i) In determining what auxiliary aids are necessary, the recipient shall give primary consideration to the requests of the individual with handicaps.

(ii) The recipient is not required to provide individually prescribed devices, readers for personal use or study, or other devices of a personal nature.

(2) Where a recipient communicates with applicants and beneficiaries by telephone, telecommunication devices for deaf persons (TDD's) or equally effective communication systems shall be used.

(b) The recipient shall adopt and implement procedures to ensure that interested persons (including persons with impaired vision or hearing) can obtain information concerning the existence and location of accessible services, activities, and facilities.

(c) This section does not require a recipient to take any action that the recipient can demonstrate would result in a fundamental alteration in the nature of a program or activity or in undue financial and administrative burdens. If an action would result in such an alteration or burdens, the re-

cipient shall take any other action that would not result in such an alteration or such burdens but would nevertheless ensure that, to the maximum extent possible, individuals with handicaps receive the benefits and services of the program or activity receiving HUD assistance.

Subpart B—Employment

§ 8.10 General prohibitions against employment discrimination.

(a) No qualified individual with handicaps shall, solely on the basis of handicap, be subjected to discrimination in employment under any program or activity that receives Federal financial assistance from the Department.

(b) A recipient may not limit, segregate, or classify applicants or employees in any way that adversely affects their opportunities or status because of handicap.

(c) The prohibition against discrimination in employment applies to the following activities:

(1) Recruitment, advertising, and the processing of applications for employment;

(2) Hiring, upgrading, promotion, award of tenure, demotion, transfer, layoff, termination, right of return from layoff, injury or illness, and rehiring;

(3) Rates of pay or any other form of compensation and changes in compensation;

(4) Job assignments, job classifications, organizational structures, position descriptions, lines of progression, and seniority lists;

(5) Leaves of absence, sick leave, or any other leave;

(6) Fringe benefits available by virtue of employment, whether or not administered by the recipient;

(7) Selection and financial support for training, including apprenticeship, professional meetings, conferences, and other related activities, and selection for leaves of absence for training;

(8) Employer sponsored activities, including social or recreational programs; and

(9) Any other term, condition, or privilege of employment.

(d) A recipient may not participate in a contractual or other relationship

87

§8.11

that has the effect of subjecting qualified applicants with handicaps or employees with handicaps to discrimination prohibited by this subpart. The relationships referred to in this paragraph (d) include relationships with employment and referral agencies, labor unions, organizations providing or administering fringe benefits to employees of the recipient, and organizations providing training and apprenticeship programs.

§8.11 Reasonable accommodation.

(a) A recipient shall make reasonable accommodation to the known physical or mental limitations of an otherwise qualified applicant with handicaps or employee with handicaps, unless the recipient can demonstrate that the accommodation would impose an undue hardship on the operation of its program.

(b) Reasonable accommodation may include:

(1) Making facilities used by employees accessible to and usable by individuals with handicaps and

(2) Job restructuring, job relocation, part-time or modified work schedules, acquisitions or modification of equipment or devices, the provision of readers or interpreters, and other similar actions.

(c) In determining, under paragraph (a) of this section, whether an accommodation would impose an undue hardship on the operation of a recipient's program, factors to be considered include:

(1) The overall size of the recipient's program with respect to number of employees, number and type of facilities, and size of budget;

(2) The type of the recipient's operation, including the composition and structure of the recipient's workforce; and

(3) The nature and cost of the accommodation needed.

(d) A recipient may not deny any employment opportunity to a qualified handicapped employee or applicant if the basis for the denial is the need to make reasonable accommodation to the physical or mental limitations of the employee or applicant.

§8.12 Employment criteria.

(a) A recipient may not use any employment test or other selection criterion that screens out or tends to screen out individuals with handicaps or any class of individuals with handicaps unless:

(1) The recipient demonstrates that the test score or other selection criterion, as used by the recipient, is job-related for the position in question; and

(2) The appropriate HUD official demonstrates that alternative job-related tests or criteria that tend to screen out fewer individuals with handicaps are unavailable.

(b) A recipient shall select and administer tests concerning employment to ensure that, when administered to an applicant or employee who has a handicap that impairs sensory, manual, or speaking skills, the test results accurately reflect the applicant's or employee's job skills, aptitude, or whatever other factor the test purports to measure, rather than the applicant's or employee's impaired sensory, manual, or speaking skills (except where those skills are the factors that the test purports to measure).

§8.13 Preemployment inquiries.

(a) Except as provided in paragraphs (b) and (c) of this section, a recipient may not make a preemployment inquiry or conduct a preemployment medical examination of an applicant to determine whether the applicant is an individual with handicaps or the nature or severity of a handicap. A recipient may, however, make preemployment inquiry into an applicant's ability to perform job-related functions.

(b) When a recipient is undertaking affirmative action efforts, voluntary or otherwise, the recipient may invite applicants for employment to indicate whether and to what extent they are handicapped, if the following conditions are met:

(1) The recipient states clearly on any written questionnaire used for this purpose, or makes clear orally if no written questionnaire is used, that the information requested is intended for

88

Office of the Secretary, HUD   **§8.21**

use solely in connection with its remedial action obligations, or its voluntary or affirmative action efforts;
and

(2) The recipient states clearly that
the information is being requested on a
voluntary basis, that it will be kept
confidential (as provided in paragraph
(d) of this section), that refusal to provide the information will not subject
the applicant or employee to any adverse treatment, and that the information will be used only in accordance
with this part.

(c) Nothing in this section shall prohibit a recipient from conditioning an
offer of employment on the results of a
medical examination conducted before
the employee's entrance on duty if all
entering employees in that category of
job classification must take such an
examination regardless of handicap,
and the results of such examination are
used only in accordance with the requirements of this part.

(d) Information obtained under this
section concerning the medical condition or history of the applicant is to be
collected and maintained on separate
forms that are accorded confidentiality
as medical records, except that:

(1) Supervisors and managers may be
informed of restrictions on the work or
duties of individuals with handicaps
and informed of necessary accommodations;

(2) First aid and safety personnel
may be informed if the condition might
require emergency treatment; and

(3) Government officials investigating compliance with section 504 shall
be provided relevant information upon
request.

Subpart C—Program Accessibility

§8.20 General requirement concerning
    program accessibility.

Except as otherwise provided in
§§8.21(c)(1), 8.24(a), 8.25, and 8.31, no
qualified individual with handicaps
shall, because a recipient's facilities
are inaccessible to or unusable by individuals with handicaps, be denied the
benefits of, be excluded from participation in, or otherwise be subjected to
discrimination under any program or
activity that receives Federal financial
assistance.

§8.21 Non-housing facilities.

(a) New construction. New non-housing facilities shall be designed and constructed to be readily accessible to and
usable by individuals with handicaps.

(b) Alterations to facilities. Alterations
to existing non-housing facilities shall,
to the maximum extent feasible, be
made to be readily accessible to and usable by individuals with handicaps. For
purposes of this paragraph, the phrase
to the maximum extent feasible   shall not
be interpreted as requiring that a recipient make a non-housing facility, or
element thereof, accessible if doing so
would impose undue financial and administrative burdens on the operation
of the recipient's program or activity.

(c) Existing non-housing facilities   Ð(1)
General . A recipient shall operate each
non-housing program or activity receiving Federal financial assistance so
that the program or activity, when
viewed in its entirety, is readily accessible to and usable by individuals with
handicaps. This paragraph does notÐ

(i) Necessarily require a recipient to
make each of its existing non-housing
facilities accessible to and usable by
individuals with handicaps;

(ii) In the case of historic preservation programs or activities, require the
recipient to take any action that would
result in a substantial impairment of
significant historic features of an historic property; or

(iii) Require a recipient to take any
action that it can demonstrate would
result in a fundamental alteration in
the nature of its program or activity or
in undue financial and administrative
burdens. If an action would result in
such an alteration or such burdens, the
recipient shall take any action that
would not result in such an alteration
or such burdens but would nevertheless
ensure that individuals with handicaps
receive the benefits and services of the
program or activity.

(2) Methods Ð(i) General . A recipient
may comply with the requirements of
this section in its programs and activities receiving Federal financial assistance through such means as location of
programs or services to accessible facilities or accessible portions of facilities, assignment of aides to beneficiaries, home visits, the addition or
redesign of equipment (e.g., appliances

89

§ 8.22

or furnishings) changes in management policies or procedures, acquisition or construction of additional facilities, or alterations to existing facilities on a selective basis, or any other methods that result in making its program or activity accessible to individuals with handicaps. A recipient is not required to make structural changes in existing facilities where other methods are effective in achieving compliance with this section. In choosing among available methods for meeting the requirements of this section, the recipient shall give priority to those methods that offer programs and activities to qualified individuals with handicaps in the most integrated setting appropriate.

(ii) Historic preservation programs or activities. In meeting the requirements of § 8.21(c) in historic preservation programs or activities, a recipient shall give priority to methods that provide physical access to individuals with handicaps. In cases where a physical alteration to an historic property is not required because of § 8.21(c)(1)(ii) or (iii), alternative methods of achieving program accessibility include using audio-visual materials and devices to depict those portions of an historic property that cannot otherwise be made accessible; assigning persons to guide individuals with handicaps into or through portions of historic properties that cannot otherwise be made accessible; or adopting other innovative methods.

(3) Time period for compliance . The recipient shall comply with the obligations established under this section within sixty days of July 11, 1988, except that where structural changes in facilities are undertaken, such changes shall be made within three years of July 11, 1988, but in any event as expeditiously as possible.

(4) Transition plan . If structural changes to non-housing facilities will be undertaken to achieve program accessibility, a recipient shall develop, within six months of July 11, 1988, a transition plan setting forth the steps necessary to complete such changes. The plan shall be developed with the assistance of interested persons, including individuals with handicaps or organizations representing individuals with handicaps. A copy of the transition plan shall be made available for public inspection. The plan shall, at a minimumÐ

(i) Identify physical obstacles in the recipient's facilities that limit the accessibility of its programs or activities to individuals with handicaps;

(ii) Describe in details the methods that will be used to make the facilities accessible;

(iii) Specify the schedule for taking the steps necessary to achieve compliance with this section and, if the time period of the transition plan is longer than one year, identify steps that will be taken during each year of the transition period;

(iv) Indicate the official responsible for implementation of the plan; and

(v) Identify the persons or groups with whose assistance the plan was prepared.

(Approved by the Office of Management and Budget under control number 2529±0034)

[53 FR 20233, June 2, 1988; 53 FR 28115, July 26, 1988, as amended at 54 FR 37645, Sept. 12, 1989]

§ 8.22 New constructionÐhousing facilities.

(a) New multifamily housing projects (including public housing and Indian housing projects as required by § 8.25) shall be designed and constructed to be readily accessible to and usable by individuals with handicaps.

(b) Subject to paragraph (c) of this section, a minimum of five percent of the total dwelling units or at least one unit in a multifamily housing project, whichever is greater, shall be made accessible for persons with mobility impairments. A unit that is on an accessible route and is adaptable and otherwise in compliance with the standards set forth in § 8.32 is accessible for purposes of this section. An additional two percent of the units (but not less than one unit) in such a project shall be accessible for persons with hearing or vision impairments.

(c) HUD may prescribe a higher percentage or number than that prescribed in paragraph (b) of this section for any area upon request therefor by any affected recipient or by any State or local government or agency thereof

90

Office of the Secretary, HUD

based upon demonstration to the reasonable satisfaction of HUD of a need for a higher percentage or number, based on census data or other available current data (including a currently effective Housing Assistance Plan or Comprehensive Homeless Assistance Plan), or in response to evidence of a need for a higher percentage or number received in any other manner. In reviewing such request or otherwise assessing the existence of such needs, HUD shall take into account the expected needs of eligible persons with and without handicaps.

[53 FR 20233, June 2, 1988, as amended at 56 FR 920, Jan. 9, 1991]

§ 8.23 Alterations of existing housing facilities.

(a) Substantial alteration. If alterations are undertaken to a project (including a public housing project as required by § 8.25(a)(2)) that has 15 or more units and the cost of the alterations is 75 percent or more of the replacement cost of the completed facility, then the provisions of §   8.22 shall apply.

(b) Other alterations. (1) Subject to paragraph (b)(2) of this section, alterations to dwelling units in a multifamily housing project (including public housing) shall, to the maximum extent feasible, be made to be readily accessible to and usable by individuals with handicaps. If alterations of single elements or spaces of a dwelling unit, when considered together, amount to an alteration of a dwelling unit, the entire dwelling unit shall be made accessible. Once five percent of the dwelling units in a project are readily accessible to and usable by individuals with mobility impairments, then no additional elements of dwelling units, or entire dwelling units, are required to be accessible under this paragraph. Alterations to common areas or parts of facilities that affect accessibility of existing housing facilities shall, to the maximum extent feasible, be made to be accessible to and usable by individuals with handicaps. For purposes of this paragraph, the phrase   to the maximum extent feasible shall not be interpreted as requiring that a recipient (including a PHA) make a dwelling unit, common area, facility or element

thereof accessible if doing so would impose undue financial and administrative burdens on the operation of the multifamily housing project.

(2) HUD may prescribe a higher percentage or number than that prescribed in paragraph (b)(1) of this section for any area upon request therefor by any affected recipient or by any State or local government or agency thereof based upon demonstration to the reasonable satisfaction of HUD of a need for a higher percentage or number, based on census data or other available current data (including a currently effective Housing Assistance Plan or Comprehensive Homeless Assistance Plan), or in response to evidence of a need for a higher percentage or number received in any other manner. In reviewing such request or otherwise assessing the existence of such needs, HUD shall take into account the expected needs of eligible persons with and without handicaps.

§ 8.24 Existing housing programs.

(a) General. A recipient shall operate each existing housing program or activity receiving Federal financial assistance so that the program or activity, when viewed in its entirety, is readily accessible to and usable by individuals with handicaps. This paragraph does notÐ

(1) Necessarily require a recipient to make each of its existing facilities accessible to and usable by individuals with handicaps;

(2) Require a recipient to take any action that it can demonstrate would result in a fundamental alteration in the nature of its program or activity or in undue financial and administrative burdens. If an action would result in such an alteration or such burdens, the recipient shall take any action that would not result in such an alteration or such burdens but would nevertheless ensure that individuals with handicaps receive the benefits and services of the program or activity.

(b) Methods. A recipient may comply with the requirements of this section through such means as reassignment of services to accessible buildings, assignment of aides to beneficiaries, provision of housing or related services at alternate accessible sites, alteration of

91

§ 8.25

existing facilities and construction of new facilities, or any other methods that result in making its programs or activities readily accessible to and usable by individuals with handicaps. A recipient is not required to make structural changes in existing housing facilities where other methods are effective in achieving compliance with this section or to provide supportive services that are not part of the program. In choosing among available methods for meeting the requirements of this section, the recipient shall give priority to those methods that offer programs and activities to qualified individuals with handicaps in the most integrated setting appropriate.

(c) Time period for compliance. The recipient shall comply with the obligations established under this section within sixty days of July 11, 1988 except thatÐ

(1) In a public housing program where structural changes in facilities are undertaken, such changes shall be made within the timeframes established in § 8.25(c).

(2) In other housing programs, where structural changes in facilities are undertaken, such changes shall be made within three years of July 11, 1988, but in any event as expeditiously as possible.

(d) Transition plan and time period for structural changes. Except as provided in § 8.25(c), in the event that structural changes to facilities will be undertaken to achieve program accessibility, a recipient shall develop, within six months of July 11, 1988, a transition plan setting forth the steps necessary to complete such changes. The plan shall be developed with the assistance of interested persons, including individuals with handicaps or organizations representing individuals with handicaps. A copy of the transition plan shall be made available for public inspection. The plan shall, at a minimumÐ

(1) Identify physical obstacles in the recipient's facilities that limit the accessibility of its programs or activities to individuals with handicaps;

(2) Describe in detail the methods that will be used to make the facilities accessible;

(3) Specify the schedule for taking the steps necessary to achieve compliance with this section and, if the time period of the transition plan is longer than one year, identify steps that will be taken during each year of the transition period;

(4) Indicate the official responsible for implementation of the plan; and

(5) Identify the persons or groups with whose assistance the plan was prepared.

(Approved by the Office of Management and Budget under control number 2529±0034)

[53 FR 20233, June 2, 1988; 53 FR 28115, July 26, 1988, as amended at 54 FR 37645, Sept. 12, 1989]

§ 8.25 Public housing and multi-family Indian housing.

(a) Development and alteration of public housing and multi-family Indian housing. (1) The requirements of § 8.22 shall apply to all newly constructed public housing and multi-family Indian housing.

(2) The requirements of § 8.23 shall apply to public housing and multi-family Indian housing developed through rehabilitation and to the alteration of public housing and multi-family Indian housing.

(3) In developing public housing and multi-family Indian housing through the purchase of existing properties PHAs and IHAs shall give priority to facilities which are readily accessible to and usable by individuals with handicaps.

(b) Existing public housing and multi-family Indian housingÐgeneral. The requirements of § 8.24(a) shall apply to public housing and multi-family Indian housing programs.

(c) Existing public housing and multi-family Indian housingÐneeds assessment and transition plan. As soon as possible, each PHA (for the purpose of this paragraph, this includes an Indian Housing Authority) shall assess, on a PHA-wide basis, the needs of current tenants and applicants on its waiting list for accessible units and the extent to which such needs have not been met or cannot reasonably be met within four years through development, alterations otherwise contemplated, or other programs administered by the PHA (e.g., Section 8 Moderate Rehabilitation or

92

Office of the Secretary, HUD

§8.26

Section 8 Existing Housing or Housing Vouchers). If the PHA currently has no accessible units or if the PHA or HUD determines that information regarding the availability of accessible units has not been communicated sufficiently so that, as a result, the number of eligible qualified individuals with handicaps on the waiting list is not fairly representative of the number of such persons in the area, the PHA's assessment shall include the needs of eligible qualified individuals with handicaps in the area. If the PHA determines, on the basis of such assessment, that there is no need for additional accessible dwelling units or that the need is being or will be met within four years through other means, such as new construction, Section 8 or alterations otherwise contemplated, no further action is required by the PHA under this paragraph. If the PHA determines, on the basis of its needs assessment, that alterations to make additional units accessible must be made so that the needs of eligible qualified individuals with handicaps may be accommodated proportionally to the needs of non-handicapped individuals in the same categories, then the PHA shall develop a transition plan to achieve program accessibility. The PHA shall complete the needs assessment and transition plan, if one is necessary, as expeditiously as possible, but in any event no later than two years after July 11, 1988. The PHA shall complete structural changes necessary to achieve program accessibility as soon as possible but in any event no later than four years after July 11, 1988. The, Assistant Secretary for Fair Housing and Equal Opportunity and the Assistant Secretary for Public and Indian Housing may extend the four year period for a period not to exceed two years, on a case-by-case determination that compliance within that period would impose undue financial and administrative burdens on the operation of the recipient's public housing and multi-family Indian housing program. The Secretary or the Undersecretary may further extend this time period in extraordinary circumstances, for a period not to exceed one year. The plan shall be developed with the assistance of interested persons including individuals with handicaps or organizations representing individuals with handicaps. A copy of the needs assessment and transition plan shall be made available for public inspection. The transition plan shall, at a minimumÐ

(1) Identify physical obstacles in the PHA's facilities (e.g., dwelling units and common areas) that limit the accessibility of its programs or activities to individuals with handicaps;

(2) Describe in detail the methods that will be used to make the PHA's facilities accessible. A PHA may, if necessary, provide in its plan that it will seek HUD approval, under 24 CFR part 968, of a comprehensive modernization program to meet the needs of eligible individuals with handicaps;

(3) Specify the schedule for taking the steps necessary to achieve compliance with this section and, if the time of the transition plan is longer than one year, identify steps that will be taken during each year of the transition period;

(4) Indicate the official responsible for implementation of the plan; and

(5) Identify the persons or groups with whose assistance the plan was prepared.

(Approved by the Office of Management and Budget under control number 2529±0034)

[53 FR 20233, June 2, 1988, as amended at 54 FR 37645, Sept. 12, 1989; 56 FR 920, Jan. 9, 1991]

§8.26 Distribution of accessible dwelling units.

Accessible dwelling units required by §8.22, 8.23, 8.24 or 8.25 shall, to the maximum extent feasible and subject to reasonable health and safety requirements, be distributed throughout projects and sites and shall be available in a sufficient range of sizes and amenities so that a qualified individual with handicaps' choice of living arrangements is, as a whole, comparable to that of other persons eligible for housing assistance under the same program. This provision shall not be construed to require provision of an elevator in any multifamily housing project solely for the purpose of permitting location of accessible units above or below the accessible grade level.

93

§ 8.27 Occupancy of accessible dwelling units.

(a) Owners and managers of multifamily housing projects having accessible units shall adopt suitable means to assure that information regarding the availability of accessible units reaches eligible individuals with handicaps, and shall take reasonable nondiscriminatory steps to maximize the utilization of such units by eligible individuals whose disability requires the accessibility features of the particular unit. To this end, when an accessible unit becomes vacant, the owner or manager before offering such units to a non-handicapped applicant shall offer such unit:

(1) First, to a current occupant of another unit of the same project, or comparable projects under common control, having handicaps requiring the accessibility features of the vacant unit and occupying a unit not having such features, or, if no such occupant exists, then

(2) Second, to an eligible qualified applicant on the waiting list having a handicap requiring the accessibility features of the vacant unit.

(b) When offering an accessible unit to an applicant not having handicaps requiring the accessibility features of the unit, the owner or manager may require the applicant to agree (and may incorporate this agreement in the lease) to move to a non-accessible unit when available.

§ 8.28 Housing certificate and housing voucher programs.

(a) In carrying out the requirements of this subpart, a recipient administering a Section 8 Existing Housing Certificate program or a housing voucher program shall:

(1) In providing notice of the availability and nature of housing assistance for low-income families under program requirements, adopt suitable means to assure that the notice reaches eligible individuals with handicaps;

(2) In its activities to encourage participation by owners, include encouragement of participation by owners having accessible units;

(3) When issuing a Housing Certificate or Housing Voucher to a family which includes an individual with handicaps include a current listing of available accessible units known to the PHA and, if necessary, otherwise assist the family in locating an available accessible dwelling unit;

(4) Take into account the special problem of ability to locate an accessible unit when considering requests by eligible individuals with handicaps for extensions of Housing Certificates or Housing Vouchers; and

(5) If necessary in order to achieve compliance with this subpart, request under 24 CFR part 882, an exception to the Fair Market Rents to allow section 8 certificate holders to rent accessible units.

(b) In order to ensure that participating owners do not discriminate in the recipient's federally assisted program, a recipient shall enter into a HUD-approved contract with participating owners, which contract shall include necessary assurances of nondiscrimination.

§ 8.29 Homeownership programs (sections 235(i) and 235(j), Turnkey III and Indian Housing Mutual Self-Help programs).

Any housing units newly constructed or rehabilitated for purchase or single family (including semi-attached and attached) units to be constructed or rehabilitated in a program or activity receiving Federal financial assistance shall be made accessible upon request of the prospective buyer if the nature of the handicap of an expected occupant so requires. In such case, the buyer shall consult with the seller or builder/sponsor regarding the specific design features to be provided. If accessibility features selected at the option of the homebuyer are ones covered by the standards prescribed by § 8.32, those features shall comply with the standards prescribed in § 8.32. The buyer shall be permitted to depart from particular specifications of these standards in order to accommodate his or her specific handicap. The cost of making a facility accessible under this paragraph may be included in the mortgage amount within the allowable mortgage limits, where applicable. To the extent such costs exceed allowable mortgage limits, they may be passed

94

Office of the Secretary, HUD

on to the prospective homebuyer, subject to maximum sales price limitations (see 24 CFR 235.320.)

§ 8.30 Rental rehabilitation program.

Each grantee or state recipient in the rental rehabilitation program shall, subject to the priority in 24 CFR 511.10(l) and in accordance with other requirements in 24 CFR part 511, give priority to the selection of projects that will result in dwelling units being made readily accessible to and usable by individuals with handicaps.

[53 FR 20233, June 2, 1988; 53 FR 28115, July 26, 1988]

§ 8.31 Historic properties.

If historic properties become subject to alterations to which this part applies the requirements of §   4.1.7 of the standards of § 8.32 of this part shall apply, except in the case of the Urban Development Action Grant (UDAG) program. In the UDAG program the requirements of 36 CFR part 801 shall apply. Accessibility to historic properties subject to alterations need not be provided if such accessibility would substantially impair the significant historic features of the property or result in undue financial and administrative burdens.

§ 8.32 Accessibility standards.

(a) Effective as of July 11, 1988, design, construction, or alteration of buildings in conformance with sections 3±8 of the Uniform Federal Accessibility Standards (UFAS) shall be deemed to comply with the requirements of §§ 8.21, 8.22, 8.23, and 8.25 with respect to those buildings. Departures from particular technical and scoping requirements of the UFAS by the use of other methods are permitted where substantially equivalent or greater access to and usability of the building is provided. The alteration of housing facilities shall also be in conformance with additional scoping requirements contained in this part. Persons interested in obtaining a copy of the UFAS are directed to § 40.7 of this title.

(b) For purposes of this section, section 4.1.6(1)(g) of UFAS shall be interpreted to exempt from the requirements of UFAS only mechanical rooms and other spaces that, because of their

intended use, will not require accessibility to the public or beneficiaries or result in the employment or residence therein of individuals with physical handicaps.

(c) This section does not require recipients to make building alterations that have little likelihood of being accomplished without removing or altering a load-bearing structural member.

(d) For purposes of this section, section 4.1.4(11) of UFAS may not be used to waive or lower the minimum of five percent accessible units required by § 8.22(b) or to apply the minimum only to projects of 15 or more dwelling units.

(e) Except as otherwise provided in this paragraph, the provisions of §§   8.21 (a) and (b), 8.22 (a) and (b), 8.23, 8.25(a) (1) and (2), and 8.29 shall apply to facilities that are designed, constructed or altered after July 11, 1988. If the design of a facility was commenced before July 11, 1988, the provisions shall be followed to the maximum extent practicable, as determined by the Department. For purposes of this paragraph, the date a facility is constructed or altered shall be deemed to be the date bids for the construction or alteration of the facility are solicited. For purposes of the Urban Development Action Grant (UDAG) program, the provisions shall apply to the construction or alteration of facilities that are funded under applications submitted after July 11, 1988. If the UDAG application was submitted before July 11, 1988, the provisions shall apply, to the maximum extent practicable, as determined by the Department.

[53 FR 20233, June 2, 1988, as amended at 61 FR 5203, Feb. 9, 1996]

§ 8.33 Housing adjustments.

A recipient shall modify its housing policies and practices to ensure that these policies and practices do not discriminate, on the basis of handicap, against a qualified individual with handicaps. The recipient may not impose upon individuals with handicaps other policies, such as the prohibition of assistive devices, auxiliary alarms, or guides in housing facilities, that have the effect of limiting the participation of tenants with handicaps in the recipient's federally assisted housing

§ 8.50

program or activity in violation of this part. Housing policies that the recipient can demonstrate are essential to the housing program or activity will not be regarded as discriminatory within the meaning of this section if modifications to them would result in a fundamental alteration in the nature of the program or activity or undue financial and administrative burdens.

Subpart D—Enforcement

§ 8.50   Assurances required.

(a) Assurances. An applicant for Federal financial assistance for a program or activity to which this part applies shall submit an assurance to HUD, or in the case of a subrecipient to a primary recipient, on a form specified by the responsible civil rights official, that the program or activity will be operated in compliance with this part. An applicant may incorporate these assurances by reference in subsequent applications to the Department.

(b) Duration of obligation.   (1) In the case of Federal financial assistance extended in the form of real property or to provide real property or structures on the property, the assurance will obligate the recipient or, in the case of a subsequent transfer, the transferee, for the period during which the real property or structures are used for the purpose for which Federal financial assistance is extended or for another purpose involving the provision of similar services or benefits.

(2) In the case of Federal financial assistance extended to provide personal property, the assurance will obligate the recipient for the period during which it retains ownership or possession of the property.

(3) In all other cases the assurance will obligate the recipient for the period during which Federal financial assistance is extended.

(c) Covenants. (1) Where Federal financial assistance is provided in the form of real property or interest in the property from the Department, the instrument effecting or recording this transfer shall contain a covenant running with the land to assure nondiscrimination for the period during which the real property is used for a purpose for which the Federal financial

assistance is extended or for another purpose involving the provision of similar services or benefits.

(2) Where no transfer of property is involved but property is purchased or improved with Federal financial assistance, the recipient shall agree to include the covenant described in paragraph (b)(2) of this section in the instrument effecting or recording any subsequent transfer of the property.

(3) Where Federal financial assistance is provided in the form of real property or interest in the property from the Department, the covenant shall also include a condition coupled with a right to be reserved by the Department to revert title to the property in the event of a breach of the covenant. If a transferee of real property proposes to mortgage or otherwise encumber the real property as security for financing construction of new, or improvement of existing, facilities on the property for the purposes for which the property was transferred, the Secretary may, upon request of the transferee and if necessary to accomplish such financing and upon such conditions as he or she deems appropriate, agree to forbear the exercise of such right to revert title for so long as the lien of such mortgage or other encumbrance remains effective.

§ 8.51   Self-evaluation.

(a) Each recipient shall, within one year of July 11, 1988, and after consultation with interested persons, including individuals with handicaps or organizations representing individuals with handicaps:

(1) Evaluate its current policies and practices to determine whether, in whole or in part, they do not or may not meet the requirements of this part;

(2) Modify any policies and practices that do not meet the requirements of this part; and

(3) Take appropriate corrective steps to remedy the discrimination revealed by the self-evaluation.

(b) A recipient that employs fifteen or more persons shall, for at least three years following completion of the evaluation required under paragraph (a)(1) of this section, maintain on file, make available for public inspection, and provide to the responsible civil rights

96

Office of the Secretary, HUD

§ 8.54

official, upon request: (1) A list of the interested persons consulted; (2) a description of areas examined and any problems identified; and (3) a description of any modifications made and of any remedial steps taken.

(Approved by the Office of Management and Budget under control number 2529±0034)

[53 FR 20233, June 2, 1988, as amended at 54 FR 37645, Sept. 12, 1989]

§ 8.52   Remedial and affirmative action.

(a) Remedial action.   (1) If the responsible civil rights official finds that a recipient has discriminated against persons on the basis of handicap in violation of section 504 or this part, the recipient shall take such remedial action as the responsible civil rights official deems necessary to overcome the effects of the discrimination.

(2) The responsible civil rights official may, where necessary to overcome the effects of discrimination in violation of section 504 or this part, require a recipient to take remedial actionÐ

(i) With respect to individuals with handicaps who are no longer participants in the program but who were participants in the program when such discrimination occurred or

(ii) With respect to individuals with handicaps who would have been participants in the program had the discrimination not occurred.

(b) Voluntary action.   A recipient may take nondiscriminatory steps, in addition to any action that is required by this part, to overcome the effects of conditions that resulted in limited participation in the recipient's program or activity by qualified individuals with handicaps.

§ 8.53   Designation of responsible employee and adoption of grievance procedures.

(a) Designation of responsible employee. A recipient that employs fifteen or more persons shall designate at least one person to coordinate its efforts to comply with this part.

(b) Adoption of grievance procedures.   A recipient that employes fifteen or more persons shall adopt grievance procedures that incorporate appropriate due process standards and that provide for the prompt and equitable

resolution of complaints alleging any action prohibited by this part. Such procedures need not be established with respect to complaints from applicants for employment or from applicants for admission to housing covered by this part.

§ 8.54   Notice.

(a) A recipient that employs fifteen or more persons shall take appropriate initial and continuing steps to notify participants, beneficiaries, applicants, and employees, including those with impaired vision or hearing, and unions or professional organizations holding collective bargaining or professional agreements with the recipient that it does not discriminate on the basis of handicap in violation of this part. The notification shall state, where appropriate, that the recipient does not discriminate in admission or access to, or treatment or employment in, its federally assisted programs and activities. The notification shall also include an identification of the responsible employee designated pursuant to §   8.53. A recipient shall make the initial notification required by this paragraph within 90 days of July 11, 1988. Methods of initial and continuing notification may include the posting of notices, publication in newspapers and magazines, placement of notices in recipients' publications, and distribution of memoranda or other written communications.

(b) If a recipient publishes or uses recruitment materials or publications containing general information that it makes available to participants, beneficiaries, applicants, or employees, it shall include in those materials or publications a statement of the policy described in paragraph (a) of this section. A recipient may meet the requirement of this paragraph either by including appropriate inserts in existing materials and publications or by revising and reprinting the materials and publications.

(c) The recipient shall ensure that members of the population eligible to be served or likely to be affected directly by a federally assisted program

97

§ 8.55

who have visual or hearing impairments are provided with the information necessary to understand and participate in the program. Methods for ensuring participation include, but are not limited to, qualified sign language and oral interpreters, readers, or the use of taped and Braille materials.

§ 8.55   Compliance information.

(a) Cooperation and assistance.   The responsible civil rights official and the award official shall, to the fullest extent practicable, seek the cooperation of recipients in obtaining compliance with this part and shall provide assistance and guidance to recipients to help them comply voluntarily with this part.

(b) Compliance reports.   Each recipient shall keep such records and submit to the responsible civil rights official or his or her designee timely, complete, and accurate compliance reports at such times, and in such form and containing such information, as the responsible civil rights official or his or her designee may determine to be necessary to enable him or her to ascertain whether the recipient has complied or is complying with this part. In general, recipients should have available for the Department data showing the extent to which individuals with handicaps are beneficiaries of federally assisted programs.

(c) Access to sources of information. Each recipient shall permit access by the responsible civil rights official during normal business hours to such of its books, records, accounts, and other sources of information, and its facilities, as may be pertinent to ascertain compliance with this part. Where any information required of a recipient is in the exclusive possession of any other agency, institution, or person and this agency, institution, or person shall fail or refuse to furnish this information, the recipient shall so certify in its report and shall set forth what efforts it has made to obtain the information.

(d) Information to beneficiaries and participants.   Each recipient shall make available to participants, beneficiaries, and other interested persons such information regarding the provisions of this part and its applicability to the program or activity under which the

recipient receives Federal financial assistance, and make such information available to them in such manner as the responsible civil rights official finds necessary to apprise such persons of the protections against discrimination assured them by this part.

(Approved by the Office of Management and Budget under control number 2529±0034)

[53 FR 20233, June 2, 1988, as amended at 54 FR 37645, Sept. 12, 1989]

§ 8.56   Conduct of investigations.

(a) Periodic compliance reviews.   The responsible civil rights official or designee may periodically review the practices of recipients to determine whether they are complying with this part and where he or she has a reasonable basis to do so may conduct on-site reviews. Such basis may include any evidence that a problem exists or that programmatic matters exist that justify on-site investigation in selected circumstances. The responsible civil rights official shall initiate an on-site review by sending to the recipient a letter advising the recipient of the practices to be reviewed; the programs affected by the review; and the opportunity, at any time prior to receipt of a final determination, to make a documentary or other submission that explains, validates, or otherwise addresses the practices under review. In addition, each award official shall include in normal program compliance reviews and monitoring procedures appropriate actions to review and monitor compliance with general or specific program requirements designed to effectuate the requirements of this part.

(b) Investigations.   The responsible civil rights official shall make a prompt investigation whenever a compliance review, report, complaint or any other information indicates a possible failure to comply with this part.

(c) Filing a complaintÐ   (1) Who may file. Any person who believes that he or she has been subjected to discrimination prohibited by this part may by himself or herself or by his or her authorized representative file a complaint with the responsible civil rights official. Any person who believes that any specific class of persons has been subjected to discrimination prohibited

Office of the Secretary, HUD   **§ 8.56**

by this part and who is a member of that class or who is the authorized representative of a member of that class may file a complaint with the responsible civil rights official.

(2) Confidentiality. The responsible civil rights official shall hold in confidence the identity of any person submitting a complaint, unless the person submits written authorization otherwise, and except to the extent necessary to carry out the purposes of this part, including the conduct of any investigation, hearing, or proceeding under this part.

(3) When to file. Complaints shall be filed within 180 days of the alleged act of discrimination, unless the responsible civil rights official waives this time limit for good cause shown. For purposes of determining when a complaint is filed under this paragraph, a complaint mailed to the Department shall be deemed filed on the date it is postmarked. Any other complaint shall be deemed filed on the date it is received by the Department.

(4) Where to file complaints. Complaints may be filed by mail with the Office of Fair Housing and Equal Opportunity, Department of Housing and Urban Development, Washington, DC 20410, or any Regional or Field Office of the Department.

(5) Contents of complaints. Each complaint should contain the complainant's name and address, the name and address of the recipient alleged to have violated this part, and a description of the recipient's alleged discriminatory action in sufficient detail to inform the Department of the nature and date of the alleged violation of this part.

(6) Amendments of complaints. Complaints may be reasonably and fairly amended at any time. Amendments to complaints such as clarification and amplification of allegations in a complaint or the addition of other recipients may be made at any time during the pendency of the complaint and any amendment shall be deemed to be made as of the original filing date.

(d) Notification. The responsible civil rights official will notify the complainant and the recipient of the agency's receipt of the complaint within ten (10) calendar days.

(e) Complaint processing procedures. After acknowledging receipt of a complaint, the responsible civil rights official will immediately initiate complaint processing procedures.

(1) Preliminary investigation.

(i) Within twenty (20) calendar days of acknowledgement of the complaint, the responsible civil rights official will review the complaint for acceptance, rejection, or referral to the appropriate Federal agency.

(ii) If the complaint is accepted, the responsible civil rights official will notify the complainant and the award official. The responsible civil righs official will also notify the applicant or recipient complained against of the allegations and give the applicant or recipient an opportunity to make a written submission responding to, rebutting, or denying the allegations raised in the complaint.

(iii) The party complained against may send the responsible civil rights official a response to the notice of complaint within thirty (30) calendar days of receiving it. With leave of the responsible civil rights official, an answer may be amended at any time. The responsible civil rights official will permit answers to be amended for good cause shown.

(2) Informal resolution. In accordance with paragraph (j) of this section, the responsible civil rights official shall attempt to resolve complaints informally whenever possible.

(f) Dismissal of complaint. If the investigation reveals no violation of this part, the responsible civil rights offical will dismiss the complaint and notify the complainant and recipient.

(g) Letter of findings. If an informal resolution of the complaint is not reached the responsible civil rights official or his or her designee shall, within 180 days of receipt of the complaint, notify the recipient and the complainant (if any) of the results of the investigation in a letter sent by certified mail, return receipt requested, containing the following:

(1) Preliminary findings of fact and a preliminary finding of compliance or noncompliance;

(2) A description of an appropriate remedy for each violation believed to exist;

99

(3) A notice that a copy of the Final Investigative Report of the Department will be made available, upon request, to the recipient and the complainant (if any); and

(4) A notice of the right of the recipient and the complainant (if any) to request a review of the letter of findings by the reviewing civil rights official.

(h) Right to review of the letter of findings. (1) A complainant or recipient may request that a complete review be made of the letter of findings within 30 days of receipt, by mailing or delivering to the reviewing civil rights official, Office of Fair Housing and Equal Opportunity, Washington, DC 20410, a written statement of the reasons why the letter of findings should be modified in light of supplementary information.

(2) The reviewing civil rights official shall send by certified mail, return receipt requested, a copy of the request for review to the other party, if any. Such other party shall have 20 days to respond to the request for review.

(3) The reviewing civil rights official shall either sustain or modify the letter of findings within 60 days of the request for review. The reviewing civil rights official's decision shall constitute the formal determination.

(4) If neither party requests that the letter of findings be reviewed, the responsibile civil rights official shall, within fourteen (14) calendar days of the expiration of the time period in paragraph (h)(1) of this section, send a formal written determination of compliance or noncompliance to the recipient and copies to the award official.

(i) Voluntary compliance time limits. The recipient will have ten (10) calendar days from receipt of the formal determination of noncompliance within which to come into voluntary compliance. If the recipient fails to meet this deadline, HUD shall proceed under §8.57.

(j) Informal resolution/voluntary complianceÐ (1) General . It is the policy of the Department to encourage the informal resolution of matters. The responsible civil rights official may attempt to resolve a matter through informal means at any stage of processing. A matter may be resolved by informal means at any time. If a letter of find-

ings making a preliminary finding of noncompliance is issued, the responsible civil rights official shall attempt to resolve the matter by informal means.

(2) Objectives of informal resolution/voluntary compliance. In attempting informal resolution, the responsible civil rights official shall attempt to achieve a just resolution of the matter and to obtain assurances where appropriate, that the recipient will satisfactorily remedy any violations of the rights of any complainant and will take such action as will assure the elimination of any violation of this part or the prevention of the occurrence of such violation in the future. The terms of such an informal resolution shall be reduced to a written voluntary compliance agreement, signed by the recipient and the responsible civil rights official, and be made part of the file for the matter. Such voluntary compliance agreements shall seek to protect the interests of the complainant (if any), other persons similary situated, and the public interest.

(k) Intimidatory or retaliatory acts prohibited. No recipient or other person shall intimidate, threaten, coerce, or discriminate against any person for the purpose of interfering with any right or privilege secured by this part, or because he or she has made a complaint, testified, assisted, or participated in any manner in an investigation, proceeding, or hearing under this part. The identity of complainants shall be kept confidential except to the extent necessary to carry out the purposes of this part, including the conduct of investigation, hearing or judicial proceeding arising thereunder.

[53 FR 20233, June 2, 1988; 53 FR 28115, July 26, 1988; 53 FR 34634, Sept. 7, 1988]

§8.57 Procedure for effecting compliance.

(a) General. If there appears to be a failure or threatened failure to comply with this part and if the noncompliance or threatened noncompliance cannot be corrected by informal means, compliance with this part may be effected by the suspension or termination of or refusal to grant or to continue Federal financial assistance, or by other means authorized by law.

100

Office of the Secretary, HUD

§ 8.57

Such other means may include, but are not limited to:

(1) A referral to the Department of Justice with a recommendation that appropriate proceedings be brought to enforce any rights of the United States under any law of the United States, or any assurance or other contractual undertaking;

(2) The initiation of debarment proceedings pursuant to part 24 of this title; and

(3) Any applicable proceeding under State or local law.

(b) Noncompliance with § 8.50. If an applicant or a recipient of assistance under a contract which is extended or amended on or after July 11, 1988, fails or refuses to furnish an assurance required under § 8.50 or otherwise fails or refuses to comply with the requirements imposed by that section, Federal financial assistance may be refused under paragraph (c) of this section. The Department is not required to provide assistance during the pendency of the administrative proceeding under such paragraph (c), except where the assistance is due and payable under a contract approved before July 11, 1988.

(c) Termination of or refusal to grant or to continue Federal financial assistance. No order suspending, terminating, or refusing to grant or continue Federal financial assistance shall become effective until:

(1) The responsible civil rights official has advised the applicant or recipient of its failure to comply and has determined that compliance cannot be secured by voluntary means;

(2) There has been an express finding on the record, after opportunity for hearing, of a failure by the applicant or recipient to comply with a requirement imposed under this part;

(3) The action has been approved by the Secretary; and

(4) The expiration of 30 days after the Secretary has filed with the committees of the House and Senate having legislative jurisdiction over the program or activity involved a full written report of the circumstances and the grounds for such action. Any action to suspend or terminate, or to refuse to grant or to continue Federal financial assistance shall be limited to the particular political entity, or part thereof,

or other applicant or recipient as to whom such a finding has been made and shall be limited in its effect to the particular program, or part thereof, in which such noncompliance has been so found.

(d) Notice to State or local government. Whenever the Secretary determines that a State or unit of general local government which is a recipient of Federal financial assistance under title I of the Housing and Community Development Act of 1974, as amended (42 U.S.C. 5301±5318) has failed to comply with a requirement of this part with respect to a program or activity funded in whole or in part with such assistance, the Secretary shall notify the Governor of the State or the chief executive officer of the unit of general local government of the noncompliance and shall request the Governor or the chief executive officer to secure compliance. The notice shall be given at least sixty days before:

(1) An order suspending, terminating, or refusing to grant or continue Federal financial assistance becomes effective under paragraph (c) of this section; or

(2) Any action to effect compliance by any other means authorized by law is taken under paragraph (a) of this section.

(e) Other means authorized by law. No action to effect compliance by any other means authorized by law shall be taken until:

(1) The responsible civil rights official has determined that compliance cannot be secured by voluntary means;

(2) The recipient or other person has been notified of its failure to comply and of the action to be taken to effect compliance; and

(3) At least 10 days have elapsed since the mailing of such notice to the applicant or recipient. During this period, additional efforts shall be made to persuade the applicant or recipient to comply with this part and to take such corrective action as may be appropriate.

However, this paragraph shall not be construed to prevent an award official from utilizing appropriate procedures and sanctions established under the program to assure or secure compliance with a specific requirement of the

101

§ 8.58

program designed to effectuate the objectives of this part.

[53 FR 20233, June 2, 1988; 53 FR 28115, July 26, 1988]

§ 8.58 Hearings.

(a) Opportunity for hearing. Whenever an opportunity for a hearing is required by § 8.57(c), reasonable notice shall be given by registered or certified mail, return receipt requested, to the affected applicant or recipient. This notice shall advise the applicant or recipient of the action proposed to be taken, the specific provision under which the proposed action against it is to be taken, and the matters of fact or law asserted as the basis for this action. The notice shall:

(1) Fix a date not less than 20 days after the date of the notice for the applicant or recipient to request the administrative law judge to schedule a hearing, or

(2) Advise the applicant or recipient that the matter has been scheduled for hearing at a stated time and place. The time and place so fixed shall be reasonable and shall be subject to change for cause. The complainant, if any, shall be advised of the time and place of the hearing. An applicant or recipient may waive a hearing and submit written information and argument for the record. The failure of an applicant or recipient to request a hearing under this paragraph or to appear at a hearing for which a date has been set is a waiver of the right to a hearing under § 8.57(c) and consent to the making of a decision on the basis of available information.

(b) Hearing procedures. Hearings shall be conducted in accordance with 24 CFR part 180.

[53 FR 20233, June 2, 1988, as amended at 61 FR 52218, Oct. 4, 1996]

PART 9—ENFORCEMENT OF NON-DISCRIMINATION ON THE BASIS OF DISABILITY IN PROGRAMS OR ACTIVITIES CONDUCTED BY THE DEPARTMENT OF HOUSING AND URBAN DEVELOPMENT

Sec.
9.101 Purpose.
9.102 Applicability.

9.103 Definitions.
9.110 Self-evaluation.
9.111 Notice.
9.112Ð9.129 [Reserved]
9.130 General prohibitions against discrimination.
9.131 Direct threat.
9.132Ð9.139 [Reserved]
9.140 Employment.
9.141Ð9.148 [Reserved]
9.149 Program accessibility: discrimination prohibited.
9.150 Program accessibility: existing facilities.
9.151 Program accessibility: new construction and alterations.
9.152 Program accessibility: alterations of Property Disposition Program multifamily housing facilities.
9.153 Distribution of accessible dwelling units.
9.154 Occupancy of accessible dwelling units.
9.155 Housing adjustments.
9.160 Communications.
9.170 Compliance procedures.

AUTHORITY : 29 U.S.C. 794; 42 U.S.C. 3535(d).

SOURCE : 59 FR 31047, June 16, 1994, unless otherwise noted.

§ 9.101 Purpose.

The purpose of this part is to effectuate section 119 of the Rehabilitation, Comprehensive Services, and Developmental Disabilities Amendments of 1978, which amended section 504 of the Rehabilitation Act of 1973 to prohibit discrimination on the basis of disability in programs or activities conducted by Executive agencies or the United States Postal Service.

§ 9.102 Applicability.

This part applies to all programs or activities conducted by the agency, except for programs or activities conducted outside the United States that do not involve individuals with disabilities in the United States.

§ 9.103 Definitions.

For purposes of this part:
Accessible: (1) When used with respect to the design, construction, or alteration of a facility or a portion of a facility other than an individual dwelling unit, means that the facility or portion of the facility when designed, constructed or altered, complies with applicable accessibility standards and can be approached, entered, and used

102

Sources for Regulations and Information

The U.S. Department of Justice offers technical assistance on the ADA Standards for Accessible Design and other ADA provisions applying to businesses, non-profit service agencies, and state and local government programs.

Homepage:
www.usdoj.gov

ADA Information Line for documents and questions
(800) 514-0301 (voice)
(800) 514-0383 (TDD)

Publications and Downloads
www.usdoj.gov/crt/ada/publicat.htm

The Access Board is an independent Federal agency that develops accessibility guidelines and provides technical assistance.

Homepage
www.access-board.gov

Telephone
(800) 872-2253 (voice)
(800) 993-2822 (TDD)

Publications and Downloads
Americans With Disabilities Act Accessibility Guidelines:
www.access-board.gov/adaag/html/adaag.htm
Uniform Federal Accessibility Standards (UFAS):
www.access-board.gov/ufas/ufas-html/ufas.htm

The U.S. Department of Housing and Urban Development, Office of Fair Housing and Equal Opportunity is responsible for enforcement of the Fair Housing Act and other civil rights laws.

Homepage:
www.hud.gov/fhe/fheo.html

Telephone
(800) 347-3739 (voice)

Publications and Downloads
www.hudclips.org

TABLE OF CONTENTS

W

NAHMA

COMMUNITIES OF QUALITY

Who We Are

Founded in 1990, the National Affordable Housing Management Association ("NAHMA") is an association representing companies and individuals involved with the management of affordable housing and, in particular, with the management of multifamily housing developments subject to requirements of federal regulatory agencies.

The management of affordable housing is a specialized business, requiring skills and programmatic knowledge not required of other real estate management professionals. The members of NAHMA strongly believe that participants in the affordable housing industry, private and public, must abide by high ethical standards in connection with their business affairs, and must strive to comply with all applicable program requirements.

As the stewards of low-and moderate-income housing, no one knows better than NAHMA's members how affordable housing operates, what works and doesn't work, and what should be done. Since the 1970s, NAHMA members have been actively involved in federally regulated housing programs. Today, as the housing environment is changing, NAHMA has repositioned its focus to include all types of affordable housing including housing developed using Low-Income Housing Tax Credits.

Our Mission

NAHMA advocates an adequate supply of multifamily, residential affordable housing by bringing nationwide attention to the necessity of preserving decent and safe housing. The foundation of NAHMA's vital mission is based upon:

- Solid partnerships with HUD, Congress, RHS, State Housing Agencies, and Housing Credit Monitoring Agencies

- Industry standards for professionals in affordable housing management: National Affordable Housing Professional (NAHP), Housing Credit Certified Professional (HCCP), Certified Professional of Occupancy (CPO), and Fair Housing Compliance (FHC).

- Commitment to Communities of Quality for families living in affordable housing.

- Preservation of existing units of affordable housing.

Our Message

Now, more than ever, it is vital that we as a nation not only protect low-income housing, but also ensure appropriate government involvement at all levels. That public/private partnership will take advantage of the best both sectors have to offer to low-income residents, and it is more efficient and less expensive to the country.

Our Members

NAHMA members manage and provide quality affordable housing to more than two million Americans with very low and moderate incomes. Presidents and executives of property management companies, owners of affordable rental housing, public agencies and national organizations involved in affordable housing and providers of supplies and services to the affordable housing industry make up the membership of NAHMA.

Benefits of Membership

NAHMA is constantly working to inform its members of issues vital to the professional management of their properties. To that end, NAHMA offers:

*   Professional development opportunities through a nationally recognized accreditation program (NAHP);

*   First-rate, informative industry news through a bimonthly newsletter, NAHMA News;

*   Up to the minute regulatory reports from HUD, RHS, State Housing Agencies, etc.;

*   Timely Legislative Updates (NAHMAnalysis) provided via email or broadcast fax offering inside information from the Nation's Capitol;

*   National exposure for managers through an annual awards program promoting Communities of Quality;

*   A national Drug Awareness Poster/Calendar Contest;

*   Partnership with NAHB's Housing Credit Group;

*   NAHP Times, a specialty publication targeting site-level professionals;

*   Local involvement and networking opportunities with local Affordable Housing Management Associations (AHMAs) across the country;

*   National peer networking with HUD, RHS and State Housing Agency officials at two meetings per year and much, much more!

Contact NAHMA

526 King Street
Suite 511
Alexandria, VA 22314
phone 703-683-8630
fax 703-683-8634
inquiries@nahma.org
www.nahma.org

Compass is a consulting partnership specializing in affordable housing policy, finance and management. Our expertise is most valuable to those with portfolios facing change. Public and private clients include apartment owners, not-for profits, trade associations, and government agencies. We provide our clients with a range of services:

- *Approach, Direction and Mission* - Identification of core values, essential strengths, and competitive advantages, and an integration of these elements into the day-to-day operations of the organization.

- *Management Level Competencies* - Assessment of key management requirements for the successful operation of multifamily properties, including methods for systematic oversight and early warning of emerging problems through operating systems, procedures, and policies designed to support performance against key indicators.

- *Management Cost Analysis* - Review management operations and recommend changes or enhancements. Areas of investigation and recommendation may include staffing, structure, cost allocation, outsourcing, as well as investment in the development of systems.

- *Property Operations Analysis* - Review and analysis of property operating costs, including Reserve for Replacement analysis, income and expense analysis, and regulatory compliance analysis.

- *Advocacy* - Compass has an extensive background in affordable housing policy and provides clients with lobbying, analysis, and guidance.

- *Regulatory Monitoring* - We monitor legislative and regulatory housing activity and provide clients with a pipeline of information.

- *Analysis* - We analyze programs at the management level, and provide guidance on establishing systems and procedures to ensure ongoing compliance with housing regulations. We also review and develop training materials.

Our expertise in housing subsidy and finance is exhaustive, creative, and provides clients with clear, strategic thinking. We can help you with an entire portfolio, or a single property. Our analysis provides the information you need to make smart, well-informed decisions.

Contact Compass Group

The Compass Group, LLC
1275 K Street, NW, Suite 925
Washington, DC 20005
phone - 703-521-9193
email - inquiries@compassgroup.net
www.compassgroup.net

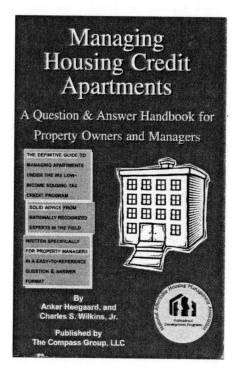

Also Available from Compass

Managing Housing Credit Apartments

A Question & Answer Handbook for Property Owners and Managers

By Anker Heegaard and Charles S. Wilkins, Jr.

ISBN: 0-9669944-0-X

The definitive handbook for anyone responsible for onsite compliance with the Low-Income Housing Tax Credit Program. Over 175 straightforward answers to tough questions about the day-to-day requirements of managing Section 42 housing. A copy of this book in the hands of each employee is your best value in compliance.

"A must have resource for Housing Credit Managers." — *Brenda McClain, Brenda McClain & Associates*

"Tax Credit Investors should make owning this Handbook a requirement for all property managers and developers seeking to do business with them." — *Michael Alexander, Vice President of Tax Credit Investments, AIMCO*

To Order

Call 800-972-1074

Retail prices range from $49.95 to $34.95 each, based on volume.

NAHMA Members enjoy a reduced price and should order through NAHMA at 703-683-8630.

Also Available from Compass

Shelter from the Storm

Successful Market Conversions of Regulated Housing
By Charles S. Wilkins, Jr.

ISBN: 0-9669944-1-8

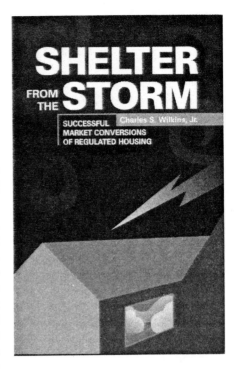

This valuable book will take you through the reasons that market conversions are imminent, the specific actions you will have to undertake to prepare, and the problems you will face along the way.

Assisted, Public and Military Housing will all undergo change, and the challenges that will confront each are discussed thoroughly and straightforwardly. This book is essential for anyone involved in the success of affordable housing, including site managers, management executives, lenders and investors, owners and potential purchasers, residents and community groups, and the public-sector leaders and managers who will have to make these conversions work.

To Order

Call 800-972-1074

Retail prices range from $65 to $32.50 each, based on volume.

Not-for-profit customers enjoy prices from $45 to $32.50 each.

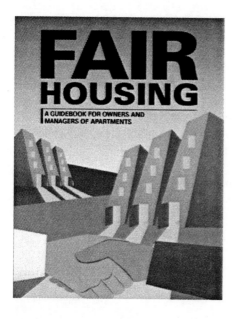

To Order Additional Copies of this Book

Fair Housing

A Guidebook for Owners and Managers of Apartments

A Joint Publication of The Compass Group, LLC & The National Affordable Housing Management Association

ISBN: 0-9669944-2-6

This invaluable reference work should be in the hands of everyone concerned with the professional management of apartments—from leasing agents to policy analysts.

Thorough research, extensive cross-referencing and indexing, clean and straightforward writing, and a quick-access question and answer format makes this the only reference of its kind on the subject.

To Order

Call 800-972-1074

Retail prices range from *only* $35 each, with substantial discounts for volume purchasers. Buy one copy for each site employee.

NAHMA Members enjoy a reduced price and should order through NAHMA at 703-683-8630.